A Plan for Evaluating the District of Columbia's Public Schools

From Impressions to Evidence

Committee on the Independent Evaluation of DC Public Schools

Division of Behavioral and Social Sciences and Education

NATIONAL RESEARCH COUNCIL
OF THE NATIONAL ACADEMIES

THE NATIONAL ACADEMIES PRESS
Washington, D.C.
www.nap.edu

THE NATIONAL ACADEMIES PRESS 500 Fifth Street, N.W. Washington, DC 20001

NOTICE: The project that is the subject of this report was approved by the Governing Board of the National Research Council, whose members are drawn from the councils of the National Academy of Sciences, the National Academy of Engineering, and the Institute of Medicine. The members of the committee responsible for the report were chosen for their special competences and with regard for appropriate balance.

This study was supported by Award No. ODCA 2010-01 and ODCA 2011-01 between the National Academy of Sciences and the Government of the District of Columbia; and Award No. 201000123 between the National Academy of Sciences and the Spencer Foundation. The study was also supported by the National Science Foundation, the CityBridge Foundation, the Philip L. Graham Fund, the Kimsey Foundation, the World Bank, and the Diane and Norman Bernstein Foundation. Any opinions, findings, conclusions, or recommendations expressed in this publication are those of the author(s) and do not necessarily reflect the views of the organizations or agencies that provided support for the project.

International Standard Book Number-13: 978-0-309-20936-6
International Standard Book Number-10: 0-309-20936-6

Additional copies of this report are available from the National Academies Press, 500 Fifth Street, N.W., Lockbox 285, Washington, DC 20055; (800) 624-6242 or (202) 334-3313 (in the Washington metropolitan area); Internet, http://www.nap.edu.

Copyright 2011 by the National Academy of Sciences. All rights reserved.

Printed in the United States of America

Cover credit: Photograph by Sabryn McDonald, seventh grade student from Cesar Chavez Middle School, District of Columbia, as part of the Critical Exposure Program, http://www.criticalexposure.org © 2011.

Suggested citation: National Research Council. (2011). *A Plan for Evaluating the District of Columbia's Public Schools: From Impressions to Evidence.* Committee on the Independent Evaluation of DC Public Schools. Division of Behavioral and Social Sciences and Education. Washington, DC: The National Academies Press.

THE NATIONAL ACADEMIES
Advisers to the Nation on Science, Engineering, and Medicine

The **National Academy of Sciences** is a private, nonprofit, self-perpetuating society of distinguished scholars engaged in scientific and engineering research, dedicated to the furtherance of science and technology and to their use for the general welfare. Upon the authority of the charter granted to it by the Congress in 1863, the Academy has a mandate that requires it to advise the federal government on scientific and technical matters. Dr. Ralph J. Cicerone is president of the National Academy of Sciences.

The **National Academy of Engineering** was established in 1964, under the charter of the National Academy of Sciences, as a parallel organization of outstanding engineers. It is autonomous in its administration and in the selection of its members, sharing with the National Academy of Sciences the responsibility for advising the federal government. The National Academy of Engineering also sponsors engineering programs aimed at meeting national needs, encourages education and research, and recognizes the superior achievements of engineers. Dr. Charles M. Vest is president of the National Academy of Engineering.

The **Institute of Medicine** was established in 1970 by the National Academy of Sciences to secure the services of eminent members of appropriate professions in the examination of policy matters pertaining to the health of the public. The Institute acts under the responsibility given to the National Academy of Sciences by its congressional charter to be an adviser to the federal government and, upon its own initiative, to identify issues of medical care, research, and education. Dr. Harvey V. Fineberg is president of the Institute of Medicine.

The **National Research Council** was organized by the National Academy of Sciences in 1916 to associate the broad community of science and technology with the Academy's purposes of furthering knowledge and advising the federal government. Functioning in accordance with general policies determined by the Academy, the Council has become the principal operating agency of both the National Academy of Sciences and the National Academy of Engineering in providing services to the government, the public, and the scientific and engineering communities. The Council is administered jointly by both Academies and the Institute of Medicine. Dr. Ralph J. Cicerone and Dr. Charles M. Vest are chair and vice chair, respectively, of the National Research Council.

www.national-academies.org

COMMITTEE ON THE INDEPENDENT EVALUATION OF DC PUBLIC SCHOOLS

Christopher Edley, Jr., *Cochair*, School of Law, University of California, Berkeley
Robert M. Hauser, *Cochair*, Division of Behavioral and Social Sciences and Education, National Research Council, Washington, DC, and Vilas Research Professor, Emeritus, University of Wisconsin, Madison
Beatrice F. Birman, Education, Human Development, and Workforce Program, American Institutes for Research, Washington, DC
Carl A. Cohn, School of Educational Studies, Claremont Graduate University
Leslie T. Fenwick, School of Education, Howard University
Michael J. Feuer, Graduate School of Education and Human Development, George Washington University
Jon Fullerton, Center for Education Policy Research, Harvard University
Fernando A. Guerra, Metro Health, San Antonio, Texas
Jonathan Gueverra, Office of the Chief Executive, Community College of the District of Columbia
Jonathan Guryan, Institute for Policy Research, Northwestern University
Lorraine McDonnell, Department of Political Science, University of California, Santa Barbara
C. Kent McGuire, Office of the President, Southern Education Foundation, Atlanta, Georgia
Maxine Singer, Carnegie Institution of Washington
William F. Tate IV, Department of Education, Washington University in St. Louis

Laudan Y. Aron, *Study Director* (until December 2010)
Alexandra Beatty, *Senior Program Officer*
Natalia Pane, *Visiting Scholar*
Kelly Iverson, *Senior Program Assistant*
Jeremy Flattau, *Mirzayan Fellow*
Christina Maranto, *Mirzayan Fellow*
Jessica Schibler, *Summer Intern*

Preface

The District of Columbia has struggled for decades to improve its public education system. The school system's problems in many ways reflect its context: a city whose history has been characterized by sometimes stark racial and class divides. The District is not part of any state, and, for a variety of legal and historical reasons, the U.S. Congress has control over many aspects of its affairs and budget. The city's schools have been governed differently and with more volatility than any other urban district: 17 different management structures have been tried since 1804.

The most recent change, in 2007, was surely the most dramatic. The enactment of the Public Education Reform Amendment Act (PERAA), gave primary control of the schools to the mayor and a mayor-appointed chancellor, and instituted a host of major changes to management and governance. The authors of PERAA recognized the importance of obtaining a clear, objective, politically independent, and accurate picture of the schools' progress as these reforms were pursued; and they recognized the complexity of the technical challenges associated with designing and implementing an evaluation that could yield that sort of information.

The city council, under the leadership of Chairman Vincent C. Gray (who has since been elected mayor and has supported this project throughout) approached the National Research Council (NRC) of the National Academies to carry out this charge. Assembling an expert panel required special attention to local, national, and other demographic factors; expertise in the myriad relevant research fields that inevitably must be included in a comprehensive effort; political and ideological balance; and, given the ambitious timeline, sufficient prior experience among participants to ensure efficiency in deliberations and the preparation of a final report.

Perhaps most important was the decision about just how ambitious to allow the first phase of this initiative to become. Following negotiations with the DC government, the Committee on the Independent Evaluation of DC Public Schools was charged to develop a plan for the multiyear evaluation of DC's public school system; identify available data and assess its quality and utility; consider preliminary indicators; and engage with a wide cross-section of local stakeholder groups to explore the feasibility and scope of the next phases of an evaluation. In accepting this unusual assignment, the NRC recognized that there is no well-established model for evaluating the progress of school reform, and that reform in an urban district is a moving target. Understanding a school district's progress—and isolating the effects of a complex policy—entails answering an array of questions large and small.

The committee spent much of its time deepening its understanding of the unique features of Washington, DC, and its public school system, examining research and key parts of a large literature on school reform, conferring widely with experienced educators and evaluators, and identifying the most essential elements to be included in a sustainable and robust system of evaluation. In the course of this phase of the initiative, and based on careful study and deliberations, the committee developed preliminary impressions of DC schools under PERAA, which reinforced the committee's position that sound policy and practice will, indeed, necessitate more than "impressions." The fragility of inferences that are derived from first looks at data is our principal rationale for designing and advocating a rigorous long-term program. The main output of this first phase, then, is a framework for such a program.

We hope the report opens and facilitates new dialogue about the current and future prospects for infusing in the city's ongoing school reform efforts the best that scientific evidence can offer, and that this dialogue will reverberate in other cities confronting the challenge of improving their children's educational opportunities.

This study could not have happened without the support and contributions of many people. In addition to the basic financial support provided by the Government of the District of Columbia, for which we are grateful, we acknowledge the U.S. National Science Foundation for its contribution of an important planning grant. We also acknowledge grants from the CityBridge Foundation, the Spencer Foundation, the Philip L. Graham Fund, the Kimsey Foundation, the World Bank, and the Diane and Norman Bernstein Foundation. Michael Gewirz and Debbi Yogodzinski provided much needed moral support and were instrumental in facilitating connections to leading business figures in the city, without whose support the prospects for a successful initiative would have been questionable. These organizations and individuals sensed the potential for this venture, and we are extremely grateful.

We are also grateful for the assistance of many other individuals, too numerous to name here. Many city officials, private citizens, business executives, parents, teachers, principals, and others made presentations to the committee, met with staff and individual members, and supplied information and materials. A group of accomplished researchers; DC Government officials; civic, business, and labor leaders; parents; experienced evaluators; and others participated in a critically important planning conference that helped shape—and contain—the parameters of our initiative.

We thank Brenda Turnbull of Policy Associates Inc. who developed a thoughtful background paper on education indicators. The committee is also very grateful to Sol and Diane Pelavin, emeriti president and vice president of the American Institutes for Research, for donating the time, wisdom, and service of Natalia Pane, who served as a visiting scholar for the study. We benefited greatly from the assistance of two National Academies Mirzayan Fellows, Jeremy Flattau and Christina Maranto, and a very capable summer intern, Jessica Schibler. A special thank you goes to the NRC staff who supported every aspect of this ambitious study, Michael J. Feuer, executive director of NRC's Division of Behavioral and Social Sciences and Education (until August 2010); Patricia Morison, director of DBASSE's Office of Communications and Reports; Jean Moon, scholar; Laudan Aron, study director (until December 2010); Alexandra Beatty, senior program officer; and Kelly Iverson, senior program assistant. Finally, we thank our fellow committee members who volunteered their valuable time and intellectual efforts. Without their critical expertise and guidance, this report would not have been possible.

This report has been reviewed in draft form by individuals chosen for their diverse perspectives and technical expertise, in accordance with procedures approved by the NRC's Report Review Committee. The purpose of this independent review is to provide candid and critical comments that will assist the institution in making its published report as sound as possible and to ensure that the report meets institutional standards for objectivity, evidence, and responsiveness to the study charge. The review comments and draft manuscript remain confidential to protect the integrity of the deliberative process.

We thank the following individuals for their review of this report: Richard A. Berman, Licas.net; Lawrence D. Bobo, Department of African and African American Studies, Harvard University; Mark Dynarski, Pemberton Research, East Windsor, New Jersey; Robert F. Floden, Institute for Research on Teaching and Learning, College of Education, Michigan State University; Margaret E. Goertz, Graduate School of Education, University of Pennsylvania; Jane Hannaway, Education Policy Center, Urban Institute; Ernest R. House, School of Education, University of Colorado; Alan J. Ingram, Springfield Public Schools; Robert L. Johnson, Adolescent and Young Adult Medicine, University of Medicine and Dentistry of New Jersey-New Jersey Medical School; Richard C. Larson, Center for Engineering Systems Fundamentals, Learning International Networks Consortium, Massachusetts Institute of Technology; Robert Rothman, Alliance for Excellent Education, Washington, DC; Allan Sessoms, University of the District of Columbia; William T. Trent, Department of Educational Policy Studies, College of Education, University of Illinois.

Although the reviewers listed above have provided many constructive comments and suggestions, they were not asked to endorse the conclusions or recommendations nor did they see the final draft of the report before its release. The review of this report was overseen by Adam Gamoran, Wisconsin Center for Education Research, University of Wisconsin, and Caswell A. Evans, College of Dentistry, University of Illinois at Chicago. Appointed by the NRC, they were responsible for making certain that an independent examination of this report was carried out in accordance with institutional procedures and that all review comments were carefully considered. Responsibility for the final content of this report rests entirely with the authoring committee and the institution.

Christopher Edley, Jr., *Cochair*
Robert M. Hauser, *Cochair*
Committee on the Independent
Evaluation of DC Public Schools

Contents

SUMMARY 1

1 INTRODUCTION 11
   The City and Its Schools, 11
   The Committee's Charge and Its Work, 14
   References, 17

2 EDUCATION REFORM IN THE UNITED STATES 19
   Reform in Urban Districts, 21
   Mayoral Control, 23
   The Context of Reform, 25
   References, 27

3 THE DISTRICT OF COLUMBIA AND THE REFORM ACT:
   HISTORICAL OVERVIEW 31
   A History of Reform and Criticism, 31
   The Racial History of DC Schools, 33
   School Politics and the Legacy of Congressional Control, 36
   Weak Central Office Leadership and Capacity, 39
   Responses to the System's Problems, 41
   The Enactment of PERAA, 42
   References, 44

4 RESPONSES TO PERAA: INITIAL IMPLEMENTATION 47
   A New Structure, 48
   Mayoral Control: The Chancellor and the Budget, 48
   State Superintendent and State Board of Education, 52
   Department of Education and Deputy Mayor, 54
      The Ombudsman, 54
      Facilities, 55
      Structures for Charter Schools, 56
   Interagency Commission, 57
   Ongoing Questions, 58
   References, 60

5 STUDENT ACHIEVEMENT UNDER PERAA:
   FIRST IMPRESSIONS 63
   Student Achievement and Test Data, 64
   The Data Sources, 65
   Test Score Trends, 67
   Issues for Interpreting Test Scores, 77
      Evidence Needed for Conclusions of Causation, 77
      Looking Beyond Proficiency Rates, 82
      Disaggregating Test Results, 83
      Comparing Test Results, 85
   References, 86

6 SCHOOL QUALITY AND OPERATIONS UNDER PERAA:
   FIRST IMPRESSIONS 89
   Data—Looking Beyond Test Scores, 90
      Sources for This Chapter, 90
      The District's Data Collection Efforts, 91
   The DCPS Effective Schools Framework, 96
   Areas of District Responsibility, 98
      Quality of Personnel, 98
         Teachers, 98
         Principals and District Leaders, 99
         What Districts Can Do, 99
         Efforts in the District of Columbia, 100
      Quality of Classroom Teaching and Learning, 103
         The Role of Standards, 103
         Implementing Coordinated Standards, Curriculum, and
            Assessments, 104
         Efforts in the District of Columbia, 105

Serving Vulnerable Children and Youth, 108
  Beyond the School System, 109
  Students with Disabilities and English Language Learners, 109
  Efforts in the District of Columbia, 110
    Special Education, 110
    Other Vulnerable Youth, 110
Family and Community Engagement, 113
  Approaches to Engagement, 114
  Efforts in the District of Columbia, 114
Operations, Management, and Facilities, 116
  Measuring Performance, 117
  Efforts in the District of Columbia, 117
Conclusion, 119
References, 120

7   FROM IMPRESSIONS TO EVIDENCE: A PROGRAM FOR EVALUATION   129
A Framework for Evaluation, 130
  Element 1: Structure and Roles, 132
  Element 2: Strategies, 133
  Element 3: Conditions for Student Learning, 133
  Element 4: Outcomes, 134
  The Evaluation Goal, 135
  A Combination of Ongoing Indicators and In-Depth Studies, 135
    Ongoing Indicators, 135
    In-Depth Studies, 136
  Reporting, 138
An Example of Integrating Evaluation Activities: Improving Teacher Quality, 138
  Strategies, 139
  Ongoing Indicators, 140
    Teacher Quality, 142
    Recruitment, Retention, and Professional Support, 143
  In-Depth Studies, 143
Determining Priorities for Evaluation, 145
  Primary Responsibilities to Be Evaluated, 146
  Criteria for Setting Priorities, 149
Establishing Long-Term Evaluation Capacity, 151
  Evaluation Programs: Resources and Examples, 152
  The Committee's Goal, 156
References, 157

APPENDIXES

A	Public Community Forum Agenda and Summary	161
B	Student Achievement and Attainment Indicators Collected by DC and Three Other Districts	165
C	Education Data for the District of Columbia	169
D	Biographical Sketches of Committee Members	183

Summary

In 2007, the District of Columbia made a bold change in the way it governs public education with the goal of shaking up the system and bringing new energy to efforts to improve outcomes for students. The Public Education Reform Amendment Act (PERAA) shifted control of the city's public schools from an elected school board to the mayor, created a new state department of education, created the position of chancellor, and made other significant management changes. PERAA also mandated an independent, comprehensive, 5-year evaluation to determine "whether sufficient progress in public education has been achieved to warrant continuation of the provisions and requirements of this act or whether a new law, and a new system of education, should be enacted by the District government. . . ."

To plan that evaluation, the Committee on the Independent Evaluation of DC Schools was convened by the National Research Council in response to a request from the City Council of the District of Columbia. The committee was asked not to conduct the evaluation, but to provide initial guidance on the focus and structure of the required evaluation. The work included identifying available data and assessing its quality and utility; developing a preliminary set of indicators; engaging with various stakeholder groups, including civic leaders, parents, researchers, and national and local reform experts; and exploring the desirability, feasibility, and scope of the optional next phases of the evaluation.

This report documents the committee's plan for the evaluation. It lays out a plan for a comprehensive, long-term program of evaluation that is designed not only to examine short-term effects of the changes made under PERAA, but also to provide the District with a structure for continuous, independent monitoring of important features of its school system. The plan is based on the committee's review of preliminary data and on its conclusion that first impressions of the implementation of PERAA and its effects, though informative, are not sufficient as a basis for decisions about PERAA or continued improvement of the city's education system.

The committee agreed on several basic assumptions and goals that have guided our work. First, although many U.S. cities have undertaken significant reforms to change their schools and researchers have examined what they have done, there is no established model for evaluating a district involved in reform—or, for that matter, any district. Second, school districts are judged primarily on the academic achievement of their students, but achievement depends on how effectively a school district accomplishes its many responsibilities and pursues many valued educational outcomes. Third, we interpreted PERAA's requirement for an evaluation broadly: to establish for the residents and leaders of DC a sustainable ongoing program of evaluation that provides reliable information they can use to improve the school system continuously, regardless of future political or personnel changes. Last, the committee approached the most challenging part of its charge—to explore the effects of the reform legislation itself—by distinguishing among the *intent* of the reform, as articulated in the law; its *implementation*, that is, the actions taken by the DC Public Schools (DCPS) and other responsible city agencies; and its *effects* on student learning and other valued outcomes.

CONTEXT

PERAA is the latest in a long line of changes in the way the city's public schools are governed. Since 1804, there have been 17 different governance and administrative structures, and PERAA was the second new approach since 2000. Many of these changes were responses to concerns about students' academic performance, the quality of the schools and the teachers, and an ineffective central bureaucracy, as well as the perception that many DC residents were indifferent to the persistent problems.

The city's education problems have been intensified by a history of segregation, and the city continues to struggle with many challenges related to race, poverty, and geography. Those challenges include inequitable distribution of resources and supports to schools in the lowest-income sections of the city, which are largely black, tensions over demographic shifts that change the character of neighborhoods, and a strong charter school movement. They have made reform efforts more urgent while complicating the city's response to them.

Another factor in DC has been the city's distinctive political status as a small geographic area under the jurisdiction of the federal government.

Because DC is not part of any state and elected its first mayor and city council only in 1973, it does not have a long tradition of self-governance. The U.S. Congress retains considerable authority over its affairs and budget.

PERAA was a response in part to these historical circumstances, but it was also spurred by impressions of the effectiveness of reforms in other urban districts facing at least somewhat similar economic, social, and historical challenges. Districts in Boston, Chicago, Cincinnati, Minneapolis, and New York City (among others) have focused on the alignment of content and performance standards with curricula, instruction, and other aspects of the school system. They have used data to guide their decisions, emphasizing such goals as improved professional development for teachers and principals; more frequent formative assessments; and the development of a culture of learning and collaboration among teachers. These approaches are widely used and are supported by some promising evidence, but the research literature is not yet settled enough to provide firm guidance on best practices for district reform or evaluation.

Some districts have also focused on the governance of schools, and a few (e.g., Boston, Chicago, Cleveland, and New York City) have given their mayors control over the public schools. Such reforms are designed to "jolt" the system by changing dysfunctional institutional relationships and giving leaders new lines of authority and accountability. Evaluation of these governance reforms is critical to knowing what really works and what does not, but few cities have made this a priority, so there are neither clear exemplars nor substantial evidence to guide the District as it implements PERAA.

IMPLEMENTATION OF PERAA

The District of Columbia has made many changes called for in PERAA. Thoroughly documenting the city's efforts will be a critical component of the comprehensive evaluation the law requires, and until this is done, no firm conclusions should be drawn about how well the city has implemented PERAA and fulfilled its intentions. As a first step, however, we offer an outline of the city's response to PERAA.

The new structures mandated in PERAA have largely been put into place. The mayor now has responsibility for most key aspects of the school system, including appointment of a chancellor who establishes educational priorities, adopts curricula and assessments, and ensures that the schools are appropriately staffed and managed. Also in place are the Department of Education, the Deputy Mayor for Education, the Office of the State Superintendent of Education (OSSE), the State Board of Education, and the Public Charter School Board. Not currently in place are the Office of Ombudsman for Public Education (a position that had been filled but was later eliminated) and the comprehensive data system.

DCPS has also adopted strategies to meet the goals of PERAA. Among them are efforts intended to improve the quality of teachers, principals, and administrators, including a new system for evaluating teacher performance; a new teaching and learning framework, which describes the specific instructional practices the district has identified as most likely to promote student learning; and improvements to school facilities.

FIRST IMPRESSIONS OF THE DC SCHOOL SYSTEM UNDER PERAA

Student Achievement

Public attention frequently is focused on fluctuations in student achievement scores, in DC as in the rest of the nation. First impressions offer a mixed picture: in general, scores on the District of Columbia Comprehensive Assessment System (DC CAS) have continued on an upward trajectory (which began before PERAA was enacted), and they have flattened slightly during the most recent 2 school years. However, definitive conclusions about PERAA's effects cannot be drawn from these preliminary results for three major reasons:

1. The DC CAS is designed to measure students' mastery of specific academic skills, but determining whether and how the changes in district policies or strategies have contributed to those skills requires additional empirical evidence: the scores themselves do not provide evidence about what accounts for them.
2. The available scores are averaged across the entire student population, and do not provide information on the status or progress of specific groups: some may be making sharp gains while others are not.
3. Because DC is a highly mobile district and the student population changes every year, score fluctuations may be the result of changes in the characteristics of the students taking the test, rather than improvements or declines in students' knowledge and skills.

Thus, in order to draw any conclusions about the effect of PERAA on student achievement as measured by DC CAS, further study of patterns for types of schools, individual schools, grade levels, neighborhoods, wards, and population subgroups is needed, and this should include longitudinal studies of cohorts of students within the District.

Scores from the National Assessment of Educational Progress (NAEP) provide independent information about achievement trends in all 50 states and DC, and these results also suggest that, in general, DC students' performance has been improving. However, as with the DC CAS scores, more study is needed to understand the reasons for trends. Like DC CAS, NAEP does not account for changes in the demographics of the population, so it is not possible to tell from these scores alone whether the improvements are the result of demographic shifts rather than changes in educational policies, programs, or practices.

School Quality and Operations

Like any district, DC is responsible for setting high expectations for all students and providing them with the instruction and resources necessary to meet them. Test scores only provide evidence, partial at that, about one aspect of the system. A school system's responsibilities are more complicated, and can be categorized in five broad areas:

1. quality of personnel (teachers, principals, and others),
2. quality of classroom teaching and learning,
3. capacity to serve vulnerable children and youth,
4. promotion of family and community engagement, and
5. quality and equity of operations, management, and facilities.

The District seems to have made changes in these areas, but a comprehensive evaluation would be needed to determine whether, how, and where conditions are improving. The District is already collecting data on many of these functions, and a first step in the evaluation will be to systematically assess these measures, determine which will be useful for the evaluation program, and identify priorities for new data collection—a task that was beyond the resources of this committee.

FROM IMPRESSIONS TO EVIDENCE: AN EVALUATION PLAN

RECOMMENDATION 1 We recommend that the District of Columbia establish an evaluation program that includes long-term monitoring and public reporting of key indicators as well as a portfolio of in-depth studies of high-priority issues. The indicator system should provide long-term trend data to track how well the programs and structure of the city's public schools are working, the quality and implementation of key strategies undertaken to improve education, the conditions for student learning, and the capacity of the system to attain valued outcomes. The in-depth studies should build on indicator data. Both types of analysis should answer specific questions about each of the primary aspects of public education for which the District is responsible: personnel (teachers, principals, and others); classroom teaching and learning; vulnerable children and youth; family and community engagement; and operations, management, and facilities.

Figure S-1 depicts our proposed evaluation framework. It begins with the goals the district has set for itself, as shown in the horizontal box that appears at the top of the figure. The logic of this framework reflects the point that passing a law does not automatically result in increased student learning, reduced achievement gaps, increased graduation rates, or other valued outcomes. To achieve these outcomes, the new structures and relationships that PERAA mandated have to be established and working as intended; school system leaders have to have implemented strategies that are likely to be effective; those strategies have to be well implemented; and the conditions for student learning—such as the quality of school staff and instruction—have to have improved.

In addition to the elements of reform, the evaluation has to cover the broad areas of the school district's responsibility: see the shaded horizontal stripes that cut across the elements of reform in Figure S-2. In this elaboration of Figure S-1, the elements of reform and the broad evaluation questions pertaining to them are depicted in the vertical boxes, and the substantive areas of responsibility are depicted with shaded horizontal bands. This framework is designed to guide the evaluation so that it is comprehensive: even if resources limit the specific analyses that can be undertaken at a given time, use of the framework will ensure that the most important aspects of the system are examined.

The framework is a depiction of the primary components of reform and of the district's responsibilities. The basic questions to be asked under each of the four elements and across the five areas of responsibility will need to be answered using many different study designs, data collection methods, and types of analysis. Thus, the evaluation framework provides a guide to the kinds of information that are needed to fully inform policy makers and the public. The indicators—which should be developed in conjunction with OSSE and DCPS and members of the community—should provide long-term disaggregated trend data to track how well district roles and structures are working, the quality and implementation of key strategies undertaken to improve education, the conditions for student learning, and valued outcomes. The in-depth studies should draw from the indicators, as well as other data, to provide detailed answers to specific questions about key aspects of public education in the District.

It will be critical to establish stable indicators as soon as possible, supplementing and refining those the District is already collecting as needed; however, the program of focused evaluation studies will evolve over time as changes in the city's policies, challenges, and circumstances require. Many empirical questions are subsumed in the elements of reform and

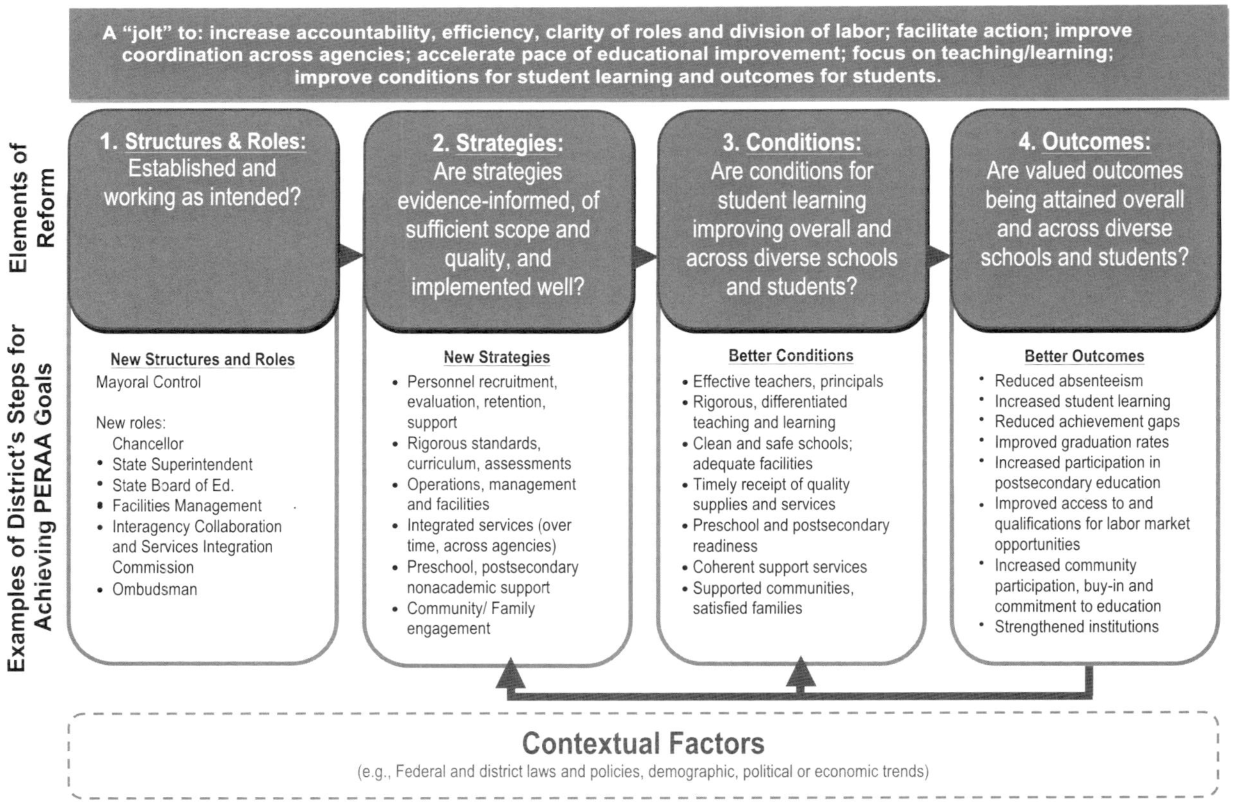

FIGURE S-1 A framework for evaluating DC public education under the Public Education Reform Amendment Act.

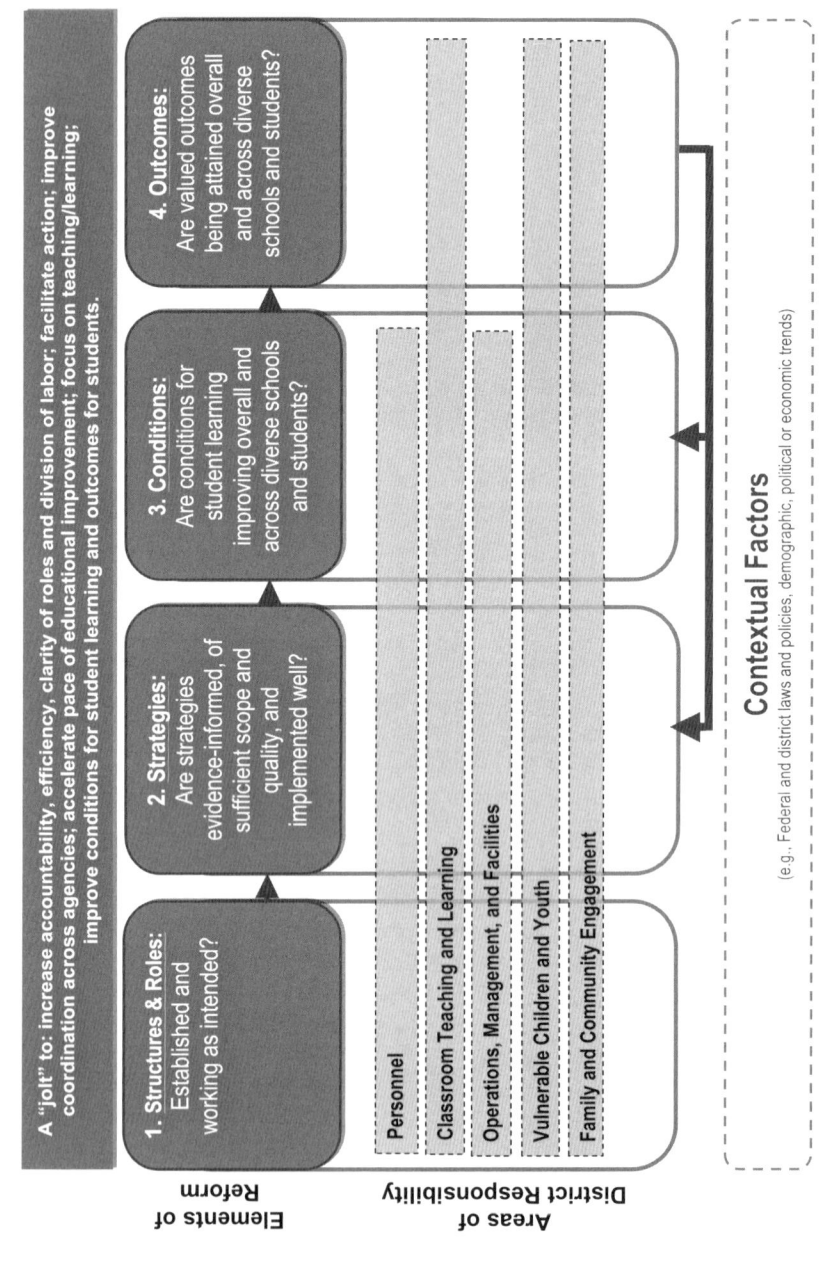

FIGURE S-2 Evaluation priorities in key areas of distinct responsibility.

the broad categories of district responsibility. The evaluators will look to District leaders and other members of the community to establish the priorities and available resources that will guide the choice of specific indicators and studies, and the long-term indicator system will build on data collection efforts already in place in the District. The evaluation needs to engage the perspectives, concerns, and needs of all who are part of and care about the system: students (and youth who are disconnected from school), families, educators, administrators, and the community. The key evaluation questions, the data used to answer them, and how these answers are shared and used need to be designed with the concerns and goals of the community in mind.

RECOMMENDATION 2 The Office of the Mayor of the District of Columbia should produce an annual report to the city on the status of the public schools, drawing on information produced by the District of Columbia Public Schools and other education agencies and by the independent evaluation program that includes

- summary and analysis of trends in regularly collected indicators,
- summary of key points from in-depth studies of target issues, and
- an appendix with complete data and analysis.

Building and maintaining a high-quality indicator system, designing studies that address pressing issues, and presenting and disseminating findings so that all stakeholders can act on them will require deliberate and skillful management. An independent evaluation program that is an ongoing source of objective information and analysis will be an invaluable resource for the city under changing political circumstances. To make such a program work, the District of Columbia will need to engage potential research partners and funders in planning and developing an infrastructure for ongoing independent evaluation of the city's public schools.

Urban districts face some of the most difficult challenges in U.S. public education, and many have pursued ambitious reforms. Valuable lessons have begun to emerge from their experiences; systematically evaluating these efforts and their effects is a critical part of education reform. Objective evidence derived from multiple sources of data is a tool for monitoring progress and guiding continuous improvement in a city's schools—and also for ensuring that their benefits can be sustained and replicated in other districts. It is our hope that this model will be of use to districts around the country.

1

Introduction

THE CITY AND ITS SCHOOLS

The nation's capital is a small city with big challenges. Home to the government of the richest and most powerful country on earth, the District of Columbia has a population of about 600,000 (excluding its ever widening suburban ring), which makes it roughly comparable in size to Boston and about 1/13th the size of New York City.[1] The fiscal 2010 operating budget for the city government was about $10 billion, and it employs more than 32,000 full-time staff.

Washington is a diverse city. Over half the residents are black, and almost one in five speaks a language other than English in the home. It is home to the nation's largest concentration of college-educated blacks, and black residents hold prominent leadership positions in corporations, universities, and federal, state, and municipal government agencies. However, blacks also make up the largest group of economically disadvantaged residents in the city.

Although median household income and the share of residents who are college educated are higher than national averages, poverty rates are also higher (17 percent compared to 13 percent nationally), and there is large variation in economic well-being by neighborhood. The city includes neighborhoods that have been impoverished for decades, extremely affluent sections similar to the most well-to-do suburbs of nearby Maryland

---

[1] The city of Washington, District of Columbia, is commonly referred to as Washington, the District, or simply DC, and we use all three names in this report. Where the word district is not capitalized, we are using it to refer to school districts in general.

and Virginia, and many in between. The most affluent section (the city's Ward 3) has a median household income that is almost 200 percent of the citywide average; in contrast, the poorest neighborhoods have incomes that are 37 percent below the citywide average. The phrases "east of the river" (the Anacostia) and "west of the park" (Rock Creek Park) are understood by DC residents as euphemisms for the city's enduring race and class divide, a divide mirrored in the city's public schools.

The city's most significant political peculiarity is that it was designated in the U.S. Constitution (Article One, Section 8) as a district under the jurisdiction of the federal government and is not part of any state. Until 1973, the city had no independent governing authority, with virtually all municipal functions under the control of the U.S. Congress. In that year the Home Rule Act granted the District limited governance authority, but Congress still retains considerable authority over its affairs and budget, and the city's elected Representative to Congress does not have a vote in that body. This situation has long been a flash point for DC residents, and many car owners have license plates with the slogan "taxation without representation," to echo Patrick Henry's famous phrase about tyranny.

The public policy arena under the purview of the DC government that is most fraught, most politically contested, and most socially complex is education. The city has a relatively small public school system, with about 45,000 students enrolled in traditional elementary and secondary schools and another 28,000 in public charter schools.[2] Formally segregated until 1954, the schools serve a city in which residential patterns continue to play a prominent role in the politics of education. In the 2006-2007 school year, for example, less than 33 percent of all white school-age children attended DC public schools (including charter schools), while more than 90 percent of all black and 88 percent of all Hispanic school-age children did so. Looking at it another way, white children made up over 13 percent of the city's school-age population, but accounted for only 5 percent of all students in public or charter schools.[3]

Reforms to the education system, then, inevitably evoke concerns about neighborhood cohesion, gentrification, and the power of commercial and economic development interests, as well as the potentially negative effects that change may have on the city's poor and minority populations.

Given the city's uniquely complicated historical, political, and economic history, the governance of the DC Public Schools (DCPS) has necessarily

---

[2] For contrast, New York City has more than 1 million children enrolled in public schools and about 40,000 in charter schools.

[3] For 2006-2007 (the latest year for which complete data are available), 3,521 of 11,298 white school-age children were in public or charter schools, 57,706 of 63,861 black children, and 7,130 of 8,017 Hispanic children (21st Century School Fund, Brookings Institution, and Urban Institute, 2008).

been significantly different from that of any other school district in the country. Rather than being one of a number of school districts governed by a state department of education, DCPS has been overseen by a changing combination of entities and individuals, including Congress and local officials. As summarized by two experts who have studied the system closely (Hannaway and Usdan, 2008, p. 116):

> In recent years, the Board of Education (both appointed and elected), a number of U.S. Senate and U.S. House of Representative committees, the DC City Council, DC Financial Control Board, a state education office, the mayor, the DC Chief Financial Officer, two charter school boards, many superintendents (appointed by different authorities), and unions have all played key roles in education policy making and school management. At almost any point in time, overlapping areas of responsibility provided all players with reason to blame each other when things went wrong, and they left none of the players with sufficient power to demand quality performance.

The school system is well known not only for its struggles with governance, but also for its students' persistently low average achievement, and particularly the achievement of poor and minority students. Although recent data from the National Assessment of Educational Progress (NAEP) show modest gains in student achievement for some DC students between 2007 and 2009, the district's average test performance historically has been poor, contributing to the system's dismal reputation for at least three decades.

Since state-by-state comparisons of student achievement on NAEP first became available in the 1990s, DC schools have performed at the low end of the scale; numerous reports prior to that time had also documented DC students' low average performance and other shortcomings. On the District's own assessments, average performance has fluctuated, although there have been pockets of excellence. DCPS has frequently been publicly criticized not only for its students' low achievement, but also for its poor financial management, dilapidated facilities, inadequate resources, and other failings. Mounting frustration about the quality of the public schools has led DC (like other cities confronting similar challenges) to approve 60 public charter schools, now serving roughly 28,000 students. Some local activists have urged an even more dramatic change by supporting school vouchers that can be used toward tuition costs at private schools (District of Columbia Charter School Board, 2010). As this report goes to press, there is a movement in the U.S. Congress to restore the city's voucher program, which was suspended in 2006.

It was in this context that the DC City Council passed the Public Education Reform Amendment Act (PERAA) of 2007, which established mayoral control of the city's public schools and a state department of education and instituted other significant management changes (Office of the Chief Financial Officer, 2007). PERAA also mandated an independent, comprehensive, 5-year evaluation to determine "whether sufficient progress in public education has been achieved to warrant continuation of the provisions and requirements of this act or whether a new law, and a new system of education, should be enacted by the District government . . ." (p. 9).

THE COMMITTEE'S CHARGE AND ITS WORK

In response to PERAA's requirement for an independent evaluation, the DC City Council, with the concurrence and cooperation of the mayor, the chancellor of DCPS, and the new State Superintendent of Education (a position created by PERAA), turned to the National Research Council (NRC) of the National Academies. This report, the first in what is expected to be a series issued during the next 5 years, is the product of an expert panel convened by the NRC in response to that request.

Although the design and oversight of an evaluation is an unusual assignment for the NRC, which does not routinely conduct program evaluations or address the circumstances of a single jurisdiction, the institution recognized both the special circumstances motivating the request and the extraordinary opportunity the initiative represents. The financial and moral support of local business and civic leaders reinforced the NRC's vision that the initiative could provide a valuable contribution to the ongoing public debate about public education in the District.

The committee's charge for the first phase of the project was not to conduct an evaluation but to design a potential multiyear, multiphase evaluation of the District of Columbia Public Schools. The committee was asked to identify available data and assess its quality and utility; develop a preliminary set of indicators; engage with various stakeholder groups, including researchers, national and local reform experts, and civic leaders; and explore the desirability, feasibility, and scope of the optional next phases of the initiative. The committee has aspired to provide as comprehensive a response as possible, and our interpretation of the charge is based on a number of basic assumptions, shown in Box 1-1.

The committee addresses all aspects of its charge in this report, but we do so with varying degrees of analytical depth as allowed by existing and accessible information. Constraints of budget, time, and data availability limited what we could accomplish. Indeed, our experience developing this foundational evaluation plan demonstrated that answering complex questions about a rapidly changing urban school reform requires a sustainable program that takes into account ongoing community input.

> **BOX 1-1**
> **Committee's Assumptions**
>
> In carrying out its work and writing this report, the committee made four fundamental assumptions about an evaluation program. We believe that an evaluation with these characteristics is applicable not only for the District of Columbia Public Schools, but also for many other school districts.
>
> 1. Conscientious evaluation of a school district with an ambitious reform program requires comprehensive thinking about its goals and its many responsibilities to students, the education workforce, and the community.
> 2. Readily available quantitative data, such as standardized test scores, provide one source of valuable information for an evaluation, but they do not substitute for a thorough examination of important questions about the overall performance of a public school system. A significantly wider range of information is required.
> 3. Although PERAA requires a specific evaluation, we interpret its purpose more broadly: to establish for the residents and leaders of DC a sustainable ongoing program of evaluation that provides reliable information they can use to continually improve the school system.
> 4. Although much attention has been focused on the actions of the mayor and chancellor who began the process of implementing PERAA, neither the provisions of the law nor their actions are likely to provide the principal explanations for all the changes in teaching, learning, and student progress. Thus, an independent evaluation program, designed to provide stable, ongoing information, is needed to track and analyze long-term, meaningful changes in the system. It should be robust and resilient in order to withstand whatever personnel and political changes may occur in the city and the school system and provide a stable basis for evidence-informed decision making.

We learned a great deal about the circumstances in the DC school system from our review of preliminary data, but the committee had neither the time nor the resources to conduct a thorough analysis of available data or to collect new data. However, even a more systematic analysis of the information that is available would likely not provide a sufficient basis for conclusions about the effects of PERAA or about how well the system is faring more generally. Moreover, even as this first report goes to press, the situation in DC has changed significantly from when the committee first met: although much attention was focused as this project began on the decisions of the first mayor and chancellor who served under PERAA, both offices have since changed hands.

Thus, our focus was the development of a plan for a sustained, independent evaluation program. We hope that this plan will be of use to other districts but it was developed specifically for Washington, DC. Our report begins with a review of the historical background and context in which PERAA was enacted and a discussion of what we have learned about the public education system in the city—all of which influenced our plan for the evaluation.

Planning for the committee's work began with a public meeting in July 2009, which approximately 80 people attended. Many spoke about what they saw as the most important educational outcomes for DCPS. Perspectives were offered by DC government officials (the chair of the city council, the deputy mayor, the chancellor and the state superintendent all spoke), as well as civic, business, and labor leaders, and DCPS parents. Expert input was also obtained from education researchers and evaluators.

The committee was formally appointed in early 2010, and it held three meetings that year, as well as a public forum through which we again sought the views of stakeholders from across the city. At that forum, principals and school administrators; teachers; charter school representatives; special education providers; education providers for children and youth; representatives of colleges, universities, and job training programs; students; and parents were asked to discuss the education issues they viewed as most important for the city.

We also commissioned two background papers and have sought input from researchers, DCPS officials, national and local experts in education reform, civic leaders, and members of the school community. On behalf of the committee, staff attended DCPS hearings and community meetings. We have also reviewed much of the published literature on recent reforms in the District, as well as other relevant research on reforms elsewhere and have examined available accounts of developments in the history of PERAA.

The primary result of the committee's work is the design for a comprehensive and continuing program for evaluating the District's schools. Our recommended design is presented and discussed in Chapter 7. We note the logic that leads us to this conclusion. In general terms we differentiate among the *intent* of the reform (as articulated in the law), its *implementation* (actions taken by DCPS and the city government), and its *effects* (on student learning and other valued outcomes). Though questions about the reform's effects on learning are perhaps the most important and the ones with greatest long-term impact, they also require the most data, the most rigorous analysis, and the most patience.

The structure of this report reflects that logic and those three elements. We begin in the next two chapters with the background needed to understand the District of Columbia's schools and the intents underlying the passage of PERAA. Chapter 2 provides a brief overview of education reform nationally; Chapter 3 provides the historical context for PERAA. Chapter 4 describes the city's response thus far (up to the end of 2010, when this report went into final production) to the requirements of PERAA, focusing on its implementation. The next two chapters provide a preliminary look at the very limited evidence that is available about effects on learning and other valued outcomes: Chapter 5 looks at student achievement, and Chapter 6 considers a wide array of other issues that need to be considered in any evaluation. In both these chapters we offer the committee's cautions and caveats about how to interpret this kind of early evidence. Chapter 7 presents the committee's consensus regarding the fragility of existing information as a basis for reaching summative judgments—positive or negative—about the effectiveness of the reform, and our recommendation for a robust, sustainable, and independent program of evaluation and research.

REFERENCES

District of Columbia Public Charter School Board. (2010). *SY2009 to 2010 Charter School Profile*. Available: http://www.dcpubliccharter.com/Enrollment-and-Demographics/SY2009-to-2010-Charter-School-Profile.aspx [accessed July 2010].

Hannaway, J., and Usdan, M.D. (2008). Mayoral takeover in the District of Columbia. In W.L. Boyd, C.T. Kerchner, and M. Blyth (Eds.), *The Transformation of Great American School Districts: How Big Cities Are Reshaping Public Education* (pp. 113-188). Cambridge, MA: Harvard Education Press.

Office of the Chief Financial Officer. (2007). *Public Education Reform Amendment Act of 2007*. Washington, DC: West Group.

21st Century School Fund, Brookings Institution, and Urban Institute. (2008). *Quality Schools, Healthy Neighborhoods, and the Future of DC, Policy Report*. Washington, DC: Author. Available: http://www.21csf.org/csf-home/publications/QualitySchoolsResearchReport/QualitySchoolsPolicyReport9-18-08.pdf [accessed March 2011].

2

Education Reform in the United States

The history of efforts to reform education is likely almost as long as the history of schools and teaching, but the last few decades have been characterized by particularly active reform efforts in the United States (see, e.g., Tyack and Cuban, 1995). Dire (if possibly exaggerated) warnings about declining academic achievement in the 1980s (see, e.g., Cremin, 1990) inspired a flowering of research as well as ongoing public dialogue about ways to improve teaching and learning.

Standards-based reform—the establishment of rigorous content and performance standards for what students should know and be able to do and the alignment of curriculum, assessment, and other elements of the system to those standards—has become an organizing principle for most states' and districts' efforts to improve, as well as for federal programs and policy, beginning with the Improving America's Schools Act of 1994 (see, e.g., Goertz, 2007; Hamilton, Stecher, and Yuan, 2008; Smith and O'Day, 1991; Zavadsky, 2009). The Improving America's Schools Act of 1994 was the first to focus on standards-based reform, though that approach probably came to most people's attention when the 2001 No Child Left Behind (NCLB) Act was passed. It is central to more recent initiatives, such as the Race to the Top grant initiative.

Standards-based reform is an idea that has caught on more thoroughly than perhaps any other single strategy in the history of U.S. public schools. A combination of research, experience, and intuition about school governance and the prospects for systemic improvement have made it appealing to educators and policy makers alike. They find it compelling because it addresses concerns that a major obstacle to improvement is the fragmented nature of school governance and the frayed connections among major school functions—curriculum, instruction, assessment, and professional development. Standards-based reforms called for a more centralized approach to a school system. Though it can be argued that the absence of centralized authority has given U.S. schools an advantage in capacity to innovate and to respond to the needs of a fast-growing and diverse population (see, e.g., Cremin, 1990; Feuer, 2006), it is also clear that large numbers of students are still not meeting rigorous standards, at least as defined by current national and international benchmarks.

At the core of the standards movement is the focus on holding states, districts, and schools accountable for their students' achievement—in part by monitoring their performance using assessments aligned with rigorous standards.[1] This kind of accountability entails a commitment that is relatively new in the United States: to hold every student to high standards and to provide every student with the curricula and instruction necessary to meet them. Expectations for young people have evolved significantly over the past 100 years. At the beginning of the 1900s, only about 10 percent of students graduated from high school, yet by the second half of the century the prevalent view was that all students should not only be expected to graduate from high school, but also to aspire to college (see National Research Council, 2001). The pattern of participation in education for the second half of the 20th century was what has led some scholars to label it as "the human capital century" (Goldin and Katz, 2008). It is worth noting that this massive expansion in access began decades before any even vaguely similar expansion was implemented in most European and Asian democracies.

The idea that all students should be held to the same high standards was put to the test as a growing body of achievement data—from both the National Assessment of Educational Progress and state assessments—documented the persistent disparity in academic performance among students with different racial, ethnic, and socioeconomic backgrounds. The legal responses to these disparities have ranged from disputes over racial preferences in selection processes and the use of busing to desegregate schools to numerous school finance lawsuits, such as *Abbott v. Burke*, in which the New Jersey court ruled that the state had failed in its constitutional obligation to provide a "thorough and efficient" education to students in poor, urban school districts. The 1985 ruling led to a requirement that the state implement a variety of reforms to ensure equitable distribution

---

[1] For more information on Race to the Top, see http://osse.dc.gov/seo/frames.asp?doc=/seo/lib/seo/cos/race_to_the_top/dc_rttt_section_vi_application.pdf [accessed November 2010]. For discussions of content and performance standards and their influence on schools, see, among others, Stecher and Vernez (2010) and Goertz and Duffy (2003).

of educational resources among its districts and schools (Education Law Center, 2010).

Jurisdictions in all parts of the country have struggled to develop ways to truly hold all students to high standards while also meeting a wide range of needs. Students with disabilities, students who are not fluent in English, students who start school without having had high-quality preschool preparation, students who are living in poverty or in struggling families and neighborhoods—all require support if they are to learn to high standards. The NCLB requirement to report disaggregated data on student achievement further solidified the national commitment to understanding and attempting to close the achievement gap, and it has codified into law the pursuit of equity as a high-priority goal of public education.

REFORM IN URBAN DISTRICTS

Urban school districts, which frequently have high concentrations of students at risk for school failure, are at the forefront in the challenge of defining and ensuring equity, and many have also been pioneers in school reform. Persistently low levels of achievement, struggles to recruit and retain both effective teachers and principals and other leaders, and the needs of families in high-poverty neighborhoods are among the challenges that face these districts. Recent attention to seemingly chronic district-level failings has highlighted the importance of considering the advantages of district-level reforms. A focus on this level makes it possible to examine governance structures, central office performance, and districtwide policies and management—all of which make districts "potent sites and sources of educational reform" (Hightower et al., 2002, p. 1).

Studies of district management of resources and personnel, as well as case studies of the culture of school districts, have contributed to understanding of the important role of school districts in reform (see, e.g., Chait, 2009; Elmore, 2004; Loeb and Reininger, 2004; McLaughlin and Talbert, 2006; Moon, 2007; Murnane and Steele, 2007; Rivikin et al., 2005; Spillane, 1998; Steele et al., 2010; Stotko et al., 2007; Wenglinsky, 2000). Districts are also appealing to study because it is at this level that promising reforms can be brought to scale. Though districts are complex—and each has its own characteristics and challenges—they also have the power to implement more comprehensive reforms than are possible at the single-school level. Since the reform movement took hold, districts have also learned from one another, and they have explored a range of approaches to building on the standards-based approach as they work to bring about improvements in even the most challenged schools. The research that has explored the strategies they have used has begun to identify factors that have been effective.

Much of the research on district-level school reform consists of case studies. For example, a study of three districts that worked with the Institute for Learning to implement systemic reforms[2] found that although the districts' experiences and results varied, they demonstrated the possibilities for using data effectively to solve problems and make other valuable changes (Marsh, 2002; Marsh et al., 2005).[3] However, limited staff, time, and money have constrained the progress these districts could make.

For example, a study of seven urban districts[4] that received grants from the Pew Charitable Trusts to support implementation of standards-based systemic reform concluded that high standards for students, assessments, and accountability by themselves are not sufficient to produce significant improvement (David and Shields, 2001). These elements have to be accompanied by explicit guidance to teachers for implementing an equally ambitious curriculum and by explicit expectations regarding instructional practices.

Another study documented the paths taken by five urban districts[5] that have won the prestigious prize for urban education awarded by the Broad Foundation (Zavadsky, 2009). To select its winners, the Broad Foundation analyzes a range of district data, including student achievement results, graduations rates, and district management and performance data.[6] The study found that the five winners shared a long-term commitment to the reforms they adopted, and that all have "[clear definitions of] what students are to know and be able to do; teachers who feel supported and respected; and students who progress through seamless educational programs" (Zavadsky, 2009, p. xxi).

Another case study examined results for districts that pursued a "data-driven reform model" developed by the Center for Data-Driven Reform in Education (Slavin et al., 2010, p. 4), in which data are used to guide

---

[2]Systemic reform is a term used to describe one of the central aspects of standards-based reform, the idea that all of the components of the public education system (e.g., instruction, assessment, curriculum, professional development) must be thoughtfully planned so that they are integrated and can work together. The term highlights the contrast between a comprehensive, or systemic, approach and efforts to tackle one area of improvement at a time (O'Day and Smith, 1993).

[3]For more information on the Institute for Learning, see http://ifl.lrdc.pitt.edu/ifl/ [accessed March 2011].

[4]The districts were Christina, Delaware; Community District 2, New York City; Fayette County, Kentucky; Pittsburgh, Pennsylvania; Portland, Oregon; San Diego, California; and Yonkers, New York.

[5]The districts were Aldine Independent School District, Texas; Boston, Massachusetts; Garden Grove Unified School District, California; Long Beach Unified School District, California; and Norfolk, Virginia.

[6]For more information on the foundation, see http://www.broadfoundation.org/ [accessed March 2011].

districts and schools in improving. The study concluded that the use of data on student learning, students' demographic characteristics, school processes, and teacher perceptions allowed educators to identify problems and use professional development, and other interventions to solve them. The study also concluded that the collection and interpretation of data were not sufficient to yield improvement—it was necessary for schools and districts to follow up with specific actions designed to meet clearly defined goals.

In short, the literature on district reform suggests that a district can be a strong agent for reform and that districts that have achieved improvements share several attributes, such as those identified by Marsh (2002) and Marsh et al. (2005)[7]:

- a systemwide approach in which policies and practices are aligned;
- strong support and professional development for both teachers and administrators;
- clearly defined expectations for students and teachers, combined with a strong emphasis on improvement; and
- reliance on data to support instructional decisions and for accountability.

Boston, Chicago, Cincinnati, Minneapolis, and New York City are all examples of districts that have adopted rigorous content and performance standards and have aligned the curricula, instruction, and other aspects of their systems to those standards (Elmore, 2004). They have used data, including comprehensive student information management systems, to guide their decisions and have emphasized professional development for teachers and principals. They have relied on frequent formative assessments.[8] They have also developed a culture of learning and collaboration among teachers. But districts have taken very different routes even to making these sorts of changes—and these differences reflect marked differences in their circumstances.

MAYORAL CONTROL

Changing the way districts are governed, i.e., rethinking basic managerial and political structures, has long been a linchpin of reform. Policy makers have assumed that new structures of authority at the top of the

---

[7] We emphasize that defining success or improvement for an entire district is not a straightforward task, an issue we discuss in Chapters 5-7.

[8] Formative assessments are those that are designed primarily to provide immediate feedback to both teachers and students about what has been learned. They can be contrasted with summative assessments, which are usually designed primarily to provide more generalized information about student performance to administrators and policy makers.

system will facilitate the improvements that are needed to raise student achievement. Changes in governance structures alter institutional relationships, establish new lines of authority and accountability, influence the way resources are allocated, and shift patterns of influence over key policy and programmatic decisions (March and Olsen, 1989, 1995; Mazzoni, 1991; Meier, 2004). Such governance reforms focus on authority for decisions about finances, personnel, and curriculum, as well as changes in lines of accountability—who is accountable to whom for school operations and student outcomes. Reformers who have used governance structures as instruments of change believe that institutions can become calcified over time, as those who benefit from them seek to preserve the status quo (see, e.g., Henig and Rich, 2004). Consequently, reform may require that school district governance be "jolted" through new institutional rules and structures.

Mayoral control is one sort of jolt that has been tried in Boston, Chicago, Cleveland, New York City, and now, Washington, DC. Each of these cities has given the mayor increased formal authority over the school system through the power to appoint school board members and, in some cases, the district superintendent or chief executive officer of the school system. In each case, the city has decided that centralized authority will allow district leaders to better coordinate across units; recruit and manage personnel; impose tighter control over finances; and provide more equal learning opportunities for students. These cities have hoped the new structures will also solve problems associated with entrenched interest groups who gain power through school board elections in which relatively few people vote. Reformers believe that the lines of accountability will be clearer because responsibility for the schools' performance will ultimately rest with one visible official with a broad-based electoral constituency.

Although the exact form that mayoral control has taken has varied considerably, several managerial approaches have been common. In each case, reformers have emphasized the use of data in decision making and have structured accountability systems around measures of school and student performance. The extent to which curricular decisions are centralized or delegated to individual schools varies, but these systems share a focus on the professional competence of the teaching force as a critical element, and they stress the primacy of teachers in their reform strategies. Cities with mayoral control have also sought to mobilize a constituency much wider than those directly employed by or associated with the schools, so a whole community will share a stake in the public schools (Henig and Rich, 2004; Hess, 2008; Viteritti, 2009).

Researchers have begun to examine the effects of mayoral control. Most recently, a study of nine cities that implemented new school governance models was conducted by the Institute on Education Law and Policy, Rutgers University. The study found that these approaches (which included mayoral control and other models) resulted in greater efficiency and reduced corruption, and they also helped the cities gain significant funding boosts through private philanthropy and federal support (Institute on Education Law and Policy, Rutgers University, 2010).[9] The study also concluded that, while changes in governance may have a positive or neutral effect on student achievement, governance is likely not the most important factor in district change. A study of mayoral control in New York City (Hill, 2011) also noted the importance of distinguishing between a structural change in governance and the leadership approach with which it is implemented. In general, these studies have shown that "structure is not a solution; it is an enabler" (Viteritti, 2009, p. 9; see also Allen and Mintrom, 2010; Carl, 2009; Henig and Rich, 2004). That is, altered political arrangements can bring about important changes, such as new institutional relationships and lines of authority and accountability, and new ways of allocating resources. However, they do not, by themselves, bring about educational improvements.

THE CONTEXT OF REFORM

Ideas about mayoral control, charter schools, vouchers, privatization of instructional services through for-profit firms, and other managerial innovations reflect the continuation of a long-standing American quest to solve a fundamental dilemma: how to reconcile the nation's democratic ideals, its insistence on high academic standards, and its belief in the virtues of economic efficiency and productivity. Simply stated, Americans have never accepted the notion that high standards *for all* is, in any sense, an oxymoron. As the preeminent historian of American education observed (Cremin, 1990, p. 43):

> [I]f there is a crisis in American schooling it is . . . the crisis inherent in balancing [a] tremendous variety of demands Americans have made on their schools and colleges—of crafting curricula that take account of the needs of a modern society at the same time that they make provision for the extraordinary diversity of America's young people. . . .

In recent years, debates over access, efficiency, and inclusion have become refocused as Americans struggle to understand and cope with an increasingly complex global and domestic environment. Some people ask whether schools will be valued as a public good and their legitimacy measured by their capacity to educate students according to the demands of

---

[9]The cities in the Rutgers study were Baltimore; Boston; Chicago; Cleveland; Detroit; Hartford, Connecticut; New York; Philadelphia; and Washington, DC.

informed and active citizenship. Others ask whether schools reflect a more private definition and serve as training grounds for business, the labor market, and the self-interest instincts of an advanced capitalist system. Inevitably these questions evoke an especially sensitive question relevant to reform in large cities: Can the political organization and control of school systems be decoupled from the processes of urban neighborhood revitalization?

For some observers of and participants in efforts to improve urban schooling, "reform" brings a potentially unacceptable risk—exacerbating the vulnerabilities of black, Hispanic/Latino, and poor students—especially if the reform is accompanied by the gentrification of resource-poor neighborhoods that are home to those students. According to one characterization of this issue, developers use schools as the initial and critical site for boosting urban real estate values. Middle- and upper-income, mostly white, residents relocate to newly upgraded urban centers, and public housing is often abandoned, pushing poor black and Hispanic/Latino residents out of central cities (Fenwick, 2006).

In this scenario, school systems that serve high percentages of black, Hispanic/Latino, and poor students face at least three particular challenges: (1) from the perspective of real estate developers, central city schools are situated near valuable underdeveloped land; (2) from the perspective of the school district, these schools are underperforming and desperately need fiscal resources to address chronic deficiencies; and (3) from the perspective of parents with students in those schools, frustration with the inadequacies of the schools serving their children is at an all time high, and they are desperate for change (Fenwick, 2006; Lipman and Haines, 2007).

There are conflicting views about these issues and the empirical evidence regarding them is thin. However, the existence of the perception that market-driven reforms may impose severe downside risks for some communities is an important element in the complex politics of schools and schooling. It is worth noting that although it has long been argued that local control of public schools empowers parents and community residents, this empowerment has rarely occurred in poor, black and Hispanic/Latino communities (Henig et al., 1999). Some researchers suggest that political insiders sometimes short circuit the intended benefits to schools and communities, and that there is frequently a complicated racial dimension to this scenario (Henig et al., 1999). Systemic reform has not garnered much grassroots support or enthusiasm among lower- and middle-income black parents whose children attend urban schools, who often view reform initiatives as uninformed by their community and disconnected from the best interests of their children (Lipman and Haines, 2007; Vaught, 2009; Weil, 2009). These parents and community members often point to school closings as "proof" that school reform is not in their interests. Again, although there is no empirical evidence to support this claim, the perception can be strong enough to influence even the best-intentioned reforms. As districts pursue reform, they are eager to know what has worked well in other places—and what accounts for the gains that are observed. Many districts have seen periods of apparent progress followed by periods when improvement seems to stall. Researchers have raised questions about the inferences to be drawn from test scores—the most easily available measures of progress (see Chapter 5). And because districts have such broad responsibilities they may make strong progress in one area—say, improving outcomes for English language learners—while other problems, such as dropout rates, remain unsolved.

Reformers operate in an intensely political atmosphere. Their actions are scrutinized by a public that wants results. Tensions and suspicions contribute to community distrust and inertia, more so when reform is perceived as having been externally orchestrated and when its outcomes are perceived to benefit new urban residents and to hurt poor, black, and Hispanic/Latino residents. It would be naïve to expect even the most sophisticated system of research and evaluation to resolve all such political and policy issues (Cartwright, 2007), but it would be even more cynical to assume that good data and solid analysis cannot contribute usefully to improved education for all children.

REFERENCES

Allen, A., and Mintrom, M. (2010). Responsibility and school governance. *Educational Policy,* 24(3), 439-464.
Carl, J. (2009). Good politics is good government: The troubling history of mayoral control of the public schools in twentieth-century Chicago. *American Journal of Education,* 115(2), 305-336.
Cartwright, N. (2007). *Hunting Causes and Using Them: Approaches in Philosophy and Economics.* Cambridge, UK: Cambridge University Press.
Chait, R. (2009). *Ensuring Effective Teachers for All Students: Six State Strategies for Attracting and Retaining Effective Teachers in High-Poverty and High-Minority Schools.* Washington, DC: Center for American Progress.
Cremin, L.A. (1990). *Popular Education and Its Discontents.* New York: Harper & Row.
David, J.L., and Shields, P.M. (2001). *When Theory Hits Reality: Standards-Based Reform in Urban Districts: Final Narrative Report.* Available: http://policyweb.SRI.com/cep/publications/pewfinal.pdf [accessed March 2011].
Education Law Center. (2010). *About Abbott v. Burke.* Available: http://www.edlawcenter.org/ELCPublic/AbbottvBurke/AboutAbbott.htm [accessed October 2010].
Elmore, R.F. (2004). *School Reform from Inside Out: Policy, Practice and Performance.* Cambridge, MA: Harvard Education Press.
Fenwick, L.T. (2006). *Putting Schools and Community on the Map: Linking School Reform, Neighborhood Revitalization, and Community Building.* Atlanta, GA: Enterprise Community Partners.

Feuer, M.J. (2006). *Moderating the Debate: Rationality and the Promise of American Education.* Cambridge, MA: Harvard Education Press.

Goertz, M.E. (2007). *Standards-Based Reform: Lessons from the Past, Directions for the Future.* Paper presented at the Clio at the Table: A Conference on the Uses of History to Inform and Improve Education Policy, Brown University, Providence, RI.

Goertz, M., and Duffy, M. (2003). Mapping the landscape of high-stakes testing and accountability programs. *Theory into Practice, 42*(1), 4-11.

Goldin, C.D., and Katz, L.F. (2008). *The Race Between Education and Technology.* Cambridge, MA: Belknap Press.

Hamilton, L.S., Stecher, B.M., and Yuan, K. (2008). *Standards-Based Reform in the United States: History, Research, and Future Directions.* Washington, DC: Center on Education Policy.

Henig, J.R., and Rich, W.C. (2004). *Mayors in the Middle.* Princeton, NJ: Princeton University Press.

Henig, J.R., Hula, R.C., Orr, M., and Pedescleaux, D.S. (1999). *The Color of School Reform: Race, Politics, and the Challenge of Urban Education.* Princeton, NJ: Princeton University Press.

Hess, F.M. (2008). Looking for leadership: Assessing the case for mayoral control of urban school systems. *American Journal of Education, 114,* 219-245.

Hightower, A.M., Knapp, M., Marsh, J., and McLaughlin, M.J. (2002). The district role in instructional renewal: Setting the stage for dialogue. In A.M. Hightower, M. Knapp, J. Marsh, and M.J. McLaughlin (Eds.), *School Districts and Instructional Renewal* (pp. 1-6). New York: Teachers College Press.

Hill, P. (2011). *Leadership and Governance in New York City School Reform.* New York: American Institutes for Research.

Improving America's Schools Act of 1994. (1994). Report of the U.S. Congress House Committee on Education and Labor, House of Representatives on H.R. 6 together with minority, supplemental, and additional views (including cost estimate of the Congressional Budget Office), became P.L.103-382 October 20, 103rd Congress.

Institute on Education Law and Policy, Rutgers University. (2010). *Governance and Urban School Improvement: Lessons for New Jersey from Nine Cities.* Available: http://nsrc.newark.rutgers.edu/publications/research-reports-/43-governance-and-urban-school-improvement-lessons-for-new-jersey-from-nine-cities-.html [accessed March 2011].

Lipman, P., and Haines, N. (2007). From accountability to privatization and African American exclusion. *Educational Policy, 21*(3), 471-502.

Loeb, S., and Reininger, M. (2004). *Public Policy and Teacher Labor Markets. What We Know and Why It Matters.* East Lansing: Education Policy Center at Michigan State University.

March, J.G., and Olsen, J.P. (1989). *Rediscovering Institutions: The Organizational Basis of Politics.* New York: Free Press.

March, J.G., and Olsen, J.P. (1995). *Democratic Governance.* New York: Free Press.

Marsh, J. (2002). How districts relate to states, schools, and communities: A review of emerging literature. In A.M. Hightower, M. Knapp, J. Marsh, and M. McLaughlin (Eds.), *School Districts and Instructional Renewal* (pp. 25-40). New York: Teachers College Press.

Marsh, J.A., Kerr, K.A., Ikemoto, G.S., Darilek, H., Suttorp, M., Zimmer, R.W., et al. (2005). *The Role of Districts in Fostering Instructional Improvement Lessons from Three Urban Districts Partnered with the Institute for Learning.* Santa Monica, CA: RAND Corporation.

Mazzoni, T.L. (1991). Analyzing state school policymaking: An arena model. *Educational Evaluation and Policy Analysis, 13*(2), 115-138.

McLaughlin, M.W., and Talbert, J.E. (2006). *Building School-Based Teacher Learning Communities: Professional Strategies to Improve Student Achievement (Series on School Reform).* New York: Teachers College Press.

Meier, K.J. (2004). Structure, politics and policy: The logic of mayoral control. In J.R. Henig and W.C. Rich (Eds.), *Mayors in the Middle* (pp. 221-248). Princeton, NJ: Princeton University Press.

Moon, B. (2007). *Research Analysis: Attracting, Developing and Retaining Effective Teachers: A Global Overview of Current Policies and Practices.* Paris, France: United Nations Educational, Scientific and Cultural Organization.

Murnane, R.J., and Steele, J.L. (2007). What is the problem? The challenge of providing effective teachers for all children. *The Future of Children, 17*(1), 15-43.

National Research Council. (2001). *Understanding Dropouts: Statistics, Strategies, and High-Stakes Testing.* Committee on Educational Excellence and Testing Equity. A. Beatty, U. Neisser, W.T. Trent, and J.P. Heubert (Eds.). Board on Testing and Assessment, Center for Education. Division of Behavioral and Social Sciences and Education. Washington, DC: National Academy Press.

No Child Left Behind Act of 2001. U.S. Congress House Committee on Education and the Workforce. H.R. 1 became P.L. 107-110, 107th Congress. (2001).

O'Day, J.A., and Smith, M.S. (1993). Systemic reform and educational opportunity. In S.H. Fuhrman (Ed.), *Designing Coherent Education Policy: Improving the System* (pp. 250-312). San Francisco: Jossey-Bass.

Rivikin, S.G., Hanushek, E.A., and Kain, J.F. (2005). Teachers, schools, and academic achievement. *Econometrica, 73*(2), 417-458.

Slavin, R.E., Holmes, G., Madden, N.A., Chamberlain, A., and Cheung, A. (2010). *Effects of a Data-Driven District-Level Reform Model.* Baltimore, MD: Johns Hopkins University Center for Data-Driven Reform in Education.

Smith, M.S., and O'Day, J.A. (1991). *Systemic School Reform.* London, England: Falmer.

Spillane, J.P. (1998). The progress of standards-based reforms and the nonmonolithic nature of the local school district: Organizational and professional considerations. *American Educational Research Journal, 35*(1), 33-63.

Stecher, B.M., and Vernez, G. (2010). *Reauthorizing No Child Left Behind: Facts and Recommendations.* Santa Monica, CA: RAND Corporation.

Steele, J.L., Hamilton, L., and Stecher, B. (2010). *Incorporating Student Performance Measures into Teacher Evaluation Systems.* Washington, DC: Center for American Progress.

Stotko, E.M., Ingram, R., and Beaty-O'Ferrall, M.E. (2007). Promising strategies for attracting and retaining successful urban teachers. *Urban Education, 42*(1), 30-51.

Tyack, D., and Cuban, L. (1995). *Tinkering Toward Utopia: A Century of Public School Reform.* Cambridge, MA: Harvard University Press.

Vaught, S.E. (2009). The color of money: School funding and the commodification of black children. *Urban Education, 44*(5), 545-570.

Viteritti, J.P. (2009). *When Mayors Take Charge.* Washington, DC: Brookings Institution Press.

Weil, D. (2009). *The Charter School Movement: History, Politics, Policies, Economics and Effectiveness.* New York: Gray House.

Wenglinsky, H. (2000). *How Teaching Matters: Bringing the Classroom Back into Discussions of Teacher Quality.* Princeton, NJ: Educational Testing Service.

Zavadsky, H. (2009). *Bringing School Reform to Scale: Five Award-Winning Urban Districts.* Cambridge, MA: Harvard Education Press.

3

The District of Columbia and the Reform Act: Historical Overview

Washington's Public Education Reform Amendment Act (PERAA) of 2007, like other urban governance reforms, was a response to complex political and historical circumstances, but four themes are particularly important for understanding this new law: (1) the school system's long experience with expert scrutiny and institutional tinkering; (2) the continuing influence of the city's racial history and politics; (3) the effects of the city's unique jurisdictional relationship with the U.S. Congress; and (4) the school district's legacy of limited administrative capacity.

A HISTORY OF REFORM AND CRITICISM

PERAA is the latest in a long line of changes in the way the DC Public School (DCPS) system is governed. Since 1804, there have been 17 different governance and administrative structures, and PERAA was the second new approach since 2000 (see Levy, 2004; Richards, 2000). There were many changes through the 1900s, perhaps the most visible of which was the 1968 decision to make the local school board an elected body.

Two changes during the 1990s significantly altered authority patterns in the city's public schools. In 1995, the DC Public Charter School Board was established, which led to rapid growth in the number of charter schools: 2 in 1996, 19 more in 1997, and 10 more in 1998 (Hart, 2000). In 1996, the presidentially appointed DC Financial Responsibility and Management Board (informally known as the Control Board) reduced the authority of the elected school board and was given the authority to select the district superintendent. In the first major change in this century, DC voters in 2000 narrowly approved a referendum that allowed the mayor to appoint four of the nine school board members. Then, in 2007, PERAA was enacted. Although these 17 permutations in governance structures were implemented over two centuries by very different decision-making processes and under sharply contrasting political conditions, each can be viewed as an effort to balance ideals of democratic accountability and representation with efficiency goals.

Although the 2007 law was regarded as a dramatic change, school administrators working under earlier governance arrangements attempted some reform strategies similar to those being implemented under PERAA. For example, in 2003, DCPS officials outlined a plan to give principals greater autonomy in return for improved student performance (Archer, 2003). This initiative, implemented in partnership with the nonprofit New Leaders for New Schools, was announced less than 2 years after another initiative, the Principals' Leadership Academy, was implemented to transform principals into instructional leaders (Stricherz, 2001). One can infer from subsequent reports on educational quality in DCPS that these initiatives did not live up to their proponents' expectations. Nevertheless, it is important to keep in mind that while some past governance structures may have turned out to be ineffective, parts of their reform agendas mirrored those being implemented under PERAA.

Virtually all of the changes were prompted in part by the publication of myriad reports, commissioned by civic groups or other third parties, which were critical of the public schools. Beginning with a report prepared by Franklin Roosevelt's Advisory Committee on Education in 1938, most documented the same problems: low student achievement on standardized tests; the inability of the schools to retain students; and DCPS students' low rates of enrollment in postsecondary education, relative lack of success in obtaining employment, and poor performance on the armed forces induction tests.

Three decades later, in April 1967, the *Washington Post* echoed what scholarly analyses were documenting:

> The collapse of public education in Washington is now evident. Reading scores reported in this newspaper show that fully one-third of the city schools' pupils have fallen two years or more behind their proper grade level. . . . The real question is whether the city is going to have public schools, in any legitimate and useful sense, in the future. . . . Citizens, Congress and President Johnson now have an urgent obligation to face the truth that nothing at all will help, short of a massive reorganization of the Washington School system. (as quoted in Diner, 1990, p. 127)

The reports continued for the next 40 years, along with congressional hearings and media accounts documenting the failings of the District's public schools, such as incompetent management and lack of fiscal oversight, unequal and inefficient distribution of resources to schools, student discipline problems, and chronically low academic achievement. For example, in a 2006 report funded by the Federal City Council,[1] the Parthenon Group summarized five other reports, issued between 1989 and 2006, that consistently found student academic performance had worsened; no significant progress had been made in improving the teacher workforce; schools were hampered by an ineffective central bureaucracy; and the broader Washington community seemed to be indifferent to these persistent problems. On the eve of PERAA's enactment, a *Washington Post* reporter concluded that (Witt, 2007, para. 5):

> The history of D.C. school reform is filled with fix-it plans hailed as silver bullets and would-be saviors who are celebrated before being banished. The constant churn of reform has been a big part of the schools' troubles, according to school officials, community activists, and others who have watched the system for decades.

A good measure of the explanation for the District's saga of continued documentation of problems and shifting governance arrangements—with little to show for either—may lie in the politics that emerged from its unique dependence on congressional authority and the city's racial history.

THE RACIAL HISTORY OF DC SCHOOLS

The first District school for black students was founded in 1807 by three former slaves with support from private contributions. In 1862, Congress mandated that all black and white children (aged 6-14) receive 3 months of education each year and that 10 percent of the taxes collected on "Negro-owned property" be used to support schools for black students (Richards, 2000). In 1874, what had been separate governing boards for black schools and for white schools in Washington City, Georgetown, and Washington County were consolidated into a single board with the requirement that 5 of its 19 members be black. Despite the consolidated board, the district had two superintendents, one for the white and one for the black schools. The District's public schools remained segregated for the next 80 years, until the 1954 *Brown v. Board of Education* Supreme Court decision.

Despite significant disparities in the resources available to black and white schools, Washington had some of the highest quality black schools in the country during the period of legal segregation. For example, Dunbar

---

[1]The Federal City Council, established in 1954, is a nonprofit, nonpartisan organization composed of and financed by 200 business, educational, professional, and civic leaders.

(originally the M Street School), which was for many years the only high school for black students, had an illustrious history of academic achievement. Its students earned higher scores, on average, than did the students at two of the three District high schools for white students. Among Dunbar's graduates were the first blacks to graduate from the U.S. Military Academy and the U.S. Naval Academy, the first black federal judge, the first black general, the first black elected to the U.S. Senate since Reconstruction, and the first black full professor at a major research university (Hundley, 1967). Dunbar and other black schools were staffed by many teachers with excellent credentials during this period. For example, four of Dunbar's first eight principals graduated from Oberlin College and two from Harvard University. In the 1920s, its faculty included three teachers with PhDs. As Risen (2008, p. 82) notes of this period:

> Like many urban districts, Washington thrived because it could rely on a class of educators—in this case, African Americans—who were mostly kept out of other professions. But as barriers eroded in the 1950s and 1960s, experienced black teachers began leaving for better opportunities.

After the 1954 *Brown* decision, Washington differed from other southern school districts in its quick and positive response: only 8 days after the ruling, the appointed school board adopted a desegregation policy. However, that policy did not substantially change the racial composition of schools that had been part of the all-black system. Enrollment for these schools averaged 97 percent black students for each year between 1954 and 1960, and nearly two-thirds of the schools that had been legally restricted to white students before 1954 became predominantly black by 1960, as white families moved out of both the public schools and the inner city (Henig et al., 1999). Within 6 years of the *Brown* decision, the structure of racial isolation in DCPS that has persisted into this century was in place.

By 1966, more than 30,000 white students had left DCPS to attend private schools or suburban ones, and after the 1968 passage of the Fair Housing Act, middle-class black families also began to move to the Maryland and Virginia suburbs (Risen, 2008; Witt, 2007). A small number of schools, located mainly in the Northwest section of the city, remained overwhelmingly white in their enrollment, a state of affairs that, politically, worked against the building and sustaining of capacity across the entire school system. According to Henig and his colleagues (1999, p. 49):

> The emergence of an elite subset of predominantly white, upper socioeconomic status schools, combined with the deterioration and unresponsiveness that characterized the broader system, provided parents with an incentive to pursue their children's needs at a microlevel. Parents—

predominantly white—who lived in the regular attendance zones of these schools could devote their considerable energies and resources to fundraising and politics oriented around their own school, rather than system-wide reform.

To some extent, middle-class black parents also had the option of enrolling their children in an "enclave school." As white flight continued throughout the 1970s, 1980s, and 1990s, schools in affluent white neighborhoods ("west of the park") lost substantial enrollment and were in danger of being closed. The city responded partly by recruiting middle-class black students from other neighborhoods. Over time, DCPS adopted a liberal policy allowing out-of-boundary transfers to parents assertive enough to request them. By 1993, more than 30 percent of students in the 16 DCPS elementary schools in which fewer than a quarter of the students were eligible for free- or reduced-price lunch were out-of-boundary transfers, as compared with only 12 percent in the more than 100 elementary schools with higher proportions of low-income students (Henig et al., 1999, p. 200).

However, some activists sought districtwide solutions to the unequal distribution of resources across DCPS schools. Julius Hobson, a major Washington civil rights leader and later school board member, filed an innovative lawsuit against the school district for unconstitutionally depriving poor and black students of equal educational opportunities. In a 1967 decision (*Hobson v. Hansen, 269 F. Supp. 401-Dist. of Columbia*), U.S. Court of Appeals Judge J. Skelly Wright ordered major changes to equalize educational opportunities, including integrating teachers and busing students to relieve overcrowding in majority black schools.[2]

Parents United, an advocacy group organized in 1980 by the Washington Lawyers' Committee for Civil Rights Under Law, initially worked to mobilize parents from around the city to rally in support of additional resources for the public schools. Over time, Parents United depended less on mass mobilization and more on research and legal action. One example was its push in the 1990s to ensure that school facilities were safe and free from building code violations. After documenting widespread violations that were not being addressed by the school system, Parents United went to court. In 1994, the judge ruled in the group's favor and began to monitor the district's compliance. When DCPS failed to respond, the judge postponed the opening of school by 3 weeks, which prompted intervention by the Control Board, and Parents United reluctantly dropped its suit.[3]

---

[2]In a subsequent decree, Judge Wright attempted to equalize the salaries of black and white teachers. However, a later study found that it led to an unintended result because many of the most experienced black teachers transferred to white schools (Witt, 2007).

[3]Parents United members assumed that their lawsuit would help the superintendent, Franklin Smith, whom they supported, by forcing the mayor, city council, and Congress to pay to rebuild

Although the organization was able to recruit some middle-class blacks into its leadership core, its strongest membership base was concentrated in white, affluent sections of the city, and the group never gained strong credibility among lower-income black (Henig et al., 1999).

Despite the efforts of Parents United and a few other organizations, the District has lacked the deep tradition of cross-racial, grassroots mobilization over citywide education issues that have developed in some other cities (Hannaway and Usdan, 2008; Henig et al., 1999). The politics that emerged from the racial history of DCPS has been based on what have been largely racially divided neighborhoods and wards, and the goals of strengthening home rule and gaining a greater political voice have been persistent themes.

SCHOOL POLITICS AND THE LEGACY OF CONGRESSIONAL CONTROL

Washington, DC's unique status as the nation's capital limited local political power and authority for most of its history, with Congress determining how the city was to be governed and appointing its leaders. In the years before the Home Rule Act of 1973, the local government was essentially an agency of the federal government. The House and Senate committees that oversaw the District were controlled by white southern segregationists, who maintained a tight grip on the city's affairs and were unresponsive to black leaders who demanded a greater voice (Harris, 1995). Efforts to gain home rule became a focus for local civil rights leaders, who accused Congress of racism and insensitivity to the needs of an urban black population. The contrast between the demographics of its congressional overseers and District residents became particularly telling when the city's public student enrollment became predominantly black in the 1950s (the city's population was majority black by 1960).

In 1968, 6 years before the city was given significant (but not complete) home rule, Congress established an elected 11-member board of education consisting of three at-large members and one representing each of the city's eight wards (electoral districts). DCPS was now an independent agency, but it still lacked the authority to raise its own revenue. The significance of this shift to the first locally elected body in the 20th century was initially demonstrated when 53 candidates ran in the first election, and 70 percent of the District's registered voters went to the polls (Richards, 2000).

---

the schools. The result was quite different. The District's elected officials did not provide the needed resources and cut DCPS' capital funding, arguing that the code violations were evidence of DCPS mismanagement. The Control Board later fired Smith, and the executive director of Parents United could only say on the day he was dismissed, "The thing—the lawsuit, the court dates—it all backfired. Be careful what you wish for, you might get it" (as quoted in Witt, 2007).

The long-term political implications of the 6-year period between the advent of an elected school board and home rule were even more significant. As the only elected body in the District during that time, the school board became a focal point for both individuals and groups seeking to build a political power base. Many people saw the school system's thousands of well-paying jobs as a resource for strengthening the black middle class and the school district as a source of political patronage (Henig, 2004; Risen, 2008). The political coalition that emerged in response to the new institution of an elected board was largely composed of teachers represented by the Washington Teachers Union and parents active at individual schools.

In a number of cities in which the school district is the major employer, the allocation of jobs has become politicized. In the District, several factors complicated the situation: the long disenfranchisement of District residents and the growing pains of an emerging polity; the ward-based system of school board elections, which provided for better representation of local neighborhoods, but also led to a blurred line between board members' constituent service and micromanagement of school and district operations;[4] and pressure to revitalize the city's working- and middle-class neighborhoods.

Over time, DCPS became even more politicized. Levy (2004, pp. 6-7) summarized the expert, media, and public reaction to the way DCPS was governed over the almost three decades between the first elected school board and the mid-1990s:

> Conflicts and division continued unabated, and studies, news stories and editorials castigating the Board became routine and harsh. . . . The complaints were similar to those of the previous 60 years. Reports on the subject, numerous news stories and editorials, and public comments by citizens as well as government officials asserted that the Board of Education (1) lacked focus on student achievement and the "big picture" policymaking important to the health of all DCPS schools; (2) failed to provide effective oversight; (3) micro-managed the system; and (4) was prone to too much internal dissension and personal politicking.

A 1997 *Washington Post* article documented the extent to which the school board had become an employment agency based on family and personal relationships (Loeb and Casey, 1997, as cited in Henig et al., 1999, p. 124). Subsequent investigations found that the school district had been able, through accounting techniques, to obscure hiring in excess of what

---

[4]The newly elected school board became involved in what professional educators would see as micromanaging or even meddling in administrative affairs, such as calling on principals to reassign teachers or to accept a particular student transfer (Henig, 2004).

the city council and Congress had authorized (Horwitz and Strauss, 1997, as cited in Henig et al., 1999, p. 124).[5]

Between the beginning of home rule in 1974 and the early 1990s, Congress had lessened its oversight over District government and the schools. An in-depth study of DCPS cites two reasons for this benign neglect: (1) more sympathetic members now served on the committees with oversight authority for the District, and (2) members of Congress were wary of a situation in which white officials imposed their priorities on black citizens who had had no voice in electing them (Henig et al., 1999, p. 254).

However, when the Republicans gained a majority in Congress after the 1994 midterm elections, the relationship between the District and Congress changed again. Congressional Republicans saw an opportunity to test some of their ideas for privatizing the management and delivery of public education. The District's financial collapse, though it was not primarily an education issue, gave them a rationale because members could argue that Congress was acting responsibly in reasserting its fiscal authority. In 1995, Congress passed legislation establishing a presidentially appointed Control Board and a chief financial officer appointed by the mayor.[6] The chief financial officer continues to exercise supervisory authority over DCPS' budget, accounting, and payroll. Consequently, debate persists over whether this arrangement addresses the District's chronic problems of fiscal mismanagement or fragments DCPS' administration in a way that obscures accountability and enables "interagency finger-pointing" (Turque, 2010, para. 1). In 1995, Congress also created the DC Public Charter School Board, with authority to approve charter schools that operate independently of DCPS.

Early in its tenure, the Control Board issued a report whose assessment of DCPS sounded eerily like others issued over the past 30 years (District of Columbia Financial Responsibility and Management Assistance Authority, 1996, para. 1):

> The deplorable record of the District's public schools by every important educational and management measure has left one of the city's most important public responsibilities in a state of crisis, creating an emergency which can no longer be ignored or excused. . . . In virtually every area, and

---

[5]Because DCPS lacked (and still lacks) independent taxing authority, the absence of a direct connection between revenue and expenditures created an opportunity for blame-shifting and gaming between the school board and the city council. The board could argue that the city council had provided insufficient funds, and the city council could argue that DCPS was misusing funds, with the result that neither institution was truly accountable to the public.

[6]The Control Board (officially, the District of Columbia Financial Responsibility and Management Assistance Authority) was a five-member body established by Congress to oversee the city's finances. The board had the power to override decisions by Washington's mayor and city council. It suspended its activities on September 30, 2001, when the District achieved its fourth consecutive balanced budget.

for every grade level, the system has failed to provide our children with a quality education and safe environment in which to learn. . . . This failure is the result not of the students—for all students can succeed—but of the educationally and managerially bankrupt school system.

The Control Board found, for example, that neither the school board nor the superintendent knew precisely the number of employees and students in the system: the available data suggested that DCPS employed about 50 percent fewer teachers for every central office administrator than other urban districts (Vise and Horwitz, 1996). The Control Board also documented student test scores that were well below national averages, a widening achievement gap, unsafe and violent learning environments, and other examples of operational and financial mismanagement.

Using the authority vested in it by Congress, the Control Board took charge of DCPS. It transferred most of the responsibilities of the elected school board to a new board of trustees whose members it appointed; it was authorized to oversee DCPS until June 2000. The Control Board also replaced the superintendent.[7] Once again, tensions between local political focus as well as managerial effectiveness were evident, and at least part of the reason lay in the District's unique jurisdictional relationship with Congress.

WEAK CENTRAL OFFICE LEADERSHIP AND CAPACITY

Although it is not possible to empirically demonstrate causality, the racial history of DCPS and its changing governance models at least partly explain a major characteristic of the system's evolution, the limited administrative capacity of the central district office. In the 10 years prior to the establishment of mayoral control under PERAA in 2007, DCPS had had six superintendents, but the tensions among members of the DCPS governing board members and between them and superintendents extended back to the 1960s. For most of its history, DCPS has lacked stable leadership. Without stable leadership, efforts to build central office capacity and to introduce cost efficiencies were sporadic and almost impossible to implement.

As just one example, *Education Week* reported in 1991 that in an effort to reduce the size of the central office staff and to make it more efficient, a new superintendent had reassigned four assistant superintendents and 14 other noninstructional personnel to provide direct services to students, primarily as principals and assistant principals. However, some 4 months

---

[7]The board hired a retired lieutenant general with no education experience as his replacement; he resigned after only 17 months, citing differences with the board.

later, only 1 of the 19 had shown up at her new post; the rest had placed themselves on paid sick leave. This unsuccessful move to streamline the central bureaucracy came 2 years after a 1989 study of DCPS found that the district was spending more than a third of its budget on noninstructional services (Olson, 1991). Systematic initiatives aimed at improving student learning were few and were rarely fully implemented, largely because of the lack of central office direction and support. For example, a 1992 external review of DCPS by the American Association of School Administrators National Curriculum Audit Center (as cited in Henig et al., 1999, p. 69) concluded that DCPS' curriculum policies were "obsolete and incomplete," with few schools in compliance. Auditors found that DCPS had no systematic mechanisms for selecting, implementing, or evaluating ongoing programs. They concluded that special projects were ad hoc, and "the result of site-based entrepreneurship rather than part of a district thrust." The same report also criticized DCPS' poor accounting procedures, which made it difficult to track millions of dollars in expenditures and allowed "payroll ghosts" to draw salaries without any apparent responsibilities.

More broadly, most of the DCPS's superintendents had neither the time nor the political resources necessary to change teaching and learning according to their convictions (Henig, 2004). For more than two decades, no superintendent was able to design and implement a comprehensive plan to teach reading and mathematics, leaving individual teachers to teach these subjects in whatever way they knew (Witt, 2007). Clifford Janey, the last superintendent to serve prior to PERAA, was able to get the Massachusetts academic standards, considered the most rigorous in the country, adopted in DCPS and to implement an assessment measuring students' achievement on those standards. However, Hannaway and Usdan (2008, p. 120) conclude that "facilities and financial problems plagued Janey's tenure, and he never seemed to get control of the district apparatus. Observers noted that the large entrenched district administrative office dragged efforts down as they reportedly had in previous administrations." The unraveling of central oversight over the curriculum was just one example of a rudderless system. DCPS was not able to consistently keep school facilities safe and in good repair, and it had failed to invest in updated technology. Consequently, its data systems were antiquated and not integrated with each other.

Of particular concern was the condition of special education. In 2005, 20 percent of DCPS students were enrolled in special education.[8] In comparison with other jurisdictions, DC identifies significantly more students as having emotional disturbance, multiple disabilities, and mental retardation, and is much more likely to educate them in segregated public and private

---

[8]Nationwide, 13 percent of public school students received special education services in 2007-2008 (Aud et al., 2010).

placements (about 25 percent in DC compared with 5 percent nationally). About a third of those students were attending private schools or public schools in other districts at DCPS expense. About 10 percent of DCPS' entire budget is earmarked for private school tuition. There are a number of reasons for the disproportionate number of out-of-district placements (see Parrish et al., 2007), but most observers agree that two central ones have historically been DCPS' inability to offer adequate programs for students with disabilities, and parents' distrust of the district's ability to provide appropriate services for their children (Samuels, 2005).

RESPONSES TO THE SYSTEM'S PROBLEMS

DCPS' overall lack of capacity did not go unnoticed. Individuals and groups concerned about the district's problems offered a variety of solutions, including attempts to achieve a more equal distribution of resources to schools, filing of lawsuits, and efforts to elect or appoint members to the school board who would focus on DCPS as a whole and seek to implement reforms that reached into the classroom. However, by the late 1990s, as the Control Board era was coming to a close, a number of reformers concluded that the problems of DCPS went considerably beyond feuding school board members and superintendents, that they were structural in nature. They concluded that the solution needed to be an institutional one that changed the way DCPS was governed.

This perspective was represented in a 1999 report of the DC Appleseed Center, a nonpartisan public interest advocacy group. It proposed a hybrid model for the school board. The board would be reduced from 11 to 9 members, and if there continued to be elections, candidates would run in two stages: a primary conducted in each ward or other large subunit, followed by a citywide runoff election between the two top vote-getters in each ward or subunit. The report also raised the possibility of mayoral appointments made from a list of nominees provided by a broad-based commission, with the appointments then subject to city council approval. In addition to recommending altering the method for selecting board members, the Appleseed report also recommended that the division of labor between the board and the superintendent be clearly specified. The report recommended that the board articulate broad goals and objectives, ensure that the superintendent shares them, and then set benchmarks with which to monitor the superintendent's progress.

Although the Appleseed report was not widely known to the public, major stakeholders were aware of it, and it became the basis for a proposal that represented a compromise among the mayor, city council, and Control Board.[9] A citywide referendum, in June 2000, represented a middle approach: to reduce the size of the school board from 11 to 9 members, 4 of whom would be appointed by the mayor. The referendum passed by a margin of only 843 votes (just 2 percent of the 40,179 cast), and the voting patterns revealed sharp racial cleavages. Precincts with more than 50 percent white residents supported the referendum at rates two-and-a-half times greater than predominantly black precincts (Henig, 2004).

In his analysis of the 2000 referendum, Henig (2004) noted that those supporting the referendum, including leaders of the local business community, believed that structural changes, such as eliminating ward-based elections, would make the system less fragmented and allow it to develop greater capacity to focus on classroom instruction. But an alternative frame of reference shaped the perceptions of grassroots activists who opposed the referendum. This frame, according to Henig (2004, p. 204):

> put race and power, not organizational structure, front and center. The public education system had a special role in this narrative, but less as an institution for educating children than as an historically significant platform for democratic control, political clout, jobs, and social status within the local Black community. Thus, the basic themes of this broad frame were not specific to the schools. From the standpoint of citizens inclined to credit this narrative, the battle over the school board structure was just the latest installment in a long-running tale.

However, as in more recent elections, issues of class and status as well as race shaped the electoral outcome. Elite support for the referendum was biracial, and among its supporters was the black mayor, Anthony Williams. However, after the election, he acknowledged that the vote highlighted the District's racial cleavages and had put him at odds with the majority of the black community (Cottman and Woodless, 2000).

THE ENACTMENT OF PERAA

When Mayor Adrian Fenty, a former member of the city council, was elected in 2007, he put forward the plan that was eventually enacted by the council as PERAA. Fenty had made improving the public schools a primary

---

[9]The move to change the board structure gained momentum because of the impending changeover from the Control Board, but also partly because of the very public bickering among board members that included public insults and a move to replace the sitting board president, who then threatened to take her opponents to court (Wilgoren, 1999). Problems within DCPS became even more evident when the superintendent who had replaced the lieutenant general resigned after less than 2 years and, in leaving, criticized the many layers of oversight from the Control Board, Congress, and the city council, which had limited her ability to keep the system running smoothly (see Richard, 2000).

focus of his campaign, and he proposed the dramatic restructuring of school governance as the way to accomplish this goal. The ultimate provisions of the act were negotiated with the city council, which approved mayoral control in a 9-to-2 vote (Stewart and Labbé, 2007). Among the modifications made at the council's request was that it would have the power to withdraw the mayor's powers over public education if the mayor did not show "sufficient progress in education" within 5 years.

Passed by the Council of the District and then ratified by Congress, the Public Education Reform Amendment Act:

- established a Department of Education, led by a deputy mayor for education;
- redesigned the State Education Office, converting the position of chief state schools officer to state superintendent of education;
- converted the position of DC school superintendent to DC chancellor, now appointed by the mayor with the advice and consent of the city council, and granted the chancellor responsibility for the overall operations of the public school system;
- tasked the new Department of Education with various planning, promotion, coordination, and supervision duties, along with oversight of the Office of the State Superintendent of Education and the Office of Public Education Facilities Modernization;
- established the Office of the Ombudsman for Public Education to provide parents and residents an entity to which they could express their concerns;
- created the Interagency Collaboration and Services Integration Commission to coordinate the services of all agencies that serve children and youth;
- significantly altered the duties and authority of the former Board of Education, which was renamed the State Board of Education, and removed it from the local, day-to-day operation of the school system;
- authorized the Public Charter School Board as the sole chartering and entity in the District of Columbia; and
- mandated a 5-year independent evaluation to determine, among other things, whether sufficient progress in public education has been achieved to warrant continuation of the provisions and requirements of PERAA or whether a new law and a new system of education should be enacted.

We turn in Chapter 4 to an examination of the city's responses to this legislation.

REFERENCES

American Association of School Administrators National Curriculum Audit Center. (1992). *A Curriculum Audit of the District of Columbia Public Schools*. Arlington, VA: Author.
Archer, J. (2003). D.C. program promises principals freedom. *Education Week, 22*. Available: http://www.nlns.org/resources/EW2.12.03.pdf [accessed March 2011].
Aud, S., Hussar, W., and Planty, M. (2010). *The Condition of Education 2010*. Washington, DC: U.S. Department of Education, National Center for Education Statistics.
Cottman, M.H., and Woodless, Y. (2000). Mayor sees racial divide in vote; through not claiming victory, Williams vows inclusiveness in revamping schools. *Washington Post*, June 29. Available: http://www.lexisnexis.com/us/inacademic/delivery [accessed December 2010].
Diner, S.J. (1990). Crisis of confidence: Public confidence in the schools of the nation's capital in the twentieth century. *Urban Education, 25*(2), 112-137.
District of Columbia Financial Responsibility and Management Assistance Authority. (1996). *Children in Crisis: Executive Summary*. Washington, DC: Author.
Hannaway, J., and Usdan, M.D. (2008). Mayoral takeover in the District of Columbia. In W.L. Boyd, C.T. Kerchner, and M. Blyth (Eds.), *The Transformation of Great American School Districts: How Big Cities Are Reshaping Public Education* (pp. 113-188). Cambridge, MA: Harvard Education Press.
Harris, C.W. (1995). *Congress and the Governance of the Nation's Capital: The Conflict of Federal and Local Interests*. Washington, DC: Georgetown University Press.
Hart, E. (2000). *History of the Charter School Movement*. Available: http://www.dcwatch.com/lwvdc/lwv0003c.htm [accessed October 2010].
Henig, J.R. (2004). Race, definition, and school board restructuring. In J.R. Henig and W.C. Rich (Eds.), *Mayors in the Middle* (pp. 191-218). Princeton, NJ: Princeton University Press.
Henig, J.R., Hula, R.C., Orr, M., and Pedescleaux, D.S. (1999). *The Color of School Reform: Race, Politics, and the Challenge of Urban Education*. Princeton, NJ: Princeton University Press.
Hobson v. Hansen, 269 F. Supp. 401, U.S. District Court, District of Columbia (1967).
Horwitz, S., and Strauss, V. (1997). A well-financed failure: Systems protect jobs while shortchanging classrooms. *Washington Post*, Feb. 16, A1.
Hundley, M.G. (1967). *The Dunbar Story*. New York: Vantage Press.
Levy, M. (2004). *History of Public School Governance in the District of Columbia: A Brief Summary*. Available: http://www.dcpswatch.com/dcps/0401.htm [accessed March 2011].
Loeb, V., and Casey, W. (1997). Work force a family affair for many. *Washington Post*, Feb. 17, App. B.
Olson, L. (1991). Effort to cut back DC's bureaucracy proves nettlesome. *Education Week*, Nov. 20. Available: http://www.edweek.org/ew/articles/1991/11/20/12dc.h11.html [accessed March 2011].
Parrish, T., Harr, J.J., Poirier, J.M., Madsen, S., and Yonker, S. (2007). *Special Education Financing Study for the District of Columbia*. Washington, DC: American Institutes for Research.
Richard, A. (2000). Governance changes sought for D.C. schools. *Education Week*, May 31.
Richards, M.D. (2000). *Timeline of Public School Governance in the District of Columbia*. Available: http://www.dcwatch.com/richards/0002.htm [accessed March 2011].
Risen, C. (2008). The lightning rod. *The Atlantic, 302*(4), 78-87.
Samuels, C.A. (2005). Special education a chronic challenge for D.C. schools. *Education Week*, May 11.

Stewart, N., and Labbé, T. (2007). D.C. schools takeover gets initial approval. *Washington Post*, April 4. Available: http://www.washingtonpost.com/wp-dyn/content/article/2007/04/03/AR2007040301116.html [accessed December 2010].

Stricherz, M. (2001). D.C. principals' training designed to boost instructional leadership. *Education Week*, September 12.

Turque, B. (2010). D.C. teachers contract paid for through budget cuts, reallocation of funding, *Washington Post*, May 11. Available: http://www.washingtonpost.com/wp-dyn/content/article/2010/05/10/AR2010051004611.html [accessed December 2010].

Vise, D.A., and Horwitz, S. (1996). D.C. schools called a failure, control board blasts system as it readies takeover plan. *Washington Post*, Nov. 13.

Wilgoren, D. (1999). For bitterly divided D.C. school board, no business as usual. *Washington Post*, July 27.

Witt, A. (2007). Worn down by waves of change. *Washington Post*, June 11. Available: http://www.washingtonpost.com/wp-dyn/content/article/2007/06/10/AR2007061001496.html [accessed December 2010].

4

Responses to PERAA: Initial Implementation

The District of Columbia has made many changes since the Public Education Reform Amendment Act (PERAA) of 2007 was enacted. Some have received much public scrutiny: schools have been closed, principals and teachers dismissed, and a new teacher's union contract has been adopted. Other changes have received less attention, such as the formation of a new interagency commission to coordinate services available to children and young people and a new office to oversee the construction and renovation of schools. Information about many of these developments is available on the websites of various city agencies, and the local press and community-based groups have also reported on many of them.[1]

Systematically documenting the city's efforts will be a critical component of the 5-year evaluation the law itself calls for, and until this is done, few firm conclusions can be drawn about how well the city has implemented PERAA and fulfilled the intentions of the law. As a first step in that process, this chapter presents a picture of the broad outlines of the city's response to PERAA.

In assembling this information we relied primarily on information and materials supplied by city agencies and officials. We reviewed information made available to the public by DC Public Schools (DCPS), the Office of the State Superintendent of Education (OSSE), and the Department of

---

[1] Some early steps in the reform of DC schools under PERAA are described and evaluated in two reports, from the U.S. Government Accountability Office (2009), Ashby (2008); and a joint one from the 21st Century School Fund, the Urban Institute, and the Brookings Institution (2008).

Education headed by the deputy mayor of education, both in printed documents and on their websites. Officials of these agencies presented materials to the committee and staff and also answered specific questions about the school system. We also examined several reports produced by government agencies, research organizations and civic groups, as well as some media coverage. However, all these reports and other presentations were prepared for different purposes, and they used a variety of different methods: for this chapter, we used them primarily as sources of factual information not otherwise available; we discuss the sources further in Chapter 5.

We also note the potential for confusion regarding which entities in the city are responsible for which aspects of public education, because of the city's unique political status and structure. We generally refer to "the city" or "the District" when discussing areas that are not solely the responsibility of the DCPS.

A NEW STRUCTURE

The scope of PERAA is quite broad. Its first eight titles lay out requirements for the governance, organization, and management of DC's public schools; the corresponding functions of a state education agency; the management and construction of educational facilities; and the creation and oversight of charter schools. PERAA also establishes a structure to foster collaboration across agencies serving at-risk children in the city and calls for the appointment of an ombudsman so that the District's residents have a mechanism for registering concerns and resolving disputes. PERAA also requires that benchmarks be established for annual assessments of progress in four key areas of the school system: business practices, human resources, academic plans, and annual achievements. The mayor is charged with conducting these assessments and reporting on them to the city council. The mayor is also charged with submitting to the council a 5-year assessment of the public education system established by PERAA (that is, the evaluation this committee was asked to design).

Figure 4-1 shows the governance structure for the city's public schools before and after PERAA. The new structure is more complex than the old one, and the boundaries between the responsibilities of each of the new entities are not completely distinct, as shown in Table 4-1.

MAYORAL CONTROL: THE CHANCELLOR AND THE BUDGET

The most widely publicized change brought about by PERAA is the placement of DCPS directly under the oversight of the mayor. This change affords the mayor authority over most educational matters, ranging from school operations to personnel and labor relations, and grants the mayor

Before the Reform Act of 2007

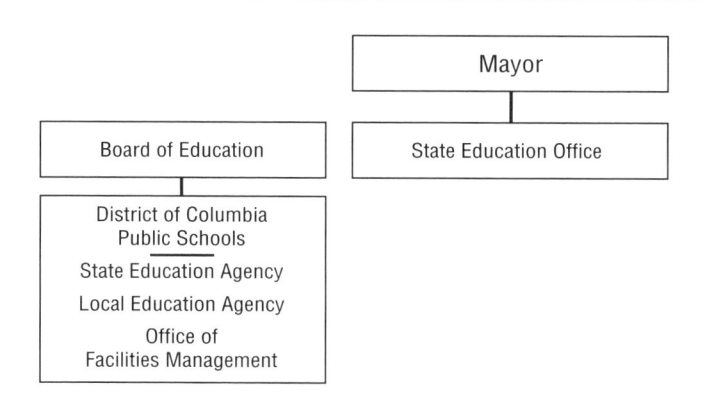

```
                        ┌──────────┐
                        │  Mayor   │
                        └────┬─────┘
    ┌──────────────────┐     │
    │ Board of Education│    │
    └────────┬─────────┘  ┌──┴──────────────────┐
             │            │ State Education Office│
    ┌────────┴─────────┐  └─────────────────────┘
    │ District of Columbia
    │   Public Schools
    │ ─────────────────
    │ State Education Agency
    │ Local Education Agency
    │ Office of
    │ Facilities Management
    └──────────────────┘
```

After the Reform Act of 2007

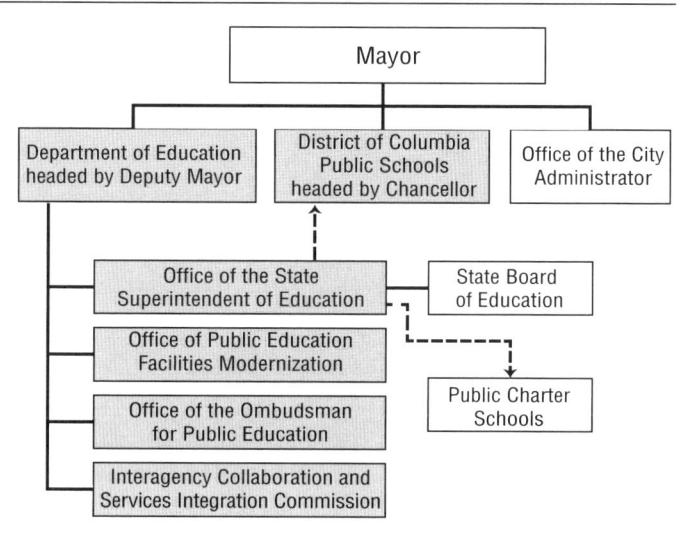

[Organizational chart: Mayor at top, with three reports: Department of Education headed by Deputy Mayor; District of Columbia Public Schools headed by Chancellor; Office of the City Administrator. Under Department of Education: Office of the State Superintendent of Education; Office of Public Education Facilities Modernization; Office of the Ombudsman for Public Education; Interagency Collaboration and Services Integration Commission. Also shown: State Board of Education; Public Charter Schools.]

- - - - - The Office of the State Superintendent of Education provides oversight, monitoring, and technical assistance to DCPS for federal and state education programs.

▭ New entities established by the Reform Act.

FIGURE 4-1 DCPS governance structure before and after PERAA.
SOURCE: U.S. Government Accountability Office (2009, p. 7).

responsibility for appointing a chancellor (to run DCPS), though the appointment has to be confirmed by the DC City Council.

The chancellor's responsibilities, like those of most district superintendents, include establishing educational priorities, adopting curri-

TABLE 4-1 Offices with Responsibility for DC Public Schools

Office and Mission	Areas of Responsibility
District of Columbia Public Schools (DCPS)—Office of the Chancellor To educate all children in the District of Columbia, providing the knowledge and skills they need to achieve academic success and choose a rewarding professional path.	• Office of the Chief Academic Officer • Office of Human Capital • Office of Special Education • Office of the Chief Operating Officer • Office of Data and Accountability Office of Family and Public Engagement
Office of the Deputy Mayor for Education (DME) Support the mayor in developing and implementing a world-class education system that enables children, youth, and adults to compete locally and globally.	• Leadership/support for education functions under mayor's office • Districtwide education strategy • Interagency coordination • Oversight and support of OSSE and OPEFM
Office of the State Superintendent of Education (OSSE) Act as the state education agency for DC; sets policies, provides resources and support, and exercises accountability for all public education in DC.	• Division of Early Childhood Education (ECE) • Postsecondary Education and Workforce Readiness Division • Department of Special Education (DSE) • Elementary and Secondary Education
DC State Board of Education (DCSBOE) Advise the state superintendent of education on educational matters, including state standards; state policies, including those governing special, academic, vocational, charter, and other schools; state objectives; and state regulations proposed by the mayor or the state superintendent of education.	• State academic standards • High school graduation requirements • Standards for high school equivalence credentials • The state accountability plan • State policies for parental involvement • Rules for residency verification • List of approved charter school accreditation organizations • Annual "report card" required by No Child Left Behind Act • Approved list of private placement accreditation organizations
Statewide Commission on Children, Youth, and Their Families (SCCYF) To improve services for vulnerable children by promoting social and emotional skills among children and youth through the oversight of a comprehensive integrated delivery system.	• Meet quarterly to discuss data and interagency collaboration • Develop pilot programs and evaluate school and community programs • Partner with directors from agencies that serve children youth, and families; the president of the Children and Youth Investment Trust Corporation, the president of the State Board of Education, and five community representatives, who participate in commission meetings

TABLE 4-1 Continued

Office and Mission	Areas of Responsibility
Office of Public Education Facilities Modernization (OPEFM) To support high-quality education by rapidly and consistently providing and maintaining safe, healthy, modern, and comfortable learning environments.	• School Modernization and Construction Program • Maintenance and Operations Program
Public Charter School Board (PCSB) To provide quality public school options for DC students, families, and communities.	• Oversee applications for new charter schools • Provide oversight in holding schools to high standards • Provide support and feedback to schools • Solicit community input

SOURCE: Compiled from the websites and fiscal 2011 annual reports of the relevant agencies and the District's CapStat website, see http://capstat.oca.dc.gov/PerfInd_Education.aspx [accessed December 2010].

cula and assessments, and ensuring that the schools are appropriately staffed and managed. Unlike many other urban school chiefs, however, the DC chancellor is not responsible for facilities construction and modernization or for transportation: these functions fall under the Department of Education and the deputy mayor for education (discussed below).

Another critical area not under the mayor's (or the chancellor's) direct control is the budget. Annual budgets have to be submitted by the mayor to the city council for review and approval, and, with a two-thirds majority, the council can change the proposed budget.

As required by PERAA, the mayor appointed a new chancellor, who was confirmed by the city council in June 2007. This action proved to be among the most high profile and contentious aspects of the changes brought about by PERAA. Beginning with the politics surrounding her selection, Chancellor Michelle Rhee's tenure was marked by controversy. It is widely understood that Mayor Fenty made a choice that reflected his view of the sort of reforms most needed to bring about change in the district: Chancellor Rhee was expected to make dramatic, rather than incremental, changes, and would focus on teacher quality (King, 2007; Turque and Cohen, 2010). (Chapter 5 provides a brief overview of the strategies Rhee and Fenty adopted.)

Other early controversies concerned school budget matters. For example, the city council held special hearings, in response to budget concerns, to review DCPS actions. A particularly heated hearing occurred in October 2009, after the chancellor announced her intention to terminate hundreds of teachers because of a projected budget shortfall. Feelings ran high after this took place; for example, WTOP, a local news radio station, characterized the action this way: "DC Schools Chancellor Michelle Rhee told the DC City Council she ignored their mandate to cut funds from next year's summer school program and instead fired hundreds of teachers" (Segraves, 2009, para. 3). Many school staff, as well as many District residents, disagreed vigorously and publicly with the decision.

Tensions between the chancellor and the council over budgetary questions and the related issues of teacher dismissals and school closures continued throughout Michelle Rhee's tenure and raise many questions about strategic management of DCPS and how budgetary matters should or should not influence management decisions. The budget approval process required in PERAA appears to have been carried out as prescribed, but some observers question the adequacy of the process. For example, the executive director of the Federal City Council, John Hill, explained to the committee:

> We believe that there needs to be a transparent budget that focuses on resources and supporting and expanding the work in terms of improving educational outcomes . . . anyone who has taken a look at the budget, even those who have studied it, it's hard to understand from outside of the government, and sometimes even hard to understand within the government. And so we believe that it should be understandable by everyone.

Although these sorts of concerns are certainly not unique to the District, they do point to a desire by some residents for clearer and more accessible information regarding school and school district financing and budgeting.

DCPS's limited authority over its own budgeting operations also has important implications for many planning, management, and operational aspects of the district. Thus, it will be important for the PERAA-required evaluation to document whether the budgetary process is working as the law intended, whether the law has resolved any long-standing problems with the budgetary process, and whether the law has introduced any unintended negative consequences.

STATE SUPERINTENDENT AND STATE BOARD OF EDUCATION

Two provisions of PERAA address the District's unique status as a city that is not part of any state but is treated like a state for some federal purposes. PERAA calls for a new state superintendent of education to serve as the chief state school officer for the District (a general title that refers to the person in charge of public education in each state, though states may have other titles for this role). Thus, this individual is responsible for functions typically handled at the state level, such as overseeing federal grants; setting standards consistent with the city's school, college, and workforce readiness goals; establishing high school graduation requirements; and early childhood and adult education programs. The OSSE is also responsible for ensuring that the District tracks and makes available accurate and reliable data that can be used to monitor compliance with both state and federal law.

Like other state education agencies, OSSE works with a state board of education to develop state education standards as well as policies governing all public schools (including charters). The DC State Board of Education is specifically charged with approving the state accountability plan for the District's schools, as well as a number of policies and regulations typically handled at the state level (e.g., who can accredit schools, rules for residency, standards for home schooling, school attendance requirements and so forth). The board has nine members: eight are elected by each of the city's eight wards and the ninth member is elected at large.

An example of OSSE's function was its role in coordinating the development and submission of two bids for federal "Race to the Top" initiative funding from the U.S. Department of Education, an effort that required the cooperation and support of many different agencies and organizations from across the city. One of the proposals won and will bring an additional $75 million in federal funds to the District's schools.[2]

OSSE is also responsible for the development of the State Longitudinal Education Data (SLED) system required by PERAA, which will be a critical tool for planning, management, reporting, instruction, and evaluation; it is not yet operational. SLED is expected to house information that can be used to track long-term trends for students in both traditional and public charter schools. The system is expected to track information related to students' educational growth and development from early care through elementary and secondary school and into college, adult education, and career pathways. After an initial release of a portion of the system in early 2009, OSSE later announced termination of the contract for the data system (Office of the State Superintendent of Education, 2010b). OSSE has solicited proposals from other firms and intends to have a new contract in place by the middle of 2011 (personal communication, February 22, 2011). OSSE staff told the committee that they have made progress in the interim, such as assigning unique identifiers to students and compiling enrollment and assessment data as they build the data warehouse.

---

[2]For details of the proposal and OSSE's goals, see Office of the State Superintendent of Education (2010a); also see Chapter 5 for a discussion of the goals.

DEPARTMENT OF EDUCATION AND DEPUTY MAYOR

PERAA established a new city Department of Education headed by a deputy mayor for education who, like the chancellor, reports directly to the mayor. The department oversees several new education-related agencies: the OSSE, the Office of Public Education Facilities Modernization (OPEFM), the Office of the Ombudsman for Public Education (OOPE), and an Interagency Collaboration and Services Integration Commission. Other important responsibilities of the Department of Education include establishing a comprehensive data system (separate from SLED) capable of aggregating and linking information across multiple city agencies, and coordinating planning and policy development related to all education and education-related activities in the District.

The Ombudsman

PERAA also spells out the requirements for the Office of the Ombudsman, who is to be nominated by the mayor and approved by the city council and report to the deputy mayor for education. The ombudsman is expected to reach out to city residents and parents, facilitate communication between residents and the mayor's office, respond to complaints, guide residents and parents to the school or agency staff who are in a position to assist them, and track complaints. This person is also charged with making recommendations for improving service delivery and responsiveness, based on the opinions and concerns of residents and parents.

An ombudsman was appointed in October 2007 and began issuing monthly reports of the office's activities in October 2008. Most of the 1,100 issues cited in the reports related to DCPS, although some referred to the city's public charter schools and the University of the District of Columbia, see http://ombudsman.dc.gov/ombudsman/site/default.asp [accessed October 2010]. The reports indicate that virtually all issues were "resolved," without providing details. The last report was dated July 2009 and announced that "funding for the Office of the Ombudsman has been eliminated for Fiscal Year 2010." The web page for the ombudsman is no longer operational (as of fall 2010).

The ombudsman was intended to be the primary channel through which public school parents could communicate with school officials and seek redress for complaints, and its absence is significant. As one person who spoke to the committee explained:

> Another thing in the legislation [PERAA] was the new State Board of Education and the ombudsman. We did not support taking away the local school board. I can just tell you my own parent and school board experience in the past is that we need some kind of locally elected or representa-

tive body that has responsibility for local education issues, which can serve as a watchdog, be a point of access for the public. That was taken away with that school board. I think [those are] unresolved issues, as is what happens with the ombudsman, which may or may not be able to cover that, but it isn't at the moment.

Facilities

The OPEFM reports to the deputy mayor; its director is appointed by the mayor and confirmed by the city council. OPEFM replaces the Office of Facilities Management that had been housed within DCPS. Thus, OPEFM is set up to operate independently of DCPS, though its director is expected to consult regularly with the chancellor, a Public School Modernization Advisory Committee, and the state superintendent of education. OPEFM has the direct authority to initiate the construction and renovation of schools in accordance with a facilities master plan. The new agency is responsible for modernizing existing DCPS schools and facilities; developing a comprehensive plan that links maintenance and modernization; and managing routine maintenance, repairs, and small capital projects on DCPS schools and facilities.

The executive director of the OPEFM was appointed in June 2007 to oversee a 15-year modernization campaign expected to cost approximately $3.5 billion dollars.[3] OPEFM's first action was a stabilization effort to address such major problems as heating, cooling, and health and safety in schools. A master facilities plan was introduced in 2008, and updated in 2010 (Office of Public Education Facilities Modernization, 2010a). It mapped out a phased modernization approach designed to provide rapid improvement to every school in the city, with priority given to the learning environments most important to the academic program. The plan also recognizes special design and planning needs for different groups of students and student and community needs, including early childhood education, special education, school-based health services, co-location with charter schools, adult and postsecondary education, and variable enrollment levels. The head of OPEFM testified in March 2010 before the city council (Office of Public Education Facilities Modernization, 2010b):

> Today, the city has an expanding portfolio of wonderful school buildings that have won praise locally from joyous students and parents, and nationally from the engineering/architectural and building industry. These modernized school buildings are evident throughout this city.

We discuss in Chapter 6 the preliminary results of these efforts.

---

[3]For more information on OPEFM, see: http://opefm.dc.gov/about.html [accessed October 2010].

Structures for Charter Schools

PERAA called for several changes in the governance of the city's public charter schools. It established the DC Public Charter School Board (DCPCSB) and charged it with (1) ensuring a comprehensive application review process for approving charter schools, (2) providing effective oversight and meaningful support to the schools, and (3) actively engaging stakeholders and the community.[4] In addition to the board role, OSSE has the authority to review charter schools to ensure that they are meeting state standards and complying with regulations.

Currently, some 39 percent of students (roughly 28,000) in public schools attend the 52 approved public charter schools on 93 campuses. Successes in some of the charter schools have received public attention (Mathews, 2006, 2007; Nanos, 2007; Turque, 2010; Wilson, 2009), but as a group they are achieving modest progress. Only five met the adequate yearly progress requirements (under the No Child Left Behind Act)[5] for 2010, and several were closed in 2010 (District of Columbia Public Charter School Board, 2009, 2010a, 2010b; Fabel, 2010).

Advocacy groups, researchers, media commentators, and others—in DC and elsewhere—have raised a number of concerns about charter schools. Some people have worried that poor-quality charter schools are not being adequately monitored or closed down when necessary and that comparisons between traditional and charter schools are misleading, in part because charter schools are not, proportionally, serving as many students with disabilities (or students with as severe disabilities) as are the traditional schools. Others have been concerned that charter schools are at a disadvantage in securing suitable buildings in which to operate, that charter schools receive fewer public funds per student than do traditional public schools, and that the high salaries teachers in traditional schools will receive under the new Washington Teachers' Union contract will make it more difficult for charter schools to recruit and retain effective teachers (see Lerner, 2010a, 2010b, 2010c, 2010d).[6]

Such questions suggest the need for evaluation of public charter schools and outcomes for students, as well as trends in enrollment patterns and the movement of students and teachers into and out of these schools.

---

[4]For more information about the DC public charter schools, see http://www.dcpubliccharter.com/About-the-Board/Board-Functions.aspx [accessed October 2010].

[5]A measure of school progress, based on student performance on standardized achievement tests, used to identify schools that are or are not meeting required improvement targets under the act.

[6]See also Friends of Choice in Urban Schools, http://www.focusdc.org/ [accessed November 2010].

INTERAGENCY COMMISSION

PERAA also created an Interagency Collaboration and Services Integration Commission to address the needs of vulnerable children and youth. The work of the commission is guided by six citywide goals the District has established for its children and youth: children are ready for school; children and youth succeed in school; children and youth are healthy and practice healthy behaviors; children and youth engage in meaningful activities; children and youth live in healthy, stable, and supportive families; and all youth make a successful transition to adulthood (District of Columbia Public Schools, 2009).

The commission is expected to articulate a vision for meeting the needs of children in the District, to set priorities for program development, and to articulate how resources can be shared across agencies. PERAA specifically calls for the development of an interagency database and integrated service plans to address such issues as juvenile and family violence, social and emotional skills, and the physical and mental health of vulnerable children. The law gives the commission authority to combine resources from different city agencies and levels of government (including federal) for the purpose of improving service integration. The commission is also expected to engage in the design and implementation of evidence-based programs for children and to evaluate these programs to gauge their effects on broad indicators of social welfare, such as levels of violence, truancy, and delinquency, as well as on academic performance.

The directors of the mandated commission (named the Statewide Commission on Children, Youth, and Their Families, although that is not its name in PERAA) (Office of the Deputy Mayor for Education, 2010b) include the heads of city agencies concerned with the health and well-being of children and youth.[7] In its first 18 months, the commission produced a "Children's Health Action Plan" and began work on a citywide school health strategy. It also created a vetting program designed to increase the quality of afterschool programs provided by community-based partners in schools, and it has launched several school-level programs.

According to an independent evaluation of the commission (Development Services Group, 2008, pp. 10-11):

---

[7]The members are the mayor, city council chair, public education officials, and the heads of the Department of Human Services, the Child and Family Services Agency, the Department of Youth Rehabilitation Services, the Department of Corrections, the Department of Health, the Department of Mental Health, and the Metropolitan Police Department. Representatives from a number of other District agencies (e.g., the Department of Employment Services, the Children and Youth Investment Trust Corporation, and the Department of Disability Services) are also asked to observe and participate in the commission's meetings.

[It has succeeded in establishing] a serious and credible process, with monthly meetings that involve the Mayor, the Deputy Mayor for Education, and the key child-serving and other agency heads . . . [and] early results of the implementation of the evidence-based programs, and of the training to support those programs, have been positive and promising.

The authors identify several areas for improvement: encouraging greater engagement of . . . school principals in the implementation of the programs; seeking ways to maintain a high level of support among teachers and other implementers, so that they can implement the programs faithfully; and involving the staff who implement the programs (e.g., school resource officers) in the planning and implementation process (Development Services Group, 2008, p. 92). They also call on the commission to provide stronger direction and coordination for the prevention programs, and to provide more services to children and families.

The commission's most recent focus has been on developing a framework that can serve as a basis for a citywide strategic education and youth development plan that will integrate existing public, private, and nonprofit plans.[8] The framework defines youth development as encompassing "health and safety, in-school-time, out-of-school time, social services, and community building, as it pertains to children, youth, and their families" (Office of the Deputy Mayor of Education, 2010a, p. 2).

ONGOING QUESTIONS

There is no question that PERAA has been the catalyst for many changes to DC's public schools. The governing structure has been significantly altered, new programs are in place, and new personnel have taken a number of actions, some bold and public and others that are less visible but perhaps equally influential. A more detailed assessment of what these new offices are accomplishing should be a primary component of the next phase of evaluation.

The structures and authorities established by PERAA do not seem to be completely settled at this point, however. In the context of the fiscal 2010 budget, for example, the city council and the mayor disagreed over whether to shift staff and funds from the deputy mayor's office to the State

---

[8]These plans include the Child and Family Services Agency 2009 Resource Development Plan; the Child Health Action Plan, 2008, Department of Health; DC Public Schools Master Education Plan for a System of Great Schools; DC Public Schools Master Facilities Plan; the District of Columbia State-Level Education Strategic Plan, Fiscal Years 2009-2013; Making Student Achievement the Focus: A Five-Year Action Plan for District of Columbia Public Schools; Race to the Top Application/Implementation Plan; and the District's Workforce Development Plan.

Board of Education. According to the *Washington Post*, this disagreement reflected "the council's discontent with what some members see as a lack of transparency and accountability in the mayor's efforts to transform the District's struggling public school system" (Turque, 2009, para. 3). The same article noted that the council wanted to bolster the power of the state board by giving it more independence because of a concern that elected officials should not report to appointed officials (meaning the State Superintendent of Education).

In response to some of these proposed changes, then Chancellor Michelle Rhee (2009) submitted a formal letter to the council asking it to reconsider a number of recommendations that "begin to erode the structure established by . . . PERAA" and "undo key components of Act" (paras. 1-2). She noted the accomplishments of the deputy mayor—especially the accomplishments of the interagency commission, which the deputy mayor oversees—and explained that:

> At this time, DCPS has neither the dedicated focus nor ability to continue this important work at this level. The Office of Youth Engagement (OYE), which the Committee of the Whole has proposed to oversee ICSIC [the interagency commission], has existed for only a few short months. OYE is building twilight programs, student attendance and truancy initiatives, and the Youth Engagement Academy. Next year, OYE will take on the mammoth task of implementing the new student discipline policy. At this time, it cannot take on the additional responsibilities of ICSIC without diverting its focus from these other important initiatives.[9]

Finally, she questioned the State Board of Education's ability to take on the Office of the Ombudsman, and noted that "I believe the transfer of the Ombudsman to an expanded State Board is likely to politicize the Ombudsman's office that has responded to over 1,000 parent and community concerns" (Rhee, 2009, para. 6).

Moreover, although PERAA has altered the way education is governed in the city, some observers suggest that it does not seem to have significantly reduced the layers of bureaucracy in the system. Without a doubt, the new arrangements are complex. The deputy mayor for education oversees every educational agency or entity in the city (OSSE, OPEFM, PCSB) *except* for the largest and perhaps most important one, DCPS. Each of the District's charter schools is considered to be its own local education agency (LEA), and these are overseen the deputy mayor. However, under PERAA, the

---

[9] The city council's Committee of the Whole is responsible for the city's annual budget and financial plan and also for matters related to public education. The Office of Youth Engagement operates under the oversight of the Office of the Chief Academic Officer and is responsible for attendance, student behavior and school culture, and health and wellness.

executive director of the Office of Public Facilities Management (OPEFM), while housed under the deputy mayor, also reports to the Executive Office of the Mayor, and issues pertaining to school modernization must also be coordinated with chancellor, though the mechanisms through which this coordination is supposed to take place are not spelled out (Lew, 2007, p. 8).

The new roles and lines of authority and accountability may not be widely understood, and it is also not completely clear whether the existing arrangements are in fact what PERAA required. People who participated in a public forum held by the committee—not a representative sample of city residents—expressed concerns about the new arrangements. "The Department of Education . . . this is totally new that there would be a Deputy Mayor for Education," one noted, adding, "I think you have to look at it. It has an immense portfolio. It's confusing to figure out what's happening there." Another questioned whether these newly created positions have been vested with the resources and authority they need to accomplish their missions.

These accounts and exchanges shed light on a city that is still trying to strike the right balance with respect to authority and oversight of its educational agencies. They also support PERAA's requirement for an independent program of evaluation that can provide detailed analysis of the effects and implementation of the new law—as well as the transparency and accountability that the community wants.

REFERENCES

Ashby, C.M. (2008). *District of Columbia Public Schools: While Early Reform Efforts Tackle Critical Management Issues, a District-Wide Strategic Education Plan Would Help Guide Long-Term Efforts.* Testimony before the Subcommittee on Oversight of Government Management, the Federal Workforce, and the District of Columbia, Committee on Homeland Security and Governmental Affairs, U.S. Senate, GAO-08-549T.

Development Services Group. (2008). *FY 2008 Annual Evaluation Report to the Interagency Collaboration and Services Integration Commission.* Washington, DC: Author.

District of Columbia Public Charter School Board. (2009). *City Collegiate Public Charter School Relinquishes Charter: Public Charter School Board Approves Other Requests & Proposals.* December 23. Available: http://www.dcpubliccharter.com/News-Room.aspx?id=132 [accessed October 2010].

District of Columbia Public Charter School Board. (2010a). *D.C. Public Charter School Board Proposes Charter Revocation of One School, Accepts Surrender of Two Others.* June 22. Available: http://www.dcpubliccharter.com/News-Room.aspx?id=156 [accessed October 2010].

District of Columbia Public Charter School Board. (2010b). *D.C. Public Charter School Board Revokes the Charter of Young America Works.* April 28. Available: http://www.dcpubliccharter.com/News-Room.aspx?id=151 [accessed October 2010].

District of Columbia Public Schools. (2009). *Working Draft: Making Student Achievement the Focus: A Five-Year Action Plan for District of Columbia Public Schools.* Washington, DC: Author.

Fabel, L. (2010). Number of DC schools meeting national standards plunges. *Washington Examiner*, August 10. Available: http://www.washingtonexaminer.com/local/Number-of-D_C_-schools-meeting-national-standards-plunges-1008721-100309699.html [accessed October 2010].

Friends of Choice in Urban Schools. (2010). *Friends of Choice in Urban Schools home page.* Available: http://www.focusdc.org/ [accessed November 2010].

King, C.I. (2007). Coming soon: The real schools battle. *Washington Post*, September 27.

Lerner, M. (2010a). The D.C. charter facility allotment saga continues. *Washington Examiner*, March 16. Available: http://www.examiner.com/charter-schools-in-washington-dc/the-d-c-charter-facility-allotment-saga-continues [accessed October 2010].

Lerner, M. (2010b). Fairness for charter schools. *Washington Examiner*, June 6. Available: http://www.examiner.com/charter-schools-in-washington-dc/fairness-for-charter-schools [accessed October 2010].

Lerner, M. (2010c). Is funding of DC charter schools linked to quality? *Washington Examiner*, June 10. Available: http://www.examiner.com/charter-schools-in-washington-dc/is-funding-of-dc-charter-schools-linked-to-quality [accessed October 2010].

Lerner, M. (2010d). PCSB revokes charter of Young America Works, more should come. *Washington Examiner*, April 29. Available: http://www.examiner.com/charter-schools-in-washington-dc/pcsb-revokes-charter-of-young-america-works-more-should-come [accessed October 2010].

Lew, A.Y. (2007). *Transition Plan: Office of Public Education Facilities Modernization.* Available: http://opefm.dc.gov/OPEFM-TRANSITION_PLAN-Final_12-04-07.pdf [accessed November 2010].

Mathews, J. (2006). A miracle in the making? KIPP turns its efforts toward elementary schools. *Washington Post Magazine*, April 2. Available: http://www.kipp.org/news/the-washington-post-a-miracle-in-the-making-kipp-turns-its-efforts-toward-elementary-schools- [accessed March 2011].

Mathews, J. (2007). Rating education gains; achievement gaps, advanced placement exams, demographic shifts and charter schools: What do they add up to for students? *Washington Post*, June 11. Available: http://pqasb.pqarchiver.com/washingtonpost/access/1285888651.html?FMT=ABS&FMTS=ABS:FT&date=Jun+11%2C+2007&author=Jay+Mathews+-+Washington+Post+Staff+Writer&pub=The+Washington+Post&edition=&startpage=B.2&desc=Rating+Education+Gains%3B+Achievement+Gaps%2C+Advanced+Placement+Exams%2C+Demographic+Shifts+and+Charter+Schools%3A+What+Do+They+Add+Up+To+for+Students%3F [accessed October 2010].

Nanos, J. (2007). Teaching kids whole-life skills; NE charter school uses innovative program to combat teen pregnancy, *The Washington Post*, December 6. Available: http://pqasb.pqarchiver.com/washingtonpost/access/1393806781.html?FMT=ABS&FMTS=ABS:FT&date=Dec+6%2C+2007&author=Janelle+Nanos&pub=The+Washington+Post&edition=&startpage=T.1&desc=Teaching+Kids+Whole-Life+Skills%3B+NE+Charter+School+Uses+Innovative+Program+to+Combat+Teen+Pregnancy [accessed October 2010].

Office of Public Education Facilities Modernization. (2010a). *Master Facilities Plan.* Available: http://dc.gov/DCPS/About+DCPS/Strategic+Documents/Master+Facilities+Plan/Master+Facilities+Plan [accessed October 2010].

Office of Public Education Facilities Modernization. (2010b). Testimony of Allen Y. Lew, Executive Director, D.C. Office of Public Education Facilities Modernization, Before the Committee of the Whole Council of the District of Columbia. Public Oversight Hearing on Master Facilities Plan for the District of Columbia Public Schools. Available: http://opefm.dc.gov/pdf/Executive%20Director%20Lew%20Testimony%20at%20MFP%20Hearing%203-24-10.pdf [accessed March 2011].

Office of the Deputy Mayor for Education. (2010a). *Framework for the Development of a Statewide Strategic Education and Youth Development Plan*. Washington, DC: Author. Available: http://dme.dc.gov/DC/DME/Programs/EYD%20Framework%20FINAL.pdf [accessed March 2011].

Office of the Deputy Mayor for Education. (2010b). *Statewide Commission on Children Youth and Their Families*. Available: http://dme.dc.gov/DC/DME/Programs+and+Services/Statewide+Commission+on+Children+Youth+and+Their+Families/Statewide+Commission+on+Children+Youth+and+their+Families [accessed October 2010].

Office of the Ombudsman for Public Education. (2009). *Office of the Ombudsman for Public Education Home Page*. Available: http://ombudsman.dc.gov/ombudsman/site/default.asp [accessed October 2010].

Office of the State Superintendent of Education. (2010a). *Section Criteria: Progress and Plans in the Four Education Reform Areas*. Available: http://osse.dc.gov/seo/frames.asp?doc=/seo/lib/seo/cos/race_to_the_top/dc_rttt_section_vi_application.pdf [accessed November 2010].

Office of the State Superintendent of Education. (2010b). *The Statewide Longitudinal Education Data System (SLED)*. Available: http://osse.dc.gov/seo/cwp/view,a,1222,q,561228,seoNav_GID,1507,seoNav,%7C31195%7C,,.asp [accessed November 2010].

Rhee, M. (2009). *Letter to City Council Chairman Vincent Gray on Committee of the Whole Recommendations on Fiscal Year 2010 Budget*. Available: http://www.dcpswatch.com/dcps/090505.htm [accessed March 2011].

Segraves, M. (2009). D.C. council grills Rhee on teacher layoffs. *WTOP*, October 30. Available: http://www.wtop.com/?sid=1798802&nid=25 [accessed October 2010].

Turque, B. (2009). Latest Fenty budget cuts funds for schools evaluation. *Washington Post*, July 21. Available: http://www.washingtonpost.com/wp-dyn/content/article/2009/07/20/AR2009072002991_pf.html [accessed October 2010].

Turque, B. (2010). Higher scores noted for KIPP program; Report finds charter students do better on math and science tests. *Washington Post*, June 22. Available: http://pqasb.pqarchiver.com/washingtonpost/access/2063430941.html?FMT=ABS&FMTS=ABS:FT&date=Jun+22%2C+2010&author=Bill+Turque&pub=The+Washington+Post&edition=&startpage=B.1&desc=Higher+scores+noted+for+KIPP+program%3B+Report+finds+charter%27s+students+do+better+on+math+and+science+tests [accessed October 2010].

Turque, B., and Cohen, J. (2010). Rhee's approval rating in deep slide. *Washington Post*, February 1. Available: http://www.washingtonpost.com/wp-dyn/content/article/2010/01/31/AR2010013102757.html [accessed March 2011].

21st Century School Fund, Brookings Institution, and Urban Institute. (2008). *Quality Schools, Healthy Neighborhoods, and the Future of DC, Policy Report*. Washington, DC: Author. Available: http://www.21csf.org/csf-home/publications/QualitySchoolsResearchReport/QualitySchoolsPolicyReport9-18-08.pdf [accessed March 2011].

U.S. Government Accountability Office. (2009). *District of Columbia Public Schools: Important Steps Taken to Continue Reform Efforts, But Enhanced Planning Could Improve Implementation and Sustainability*. Washington, DC: Author. Available: http://www.gao.gov/new.items/d09619.pdf [accessed October 2010].

Wilson, T. (2009). Tapping into students' brain power; program looks to classrooms for ideas on reducing energy use. *Washington Post*, May 14. Available: http://pqasb.pqarchiver.com/washingtonpost/access/1711568301.html?FMT=ABS&FMTS=ABS:FT&date=May+14%2C+2009&author=Timothy+Wilson&pub=The+Washington+Post&edition=&startpage=T.3&desc=Tapping+Into+Students%27+Brain+Power%3B+Program+Looks+to+Classrooms+for+Ideas+on+Reducing+Energy+Use [accessed November 2010].

5

Student Achievement Under PERAA: First Impressions

To ask how well the schools are doing under the Public Education Reform Amendment Act (PERAA) is to ask countless specific—and often complicated—questions, which is why a thorough, 5-year evaluation is called for in the law. That evaluation may be even more important than originally envisioned because—even in the short time that this committee has been developing the evaluation plan—there has been complete turnover in the primary leadership positions for education in the District. There is a new mayor, deputy mayor, chancellor, and interim state superintendent of schools. Yet, 3 years after PERAA was enacted and after many significant changes have been implemented, it is not unreasonable to consider what has happened, what we call first impressions.

In this and the next chapter, we present our first impressions on several goals of the legislation: this chapter considers student achievement data. Chapter 6 looks at the other aspects of the system that also must be measured: the quality of district staff, the quality of classroom teaching and learning, service to vulnerable children and youth, family and community engagement, and operations.

For the purposes of this first phase of the evaluation effort, the committee was able to collect only preliminary information about student achievement and the five primary areas of district responsibility we discuss in Chapter 6. We stress that these first impressions are useful only as a basis for further inquiry and not as reliable evidence about the effectiveness of the changes under PERAA or how best to fine-tune programs and strategies in the future. Those tasks require an ongoing program of evaluation and research, which we offer in Chapter 7.

STUDENT ACHIEVEMENT AND TEST DATA

The most readily available first impressions of student achievement are provided by test scores. There is a long history of relying on student test data as a measure of the effectiveness of public education, and it is tempting to simply rely on those readily available data for judgments about student achievement and about causes and effects. However, student test scores alone provide useful but limited information about the causes of improvements or variability in student performance.

The results of achievement tests provide only estimates about students' skills and knowledge in selected areas—usually, what they know and can do in mathematics and reading and sometimes other subjects. Aggregate year-to-year comparisons of test scores in the District's schools are confounded by changes in student populations that result from student moves in and out of the city and between DC Public Schools (DCPS) and charter schools, dropout and reentry, and also from variations in testing practices that may exclude or include particular groups of students.[1] For these and other reasons, therefore, it is important to remember that the consensus of measurement and testing experts has long been to use test scores cautiously.

For this discussion, it is perhaps most important to underscore that most tests are not designed to support inferences about related questions, such as how well students were taught, what effects their teachers had on their learning, why students in some schools or classrooms succeed while those in similar schools and classrooms do not, whether conditions in the schools have improved as a result of a policy change, or what policy makers should do to solidify gains or reverse declines. Answering those sorts of questions requires other kinds of evidence besides test scores. Looking at test scores should be only a first step—not an end point—in considering questions about student achievement, or even more broadly, about student learning.

Nevertheless, changes in student test scores since 2007 provide one set of impressions regarding progress in DC schools. We offer here an overview of publicly available data from both the District of Columbia Comprehensive Assessment System (DC CAS) and the U.S. Department of Education's National Assessment of Educational Progress (NAEP). We first discuss these data sources, then look at the trend data, and end the chapter with a discussion of how to interpret the data. But we note again that a systematic and comprehensive analysis of achievement data for DC was beyond the scope of this report; the readily available information provides only a useful first

---

[1]Test scores also come with measurement issues that have to be considered if they are to provide an accurate picture of even those areas they do measure (Koretz, 2008; National Research Council, 1999; Office of Technology Assessment, 1992).

look and hints about issues related to student achievement that will need to be addressed in the long-term evaluation.

THE DATA SOURCES

The District's assessment system, the DC CAS, assesses students in grades 3 through 8 in reading and mathematics and in selected grades in science and composition.[2] The assessment system, which has been in place since 2006, is designed to measure individual students' progress toward meeting the District of Columbia's standards[3] and is used to meet federal requirements under the Elementary and Secondary Education Act, as amended by the No Child Left Behind (NCLB) Act (District of Columbia Public Schools, 2010a).[4] DC CAS scores are used to determine if a given school is making sufficient progress under NCLB, and the media and the public look to them for an indication of how well district schools are doing.

DC CAS results are reported using four performance levels: advanced, proficient, basic, and below basic. Box 5-1 provides an example of the performance descriptions used in DC CAS.

The NAEP, known popularly as the Nation's Report Card, is an assessment administered by the U.S. Department of Education and overseen by the autonomous National Assessment Governing Board that provides independent data about what students know and can do in mathematics, reading, and other subjects. NAEP is valuable in part because it is not a high-stakes test—scores for individual students or schools are not reported, and there are no consequences to students, teachers, or schools associated with NAEP scores. Results are reported for states, selected urban districts, and the nation, and all students are measured against common performance expectations; consequently, the results can be used to make comparisons among jurisdictions.[5] Changes to the assessment are infrequent and come with careful studies of comparability, so NAEP is also used to track student

---

[2]Information about DC-CAS can be found at: http://www.dc.gov/DCPS/In+the+Classroom/How+Students+Are+Assessed/Assessments/DC+Comprehensive+Assessment+System-Alternate+Assessment+Portfolio+(DC+CAS-Alt) [accessed October 2010].

[3]Information about the academic standards can be found at: http://osse.dc.gov/seo/cwp/view,A,1274,Q,561249,seoNav,%7C31193%7C.asp. According to the 2011 DC CAS guide (Office of the State Superintendent of Education, 2010b), the assessments in reading and mathematics are aligned to both the District of Columbia standards and to the Common Core Standards, a set of standards that the majority of states have recently adopted to ensure greater consistency in public education from state to state (http://www.corestandards.org/ [accessed December 2010]).

[4]States must meet the requirements of the No Child Left Behind Act in order to receive federal financial assistance to support the education of poor children.

[5]The comparisons are subject to some caveats related to such issues as inclusion rates for students with disabilities and English language learners.

> **BOX 5-1**
> **DC CAS Performance Descriptions for 3rd Grade Reading**
>
> The DC CAS is a standards-based assessment. Based on performance, each student is classified as performing at one of four performance levels: below basic, basic, proficient, and advanced. The descriptions below are examples of performance descriptions for each level.
>
> **Below Basic**
>
> Students are able to use vocabulary skills, such as identifying literal or common meanings of words and phrases, sometimes using context clues. Students are able to read some 3rd grade informational and literary texts and can identify a main idea, make some meaning of text features and graphics, form questions, locate text details, and identify simple relationships (e.g., cause/effect) in texts.
>
> **Basic**
>
> Students are able to use vocabulary skills, such as identifying words with prefixes and suffixes, and distinguishing between literal and nonliteral meanings of some common words and phrases. Students are able to read some 3rd grade informational and literary texts and can identify main points and some supporting facts, locate stated facts and specific information in graphics, form questions, identify lessons in a text, make simple connections within and between texts, describe and compare characters, and make simple interpretations.
>
> **Proficient**
>
> Students are able to use vocabulary skills, such as identifying affixes and root words and using context clues to interpret nonliteral words and meanings of unknown words. Students are able to read 3rd grade informational and literary texts and can distinguish between stated and implied facts and cause/effect relationships, determine and synthesize steps in a process, connect procedures to real-life situations, explain key ideas in stories, explain relationships among characters, identify subtle personality traits of characters, and connect story details to prior knowledge.
>
> **Advanced**
>
> Students are able to use vocabulary skills, such as identifying the figurative meanings or nonliteral meanings of some words and phrases in a moderately complex text. Students are able to read 3rd grade informational and literary texts and summarize the information or story with supporting details, apply text information to graphics, identify and explain relationships of facts and cause/effect relationships, use text features to make predictions, distinguish between fact and fiction, identify a speaker in a poem or narrator in a story, explain key ideas with supporting details, use context to interpret simple figurative language, and determine simple patterns in poetry.
>
> SOURCE: Office of the State Superintendent of Education (2010a, p. 1).

performance over time. For example, the NAEP mathematics assessment scores go back to 1992, and those for reading to 1990.

DC has participated in NAEP as a "state" since the early 1990s, and the scores for grades 4 and 8 reflect the performance of all District public schools, including all public charter schools. When NAEP began the Trial Urban District Assessment (TUDA) in 2002, the District was included in this assessment as well, one of only five such districts. In 2009, 18 districts participated. Until 2009, the scores for the District were the same for both the state and district assessments. Beginning in 2009 most charter schools were excluded from the District's TUDA results, but they remained in the state score calculation. The charter schools that are excluded from DCPS's adequate yearly progress (AYP) report under NCLB were also excluded from the NAEP TUDA. This look at the data presents both state and TUDA scores together. The state scores include all DC schools and therefore serve as the basis for comparison. All NAEP data in this section refer to the state DC scores unless otherwise noted. The TUDA scores are presented in graphics for completeness, but are not discussed and should be evaluated cautiously, particularly in the context of comparisons between 2007 and 2009 because of the change in charter school exclusion in 2009.

These two assessments provide different ways of measuring student progress. DC CAS provides evidence of the progress of individual students and groups (such as 3rd graders in a school or in the district) toward mastering specific objectives in the DC standards. NAEP provides a picture of what students at each grade in the District as a whole know and can do in terms of nationwide definitions of achievement in each subject.

TEST SCORE TRENDS

The percentage of tested students who performed at or above the proficient level (proficiency rate) in all grades in the District on the DC CAS increased from 2006 to 2010. Figure 5-1 shows the upward trend prior to PERAA's passage in 2007. After 2007, the trend in both reading and mathematics increased more steeply for 2 years, then flattened out, and then declined slightly in the 2009-2010 school year.

Figure 5-2 shows the percentages of students (by grade and subject) performing at each of the four proficiency levels on DC CAS and state NAEP for 2007 and 2009. These data show that, in general, the percentages of students in both the below basic and basic categories decreased for both assessments, while the percentages of students performing at both the proficient and advanced levels increased. That is, the distribution of students shifted to higher performance levels from 2007 to 2009. Thus, the NAEP scores appear to confirm the improvement shown on the DC CAS scores. However, the percentages of students performing at the proficient

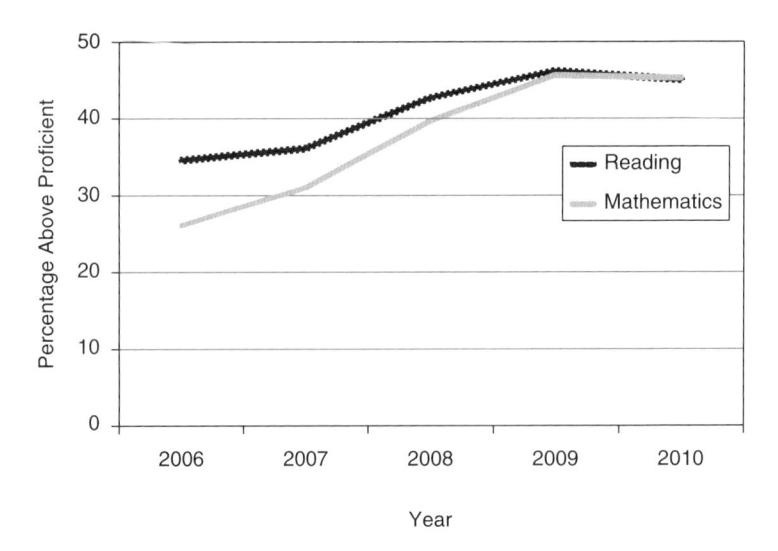

FIGURE 5-1 Percentage of District students at or above the proficient level on the DC CAS in reading and mathematics, 2006-2010.
SOURCE: Adapted from http://www.nclb.osse.dc.gov/index.asp [accessed December 2010].

level or above on NAEP is significantly smaller than the percentage who perform at those levels on DC CAS—a finding that suggests that DC CAS is a less challenging assessment than NAEP (we discuss this issue further below).

The average (scaled) score on NAEP shows a similar positive trend. The 2009 NAEP scores for DC as a state (see Figure 5-3) in grade 4 for both reading and mathematics were statistically significantly higher than they had been in all previous years (2003, 2005, and 2007). This was also true for grade 8 mathematics. In grade 8 reading, the DC state scores in 2009 were also significantly higher than those for 2003 and 2005, but not than those for 2007. That is, grade 8 reading was the only assessment in which the District did not show a significant gain from 2007 to 2009.

In comparison with states, the District's scores were notable. In grade 4 reading, only two other states improved since 2007; in mathematics, only four other states showed significant improvement at both grades 4 and 8. Only three states, Kentucky, Rhode Island, and Vermont, showed improvement in three of the four assessments, and no state improved in all four. However, in comparison with other urban districts, the District's scores were similar: many others also showed consistently significant gains.

DC CAS Grade 4 Reading

Year	Below Basic	Basic	Proficient	Advanced
2007	19	44	32	5
2009	17	38	37	8

DC CAS Grade 8 Reading

Year	Below Basic	Basic	Proficient	Advanced
2007	24	44	26	5
2009	15	40	37	8

DC CAS Grade 4 Mathematics

Year	Below Basic	Basic	Proficient	Advanced
2007	27	39	29	6
2009	18	33	37	13

DC CAS Grade 8 Mathematics

Year	Below Basic	Basic	Proficient	Advanced
2007	31	36	28	5
2009	23	34	36	6

NAEP DC State Grade 4 Reading

Year	Below Basic	Basic	Proficient	Advanced
2007	61	25	10	4
2009	56	27	12	5

NAEP DC State Grade 8 Reading

Year	Below Basic	Basic	Proficient	Advanced
2007	52	36	11	1
2009	49	37	12	1

NAEP DC State Grade 4 Mathematics

Year	Below Basic	Basic	Proficient	Advanced
2007	51	36	11	3
2009	44	39	14	3

NAEP DC State Grade 8 Mathematics

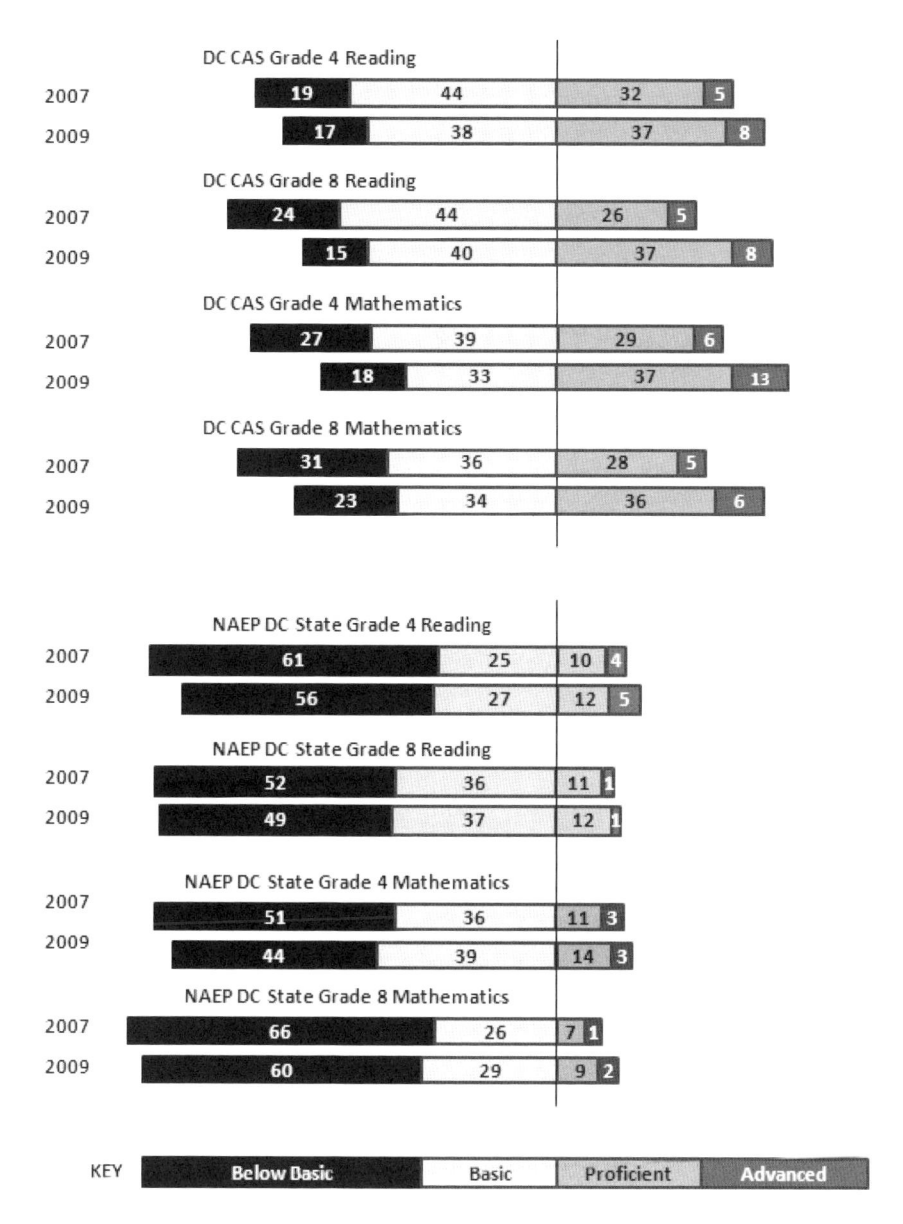

Year	Below Basic	Basic	Proficient	Advanced
2007	66	26	7	1
2009	60	29	9	2

KEY: Below Basic | Basic | Proficient | Advanced

FIGURE 5-2 Proficiency levels of District students from DC CAS and NAEP for 2007 and 2009 in reading and mathematics.
SOURCES: National Center for Education Statistics, NAEP Data Explorer, see http://nces.ed.gov/nationsreportcard/naepdata/ [accessed September 2010]; DC CAS, see http://www.nclb.osse.dc.gov/index.asp [accessed March 2011].

Grade 4 Mathematics

Grade 4 Reading

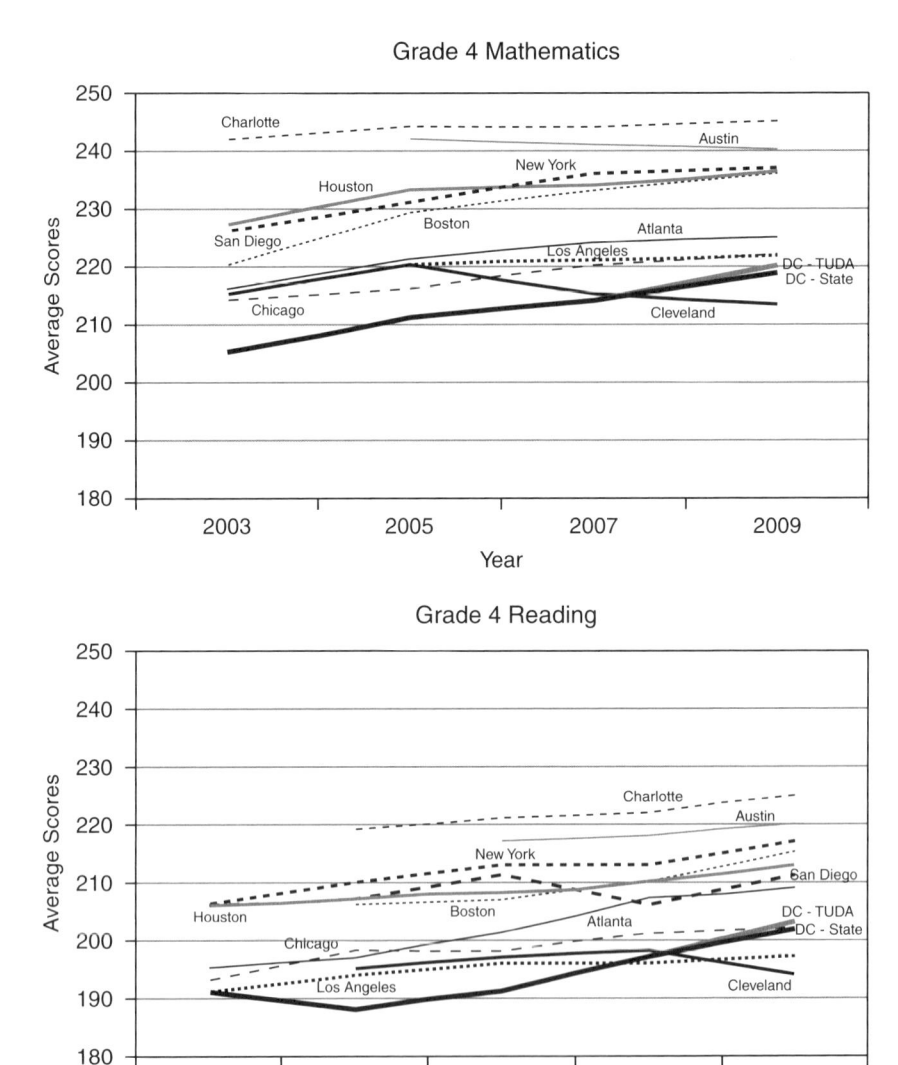

FIGURE 5-3 NAEP TUDA average scores for 10 urban districts and DC, as well as DC state NAEP, for mathematics and reading, grades 4 and 8, 2002-2009.
NOTES: State and TUDA scores are presented together for completeness. State scores include all DC schools and thus are the focus of this analysis. TUDA scores should be evaluated cautiously particularly when comparing 2007 to 2009 because most charter schools were excluded in 2009 (but included in 2007—see text).
SOURCE: National Center for Education Statistics, NAEP Data Explorer, see http://nces.ed.gov/nationsreportcard/naepdata/ [accessed September 2010].

STUDENT ACHIEVEMENT UNDER PERAA 71

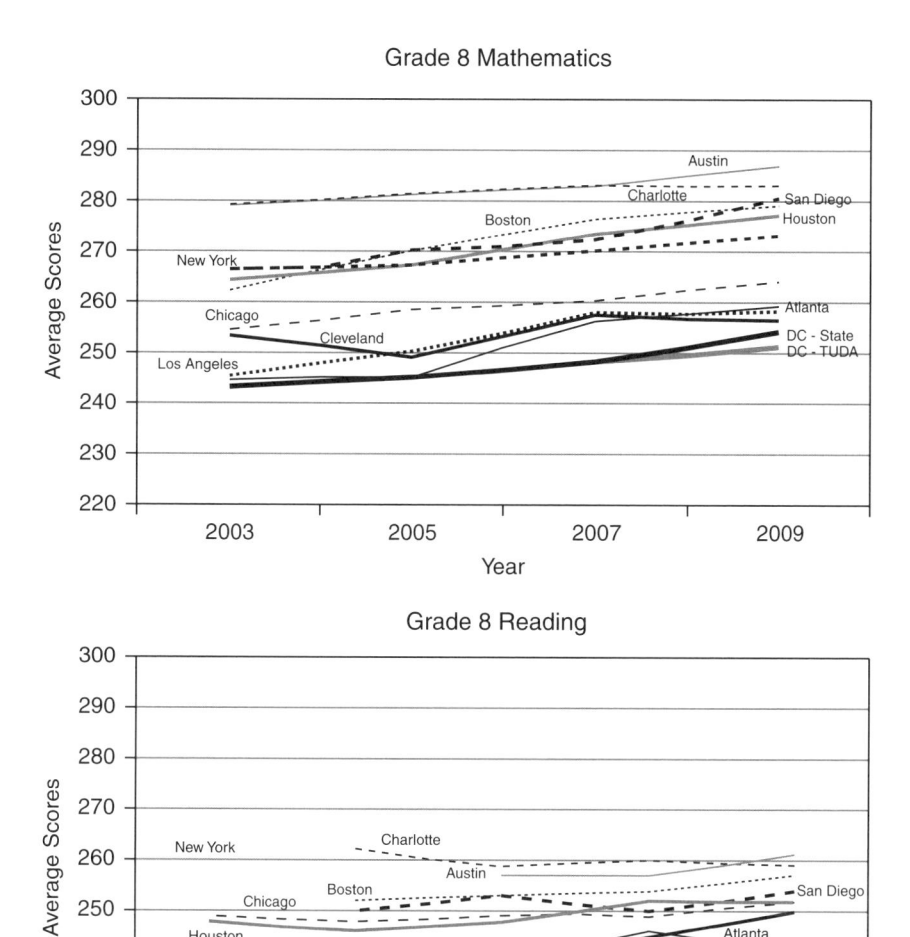

Grade 8 Mathematics

Grade 8 Reading

FIGURE 5-3 Continued.

Figure 5-3 also shows trends for other school districts assessed by NAEP in mathematics and reading.[6] Two points are worth noting: the District's average scores are low compared with those of most of the other 10 school districts in both the 2007 and 2009 TUDA (including Boston, Chicago, and New York), but DC and its peer districts are improving at similar rates. Most districts showed gains from 2007 to 2009: see Figure 5-4.[7,8]

It is important to note, however, that scores that are averaged across large numbers of students can obscure which students are improving and by how much. It may be that only a small group of students is making gains while others are not improving or may even be doing worse than previously. For example, the highest achievers may be showing gains while the lowest achievers are not, or vice versa. The committee was limited by time and resources in the number of disaggregations we could carry out for this report, but a few examples demonstrate the importance of looking beyond average scores.

It appears that students at every level in the District are gaining ground. As Figure 5-5 shows, for example, in DC state NAEP grade 4 reading, students in the lowest, middle, and highest groups all made gains, with the lowest scoring students gaining at a faster rate than the others. We note, too, that black, Hispanic and white 4th graders on average scored higher on the DC CAS mathematics in 2010 than in 2007, while English language learners and students with disabilities also showed some improvements relative to their peers: see Figure 5-6.

The NAEP data show different results. For grade 4 reading, there was no significant change in the performance of white 4th grade students in the District from 2005 to 2009, while scores for both black and Hispanic 4th graders showed a significant gain for 2009: see Figure 5-7. For grade 8 reading, the NAEP data show large achievement gaps when scores are broken out by the educational attainment of students' mothers: see Figure 5-8. These data show improvements for those students whose mothers did not finish high school.

---

[6] Although 18 urban districts participated in the 2009 mathematics and reading assessments, only 10 districts other than DC also participated in assessments in previous years, so it is only possible to examine changes over time for those 10.

[7] These data findings come from the test of differences in gains performed through NAEP Data Explorer, see http://nces.ed.gov/nationsreportcard/naepdata/ [accessed September 2010].

[8] Although the DC state scores are the focus of this analysis because they reflect all public schools, the TUDA scores are also presented in Figure 5-3. It should be noted that if the non-DCPS charter schools had been excluded in 2007 as they were in 2009 (i.e., if NAEP had used comparable samples in both years), the District would have also shown a statistically significant increase from 244 in 2007 to 251 in 2009 in grade 8 mathematics, rather than the non-significant change from 248 to 251: see "comparability of samples" at http://nationsreportcard.gov/math_2009/about_math.asp [accessed December 2010].

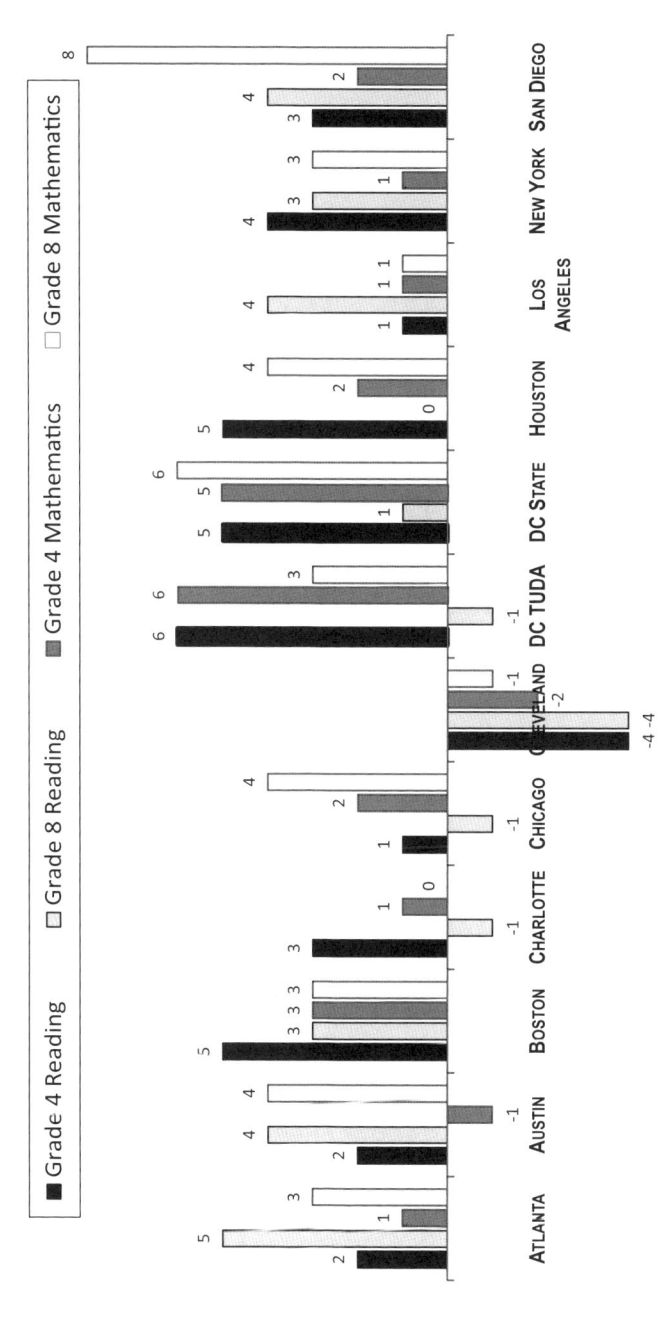

FIGURE 5-4 Changes in NAEP scores for selected urban districts, 2007-2009. Numbers indicate the amount of the increase or decrease in the average scaled score.
NOTES: State and TUDA scores are presented together for completeness. State scores include all DC schools and thus are the focus of this analysis. TUDA scores should be evaluated cautiously particularly when comparing 2007 to 2009 because most charter schools were excluded in 2009 (but included in 2007—see text).
SOURCE: National Center for Education Statistics, NAEP Data Explorer, see http://nces.ed.gov/nationsreportcard/naepdata/ [accessed September 2010].

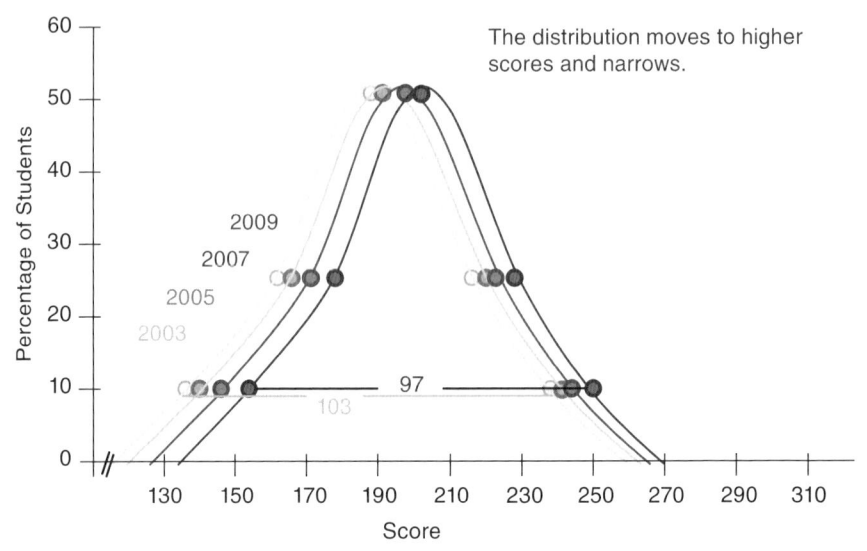

FIGURE 5-5 Changes from 2003 to 2009 in grade 4 reading score distributions on DC state NAEP.
SOURCE: National Center for Education Statistics, NAEP Data Explorer, see http://nces.ed.gov/nationsreportcard/naepdata/ [accessed September 2010].

NAEP also collects background data on students, teachers, and schools that cover general and content-specific questions (i.e., related to specific tested subjects) to provide context for the testing data. In general, these data also show improvements for DC students. For example, data collected with the grade 8 reading assessment show that the number of students reporting that they were absent more than 10 days in the month prior to testing was significantly smaller in 2009 than in 2007.[9] This finding is important because there is evidence that absenteeism by both students and teachers has a negative effect on student achievement (Allensworth and Easton, 2007; Miller et al., 2007).

Another notable finding from the background data is that the percentage of schools reporting the *smallest* percentage of teachers absent (0-2 percent) on an average day increased from 68 percent in 2007 to 85 percent in 2009, a significant decline: see Figure 5-9. These data can be crossed with the scaled scores: in 2009 the average score for students in the schools with low absenteeism (0-2 percent) was 246, while the average score in the schools with high absenteeism (6-10 percent) was

---

[9]NAEP Data Explorer analysis, see http://nces.ed.gov/nationsreportcard/naepdata/ [accessed September 2010].

STUDENT ACHIEVEMENT UNDER PERAA   75

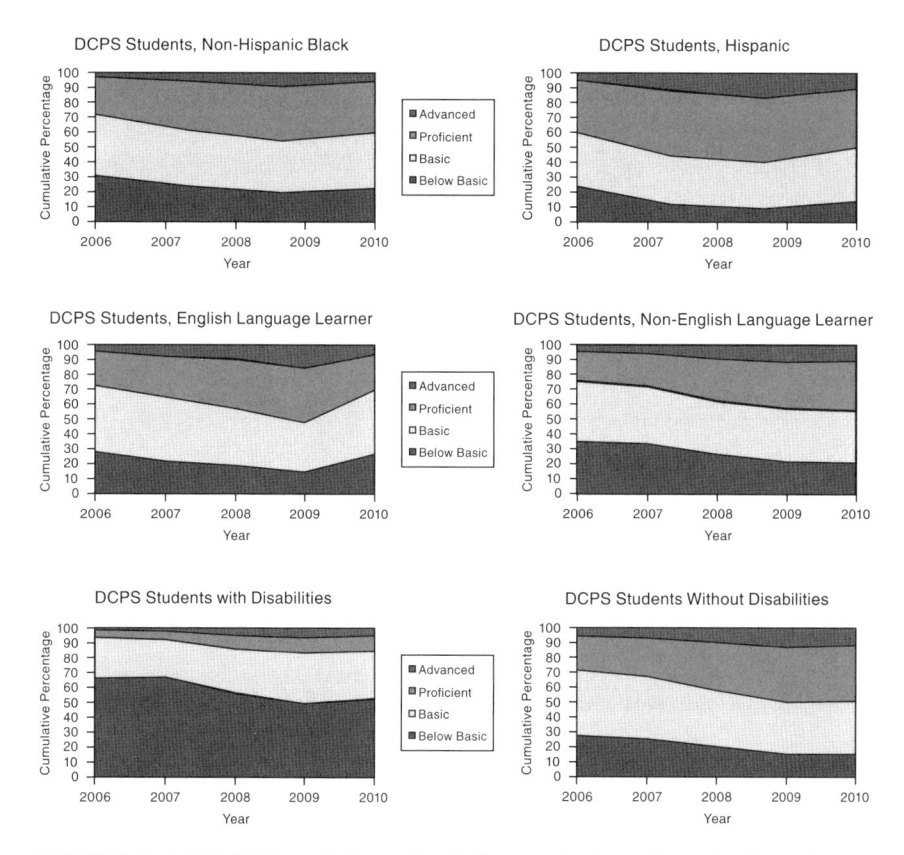

FIGURE 5-6 DC CAS proficiency levels for grade 4 mathematics by ethnicity, English language learner, and disability status, 2006-2010.
SOURCE: Compiled from http://www.nclb.osse.dc.gov/index.asp [accessed December 2010].

significantly lower, at 234.[10] It is important to note, however, that the fact that teacher absenteeism is correlated with achievement does not mean that the absenteeism causes the low achievement. There are many other factors, such as school safety, that affect both teacher absenteeism and student achievement. This is just one example of the many limitations of these data and the related qualifications that must be considered when interpreting them.

---

[10]There were insufficient data for the other categories of absentee rates to produce comparable estimates.

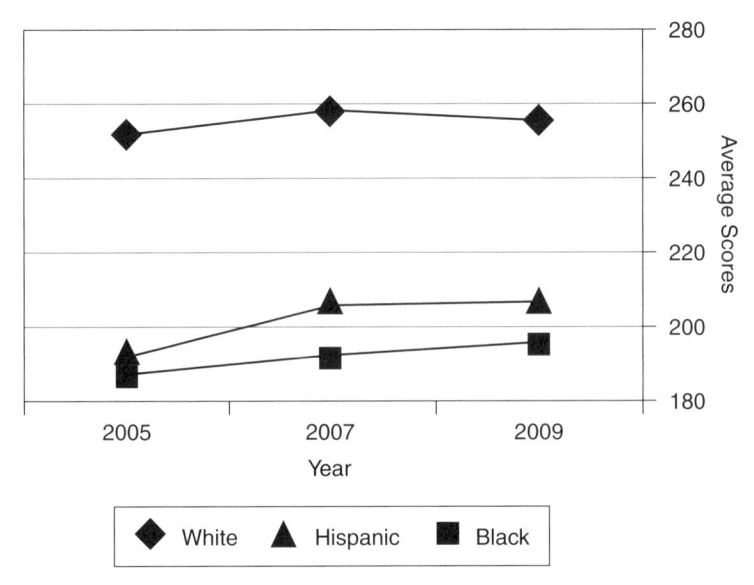

FIGURE 5-7 DC state NAEP grade 4 reading average scores by race/ethnicity, 2005-2009.
SOURCE: National Center for Education Statistics, NAEP Data Explorer, see http://nces.ed.gov/nationsreportcard/naepdata/ [accessed September 2010].

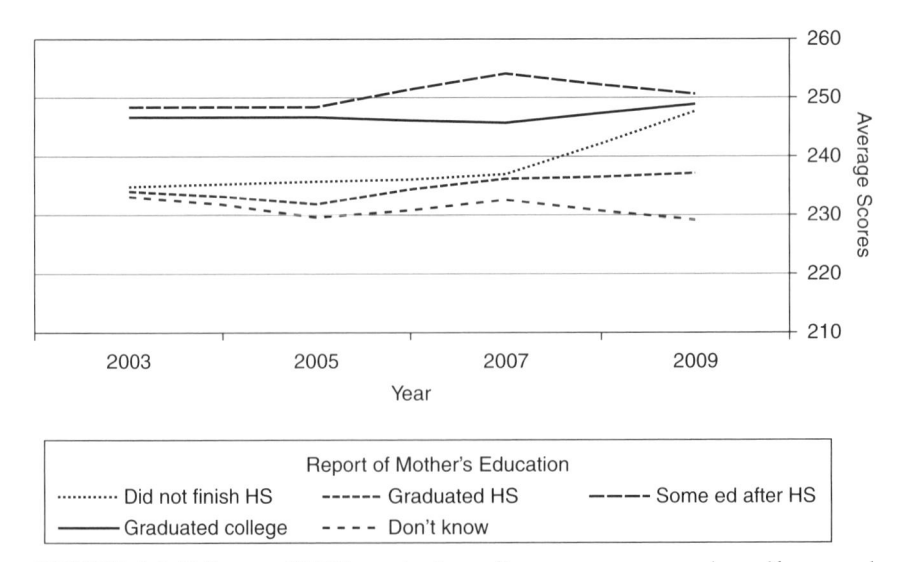

FIGURE 5-8 DC state NAEP grade 8 reading average scores by self-reported mother's education, 2003-2009.
SOURCE: National Center for Education Statistics, NAEP Data Explorer, see http://nces.ed.gov/nationsreportcard/naepdata/ [accessed September 2010].

STUDENT ACHIEVEMENT UNDER PERAA 77

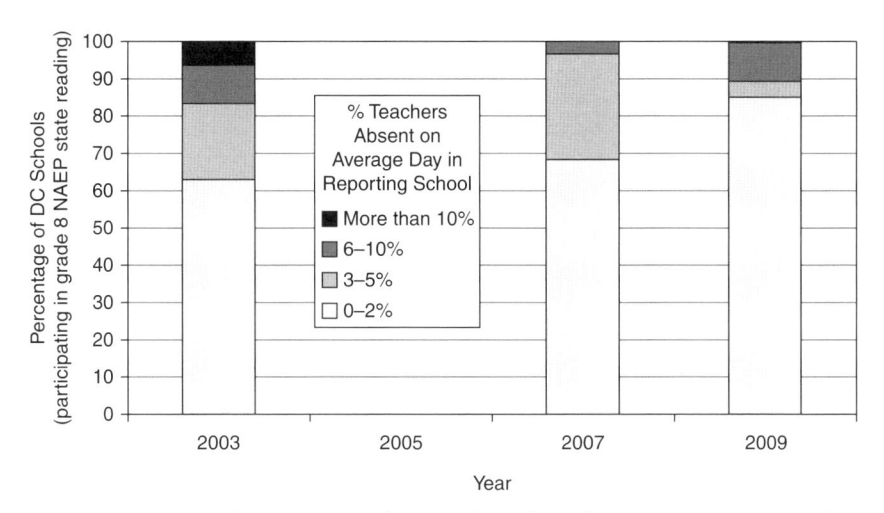

FIGURE 5-9 DC school reports of rates of teacher absenteeism, NAEP grade 8 reading, 2003-2009.
NOTE: Data are from background information on the NAEP state grade 8 reading test.
SOURCE: National Center for Education Statistics, NAEP Data Explorer, see http://nces.ed.gov/nationsreportcard/naepdata/ [accessed September 2010].

ISSUES FOR INTERPRETING TEST SCORES

Several issues must be taken into account before making inferences from results of achievement tests. There is a large technical literature on these issues; we review here a few key points of particular relevance to this report on DCPS.

Evidence Needed for Conclusions of Causation

The preliminary analysis we have provided suggests that the District's implementation of PERAA might have, overall, had a positive effect on student achievement (with some leveling off in the last year). However, these test score data are only *correlated* with the changes brought about by PERAA and cannot on their own support the idea that PERAA *caused* the scores to improve. For example, the DC CAS scores that rose during the period in question might have risen without PERAA or they might have risen more rapidly without PERAA. Alternatively, some other change that occurred at the same time might have caused the increase.

The DC CAS was introduced in 2006, and there is some evidence that when a new test is introduced scores first rise significantly and then level off (see, e.g., Linn, 2000). One hypothesis as to the reason for this pattern is that as teachers and students gradually become accustomed to the new test format and new expectations, student performance improves, but that once the test is familiar, performance stays flat (Koretz et al., 1991). Additional evidence would be needed to show whether this phenomenon might explain the observed changes in DC. In short, the DC CAS scores did rise, but there is insufficient evidence to establish the reason for the improvement.

In the case of the District, the fact that NAEP shows increases similar to those seen on the DC CAS suggests that the new-test phenomenon may not be the primary explanation; however, other changes that occurred in the same period could be responsible. Demographic shifts—changes in the composition of the student population that occur when students leave or enter the system (which will also change the groups of students being compared from year to year) are another potential source of change in test scores. Since the tests compared cohorts of students, scores will be affected if the populations are not similar. For example, if more higher-scoring 4th graders move into (or opt not to leave) the district's public schools from one year to the next, average scores would likely rise—but that rise would not reflect improved learning. Such changes could occur because of in- or out-migration from the city or transfers between public and charter schools. If there are only small differences in the composition of students being tested across years, the effect would be slight. However, if, substantially more or fewer students in one year came from families of low socioeconomic status than in the next year, test results might show substantial changes that have nothing to do with the quality of instruction in schools or improved student learning. This is a serious issue in DC, which has a highly mobile student population, where many students move into and out of the charter school system, and which has a history in which the most disadvantaged residents have sometimes been forced by changing political and economic forces to move within the city or into neighboring jurisdictions.

This issue is not just theoretical. The composition of students in tested grades in the District of Columbia's public schools, has changed markedly since 2007 (see Table 5-1).[11] The number of students in all tested grades in DCPS has dropped by almost 21 percent, while the number of tested students in the charters has increased.[12] However this decrease within the DCPS has not been consistent across demographic groups; in contrast the subgroup composition of students attending public charter schools in the district has remained relatively stable over this same time period—see Table 5-1.

---

[11]Table 5-1 was revised after the prepublication report was released; data are now presented separately for DCPS and charter schools (previously the combined data were presented).

[12]Discussion in this paragraph relies on data about students enrolled in the tested grades of 3-8 and 10 only and not to all students. See Table 5-1.

For example, the enrollment of students who were not economically disadvantaged fell considerably in DCPS between 2007 and 2010 while the enrollment of economically disadvantaged students also declined but not at the same rate. This means that economically disadvantaged students now make up a larger proportion of the total population of DCPS students—an increase of 8.2 percentage points; economically disadvantaged students were 62.2 percent of the DCPS tested population in 2007 and 70.4 percent in 2010. A similar pattern can be found for black students whose overall numbers fell in DCPS while those of whites and Hispanics increased slightly resulting in a shift in the overall demographic composition of the DCPS student body. The effects of families leaving the district or returning to the district are not generally factored in to summary proficiency statistics, yet these patterns could significantly bias the summary statistics (including cohort averages) either up or down. As we discussed in Chapter 3, the District has witnessed changes in movement between DCPS and charter schools and in the composition of particular neighborhoods (as well as tensions regarding school closures and school improvements) that are likely to affect local school student populations; consequently, this issue should be carefully considered when interpreting changes in student achievement data.

Dropout rates raise similar concerns. As students drop out of schools, their test scores are no longer included in their schools' data. Thus, those schools' average test scores may improve if significant numbers of low-achieving students leave, even if the remaining students' scores have not gone up and the school has not actually improved. This is an important consideration in assessing DC's test scores because a recent report from the National Center for Education Statistics found that the rate of students who enter 9th grade and later graduate from a DC school has steadily declined, from 68 percent in the 2001-2002 school year to only 56 percent in the 2007-2008 school year. The validity of data on dropout rates is, in itself, an issue of serious concern in interpreting achievement data (see, e.g., National Research Council and National Academy of Education, 2011).

For all of these reasons, reports of test score gains are complete and valid only when they include analysis of the demography of the student population—including examinations of the distribution of students by geographic area (e.g., ward) and movement into and out of charter schools, private schools, and suburban school districts. One means of factoring out the effects of population changes is to track individual students in the system over time to determine whether their performance is on an upward trajectory, that is, to follow actual cohorts of students across time. Doing so makes it possible to see the performance of the students who remain in the system without any distortion that could come from changes in demographic composition. Thus, it is important to complement the average scaled scores and demographic analyses with assessments of individual student growth over time.

TABLE 5-1 Changes in Demographic Subgroups Enrolled in Tested Grades for DCPS and Charter Schools, 2007-2010

DCPS

Year		Econ Dis	Non Econ Dis	Black	Hispanic	White[a]	LEP	Non-LEP	SPED	Non-SPED	Total
2007	subgroup%	62.2	37.8	83.5	9.5	5.3	8.2	91.8	21.8	78.2	
	#	16,283	9,916	21,881	2,487	1,376	2,185	24,422[b]	5,707	20,492	26,199
2008	%	64.2	35.8	83.7	10.1	5.7	8.4	91.6	19.7	80.3	
	#	15,125	8,440[b]	19,463	2,353	1,331	1,993	21,872[b]	4,638	18,927[b]	23,259
2009	%	68.5	31.5	80.0	11.2	6.9	11.6	88.4	20.8	79.2	
	#	14,631	6,738	17,091	2,389	1,473	2,470	18,899	4,446	16,923	21,369
2010	%	70.4	29.6	78.1	12.1	7.8	8.0	92.0	21.0	79.0	
	#	14,587	6,140	16,181	2,518	1,610	1,663	19,064	4,352	16,375	20,727
Percentage Point Change in Subgroup Composition (2010%–2007%)		8.2	-8.2	-5.5	2.6	2.5	-0.2	0.2	-0.8	0.8	
Percentage Change in Number Enrolled (2010#–2007#/2007#)		-10.4	-38.1	-26.0	1.2	17.0	-23.9	-21.9	-23.7	-20.1	-20.9

Public Charter Schools in DC

Year	subgroup	Econ Dis	Non Econ Dis	Black	Hispanic	White[a]	LEP	Non-LEP	SPED	Non-SPED	Total
2007	%	66.3	33.7	90.4	6.6	2.2	4.3	95.7	12.8	87.2	
	#	5,971	3,037	8,140	599	194	390	8,690[b]	1,155	7,853	9,008
2008	%	70.0	30.0	86.9	6.9	2.4	5.2	94.8	13.7	86.3	
	#	6,718	2,876	8,608	687	241	501	9,184	1,310	8,284	9,900
2009	%	72.0	28.0	89.6	7.6	2.2	6.0	94.0	13.4	86.6	
	#	8,174	3,183	10,173	859	251	677	10,680	1,519	9,838	11,357
2010	%	68.3	31.7	88.7	8.2	2.5	4.7	95.3	12.5	87.5	
	#	7,962	3,698	10,339	952	297	550	11,110	1,452	10,208	11,660
Percentage Point Change in Subgroup Composition (2010%–2007%)		2.0	−2.0	−1.7	1.5	0.4	0.4	−0.4	−0.4	0.4	
Percentage Change in Number Enrolled (2010#–2007#/2007#)		33.3	21.8	27.0	58.9	53.1	41.0	27.8	25.7	30.0	29.4

NOTES: Tested grades are 3-8 and 10. Econ Dis = economically disadvantaged, LEP = limited English proficient, SPED = special education.
[a] Percentages (across black, Hispanic, white) do not sum to 100 because two subgroups (with very low numbers) are not shown.
[b] The total across these two subgroups is greater than the total number of students reported for that year (see "Total" column at far right). Data are presented as they appear on the OSSE website; we were unable to determine the reason for the discrepancy. For these cases, percentages were calculated based on the sum across subgroups (not the total number from the far right column).
SOURCE: Compiled from http://www.nclb.osse.dc.gov/index.asp [accessed April 2011].

Looking Beyond Proficiency Rates

The primary data point reported for DC CAS (as for many assessment programs) is the proficiency rate, the percentage of students who perform at or above the proficient level. However, using proficiency rates has more significant limitations than using measures that more accurately reflect the spread of scores, such as averages. One limitation is that states have widely varying definitions of proficiency in core subjects. For example, a study for the U.S. Department of Education (Bandeira de Mello et al., 2009) found that the difference between the most and least challenging state standards for proficient performance in reading and mathematics was as large as the difference between the basic and proficient performance levels on NAEP. This study did not include the District because data were not available, but it is possible to compare the percentage of students at or above proficient on NAEP to that of DC CAS during the same year: see Figure 5-2, above. The reasons for the differences in the tests may be that the DC CAS is more closely aligned to the District's—not NAEP's—standards and therefore measures different things. It is also possible that the District, like many other states, has a lower bar for proficiency than does NAEP.

Another limitation to consider about data on the percentage of students performing at or above the proficient level is that this figure provides no information about students who are performing significantly above or below that level. Thus, this measure cannot reveal change that occurs at all other points on the scale—such as students who move from below basic to basic or from proficient to advanced. If a school or the district as a whole has focused on helping the students who are performing just below the proficiency cutoff point to cross that cutoff (sometimes called bubble kids), other students might receive less attention (Booher-Jennings, 2005; Neal and Schanzenbach, 2007).

Another and perhaps most important limitation is that the percent proficient statistic does not account for the weight (relative numbers of students) around the proficiency cut scores, and the fact that a slightly different choice in cut score may even reverse trends (Ho, 2008). Using proficiency scores to assess gains and gaps leads to "unrepresentative depictions of large-scale test score trends, gaps, and gap trends" and "incorrect or incomplete inferences about distributional change" (Ho, 2008, p. 1). Because of this limitation, analysts recommend statistics or summaries that accurately reflect the performance of all students, such as the average scaled scores and the distribution of these scores (Ho, 2008).

Disaggregating Test Results

Although average scores provide a measure of whole group performance, the average may mask important subgroup differences. For example, it is possible for the overall average to be increasing while some subgroup scores are decreasing. Alternatively, the average may not show a change, even though some subgroups' scores are significantly increasing. Thus, disaggregating results is essential to understanding of score trends.

A thorough evaluation of test scores in the District would examine how achievement has been changing across a number of student groups, considering:

- grade level,
- subject (and, in some cases, strands),
- types of schools (e.g., charter or traditional),
- student achievement levels (e.g., 10th, 25th, 50th, 75th, 90th percentiles),
- geography (e.g., in the District, ward),
- ethnicity,
- income level, and
- special populations, such as students with disabilities and English language learners.

We also note that policies that change the standards for classifying English language learners have potentially significant effects on the characteristics of the whole population, and, therefore, on average performance. Students who move into the proficient category, for example, are often automatically reclassified as non-English language learners (even though they may not have attained complete fluency) and, thus, are no longer counted in the subgroup. In this situation, overall scores would appear to decrease simply because the composition of the tested group changed.

Disaggregating data is complicated for DC because the city's black population is large in comparison with that of many other school districts. Significant demographic differences within the city, including differences in levels of income and education, may therefore be obscured in analyses of achievement by racial group. DC's unique population demographics make the black-white achievement gap less informative than comparisons within the demographic groups in the District and surrounding areas.

Although there is little argument about the importance of striving to eliminate long-standing achievement gaps, it would be misleading to focus on such aggregate gaps within the District population as was done, for example, in the 2008-2009 progress report of the DC Public Schools (District of Columbia Public Schools, 2009). The District's black population is very diverse, and includes both a concentration of very highly educated and successful black residents and many who are poorly educated and economically insecure. Socioeconomic differences are especially large between the northwest and southeast areas of the city, whose populations are dominated, respectively, by well-off whites and poor blacks. For example, recently released data from the American Community Survey—aggregated from 2005 to 2009—show that in northwest Washington more than 80 percent of adults have at least a bachelor's degree and more than 50 percent have at least a master's degree, while in southeast Washington fewer than 10 percent have a bachelor's degree. And in most areas of northwest Washington, the median household income is well over $100,000 per year, while in southeast Washington, the median household income is well under $50,000 (U.S. Census Bureau, 2010).

It is highly misleading to compare academic achievement between populations of such different social and economic standing. Even in the absence of improved measures of individual students' socioeconomic status (discussed below), when the new common core standards and common assessments become available, it should at least be possible to compare academic performance levels of white, black, and Hispanic students in the District with those in other, comparable student populations. In the meantime, naïve aggregate comparison of test scores among race-ethnic groups in the District should be interpreted critically and cautiously. Thus, analysts need to carefully consider student backgrounds when comparing average scores, for example, by disaggregating by socioeconomic background.

One way that is sometimes proposed to capture socioeconomic differences is to use eligibility for the National School Lunch Program (which provides free or reduced-price lunch for income-eligible students), but research suggests that this is not in fact a valid proxy (Harwell and Lebeau, 2010). Students are eligible for the lunch program if their family incomes fall below 125 percent of the official federal poverty guideline (for free lunch) or between 125 percent and 175 percent of the poverty line (for reduced-price lunch). However, the program serves only those students who apply, and not all who are eligible apply. The percentages of students identified as low-income using the NAEP lunch program are lower than the percentages identified by Census Bureau data (Booher-Jennings, 2005). Another difficulty with using the lunch program data as a measure comes from changes in policies regarding eligibility. During the past decade, the program has been offered to the entire populations of schools that meet certain criteria, as well as to individual students in any school. Thus, in some cases individual students who do not meet the criteria actually participate in the program. Moreover, the federal definition of the poverty threshold has risen significantly less than the standard of living since the 1960s, so the official poverty designation has come to refer to a relatively more deprived segment of the population over time (see National Research Council, 1995). Because of these variations, eligibility for free or reduced-price lunch has limited value as a measure of socioeconomic status. Further research is needed to establish an improved measure of socioeconomic status that will capture differences in the District.

We reiterate that DC NAEP results should be disaggregated by socioeconomic status, as well as by race and ethnicity, to support meaningful inferences about student learning. Multiple methods should be used to track income level, such as parental education and home ownership status, as reported by parents or other responsible adults.

The percentage of students tested (of all students enrolled) for DC CAS and the inclusion rates of English language learners and students with disabilities for NAEP are also factors that can affect population scores while masking subgroup scores. For example, if there were a significant decrease in the percentage of students tested, it could significantly affect test scores because the students most likely to be excluded are low-performing ones. For NAEP, state or district policies may differ on the inclusion or exclusion of students with disabilities or English language learners. If larger numbers of these students are excluded in one district or state in comparison with another, the test's results for that state or district may be inflated. For the District, the percentage of students with disabilities or who are English language learners and were excluded from the NAEP assessments dropped from 2007 to 2009: in mathematics, the exclusion rate declined from 6 to 4 percent in grade 4 and from 10 to 6 percent in grade 8; in reading, the exclusion rate dropped from 14 to 11 percent in grade 4 and from 13 to 12 percent in grade 8. This decrease in the percentage of excluded students provides additional evidence that the assessment gains for District students are real in every NAEP assessment.

Comparing Test Results

Even individual student-level data will have significant limitations. Tracking students who leave the city is a challenge for the District, which has high rates of mobility to and from neighboring jurisdictions. It is also not generally possible to compare student performance across districts unless they use the same assessments (or ones that have significant overlap; see National Research Council, 2010b, for a discussion of cross-state comparisons). Since the DC CAS is only administered to students in public schools in the District, it is not possible to assess whether students in DC are "catching up" over time with students outside of the system: one can only track the relative movement of DC students in comparison with one another.

The DC State Board of Education voted in 2010 to adopt the common core standards, a set of standards in English language arts and mathematics that have been developed cooperatively by the states and have been adopted by 40 other states.[13] Since these standards are different from the current standards used for the DC CAS, a new set of assessments will be needed to replace the DC CAS. The District currently plans to adopt a new common assessment system that will align with the common core standards; such an assessment system is being developed by a multistate consortium.[14] Once the new assessment system is operational, it will be possible to compare the progress of DC students with those in other jurisdictions, and thus to acquire additional evidence regarding changes in student performance since the passage of PERAA.

However, switching assessments also has disadvantages. If the DC CAS is not retained in some form for trend purposes, the District will no longer be able to compare current performance with that of the years prior to the implementation of a new assessment. It is possible to do a braided study (in which questions from the old test are nested within the new test) or to use the old test in a sample of schools for a few years to provide some information on trends. Since, as we noted above, performance typically falls in the first year after a new test is introduced and then rapidly improves as teachers and students become familiar with the new format and new standards, it will be important to take that into account in drawing conclusions about the results from a new test (see Koretz et al., 1991).

A second issue we note is that assessment scores are part of DCPS's teacher performance management system. There is considerable debate over pay-for-performance and the reliability of value-added measures; we note here only that attaching direct consequences to student test scores *may* provide an added incentive for teachers to focus on tested content, at the expense of other important educational goals, or even to cheat by offering students help or information they are not intended to have (see Jacob and Levitt, 2003; Lazear, 2006; National Research Council, 2010a). Comparing overall and disaggregated student performance on DC CAS and NAEP can help to provide a check on the integrity of results.

REFERENCES

Allensworth, E.M., and Easton, J.Q. (2007). *What Matters for Staying On-Track and Graduating in Chicago Public High Schools: A Close Look at Course Grades, Failures, and Attendance in the Freshman Year, Research Report.* Chicago: Consortium on Chicago School Research at the University of Chicago.

---

[13]For details, see http://www.corestandards.org/in-the-states [accessed January 2010].
[14]For the DC government press release announcing the State Board's adoption, see http://newsroom.dc.gov/show.aspx/agency/seo/section/2/release/20261 [accessed March 2011].

Bandeira de Mello, V., Blankenship, C., and McLaughlin, D. (2009). *Mapping State Proficiency Standards onto NAEP Scales: 2005-2007* (Research and Development Report, NCES 2010-456). Washington, DC: National Center for Education Statistics.

Booher-Jennings, J. (2005). Below the bubble: "Educational triage" and the Texas accountability system. *American Educational Research Journal, 42*(2), 231-268.

District of Columbia Public Schools. (2009). *Progress: Second Year of Reform.* Washington, DC: Author. Available: http://www.dc.gov/DCPS/Files/downloads/ABOUT%20DCPS/Strategic%20Documents/Progress%20Report%20-%202008-2009/DCPS-Annual-Report-7-21-2010-Full.pdf [accessed March 2011].

District of Columbia Public Schools. (2010). *Learning Standards for Grades Pre-K-8.* Available: http://dcps.dc.gov/DCPS/In+the+Classroom/What+Students+Are+Learning/Learning+Standards+for+Grades+Pre-K-8 [accessed October 2010].

Harwell, M., and LeBeau, B. (2010). Student eligibility for a free lunch as an SES measure in education research. *Educational Researcher, 39*(2), 120-131.

Ho, A.D. (2008). The problem with "proficiency": Limitations of statistics and policy under No Child Left Behind. *Educational Researcher, 37*(6), 351-360.

Jacob, B.A., and Levitt, S.D. (2003). Catching cheating teachers: The results of an unusual experiment in implementing theory. In W.G. Gale and J. Rothenberg Pack (Eds.), *Brookings-Wharton Papers on Urban Affairs 2003* (pp. 185-209). Washington, DC: Brookings Institution Press.

Koretz, D.M. (2008). *Measuring Up: What Educational Testing Really Tells Us.* Cambridge, MA: Harvard University Press.

Koretz, D.M., Linn, R.L., Dunbar, S.B., and Shepard, L.A. (1991). *The Effects of High-Stakes Testing on Achievement: Preliminary Findings About Generalization Across Tests.* Paper presented at the Annual Meetings of the American Educational Research Association (April 3-7) and the National Council on Measurement in Education (April 4-6), Chicago, IL.

Lazear, E.P. (2006). Speeding, terrorism, and teaching to the test. *The Quarterly Journal of Economics, 121*(3), 1029-1061. Available: http://www.mitpressjournals.org/doi/abs/10.1162/qjec.121.3.1029?journalCode=qjec [accessed March 2011].

Linn, R.L. (2000). Assessments and accountability. *Educational Researcher, 29*(2), 4-16.

Miller, R.T., Murnane, R.J., and Willett, J.B. (2007). *Do Teacher Absences Impact Student Achievement? Longitudinal Evidence from One Urban School District.* (NBER Working Paper No. 13356). Cambridge, MA: National Bureau of Economic Research. Available: http://www.nber.org/papers/w13356 [accessed March 2011].

National Research Council. (1995). *Measuring Poverty: A New Approach.* C.F. Citro and R.T. Michael (Eds.). Panel on Poverty and Family Assistance: Concepts, Information Needs, and Measurement Methods. Committee on National Statistics. Commission on Behavioral and Social Sciences and Education. Washington, DC: National Academy Press.

National Research Council. (1999). *High Stakes: Testing for Tracking, Promotion, and Graduation.* J.P. Heubert and R.M. Hauser (Eds.). Committee on Appropriate Test Use. Board on Testing and Assessment. Commission on Behavioral and Social Sciences and Education. Washington, DC: National Academy Press.

National Research Council. (2010a). *Getting Value Out of Value-Added: Report of a Workshop.* H. Braun, N. Chudowsky, and J. Koenig (Eds.). Committee on Value-Added Methodology for Instructional Improvement, Program Evaluation, and Accountability. Center for Education. Division of Behavioral and Social Sciences and Education. Washington, DC: The National Academies Press.

National Research Council. (2010b). *State Assessment Systems: Exploring Best Practices and Innovations, Summary of Two Workshops.* A. Beatty, Rapporteur. Committee on Best Practices for State Assessment Systems: Improving Assessment While Revisiting Standards. Center for Education. Division of Behavioral and Social Sciences and Education. Washington, DC: The National Academies Press.

National Research Council and National Academy of Education. (2011). *High School Dropout, Graduation, and Completion Rates: Better Data, Better Measures, Better Decisions.* R.M. Hauser and J.A. Koenig (Eds.). Committee for Improved Measurement of High School Dropout and Completion Rates: Expert Guidance on Next Steps for Research and Policy Workshop. Center for Education. Division of Behavioral and Social Sciences and Education. Washington, DC: The National Academies Press.

Neal, D., and Schanzenbach, D.W. (2007). *Left Behind by Design: Proficiency Counts and Test-Based Accountability.* (NBER Working Paper No. 13293). Cambridge, MA: National Bureau of Economic Research. Available: http://www.nber.org/papers/w13293.pdf [accessed March 2011].

Office of Technology Assessment. (1992). *Testing in American Schools: Asking the Right Questions.* Summary. Washington, DC: U.S. Government Printing Office. Available: http://govinfo.library.unt.edu/ota/Ota_1/DATA/1992/9236.PDF [accessed March 2011].

Office of the State Superintendent of Education. (2010a). *DC-CAS Grade 3 Performance Level Descriptors.* Washington, DC: Author. Available: http://osse.dc.gov/seo/frames.asp?doc=/seo/lib/seo/Grade_3_Performance_Level_Description.pdf [accessed November 2010].

Office of the State Superintendent of Education. (2010b). *District of Columbia Comprehensive Assessment System: Resource Guide 2011.* Washington, DC: Author. Available: http://osse.dc.gov/seo/frames.asp?doc=/seo/lib/seo/assessment_and_accountability/2011_dc_cas_resource_guide.pdf [accessed November 2010].

U.S. Census Bureau. (2010). *2005-2009 American Community Survey Five-Year Estimates.* Available: http://factfinder.census.gov/servlet/DatasetMainPageServlet?_program=ACS&_submenuId=&_lang=en&_ds_name=ACS_2009_5YR_G00_&ts= [accessed March 2011].

6

School Quality and Operations Under PERAA: First Impressions

A thorough and useful effort to ask how well DC schools—or the schools in any district—are faring needs to begin with a comprehensive picture of the district's responsibilities to students, families, and the community. School districts have many functions: some, such as procurement and management, are like those of any large organization. Others, such as the intellectual guidance of teaching and administrative staff and the responsibility for students' intellectual development, call for other capacities. To guide our examination of first impressions of the District's schools under the Public Education Reform Amendment Act (PERAA)—and also the comprehensive evaluation plan we describe in Chapter 7—we identified five broad categories to capture the broad range of responsibilities for which any school district is responsible:

1. quality of personnel (teachers, principals, and others),
2. quality of classroom teaching and learning,
3. serving vulnerable children and youth,
4. promoting family and community engagement, and
5. quality and equity of operations, management, and facilities.

Each of these categories encompasses many specific responsibilities and thus entails many possible evaluation questions. Our purpose in using these categories is to ensure that even first impressions about DC schools under PERAA are not driven by the data that happen to be most accessible, but by the questions that it is important to ask. A range of measures is needed to produce a picture of how well a district is functioning in these areas. In this chapter we discuss the general issues and research on each topic and then offer our impressions of the District's activities to date.

The five categories are convenient, if somewhat arbitrary, and there is overlap among them. For example, professional development for staff is important in thinking about the district's responsibility to attract and retain an effective workforce, and an equally critical aspect of its responsibility to ensure that students receive high-quality instruction. Our purpose is not to provide a definitive taxonomy of what districts do, but rather to impose a structure on the seemingly boundless number of important questions about DC schools' performance and progress under PERAA.

Before discussing the available information about school quality and operation in the categories, we discuss two topics related to data—the sources of data for our first impressions and the DC effective schools framework—which is the city's broad plan for improving education in the District.

DATA—LOOKING BEYOND TEST SCORES

Sources for This Chapter

For the purposes of developing our first impressions, we had three categories of data: materials published before PERAA, materials published after PERAA, and unpublished materials made available by the District of Columbia. Included in the first category are 1989 and 1995 reports by the Committee on Public Education (summarized in Parthenon Group, 2006); reports from the Council on the Great City Schools (CGCS) (2004, 2005, and 2007); a study by the Parthenon Group (2006), which was an important factual resource for the developers of the PERAA; studies focusing on special education issues by the DC Appleseed Center (2003) and the American Institutes for Research (Parrish et al., 2007); and studies on charter schools and vouchers by the Georgetown University Public Policy Institute (Stewart et al., 2007; Sullivan et al., 2008) and the U.S. Government Accountability Office (2005a, 2005b) and Ashby and Franzel (2007).

Resources published after PERAA include two reports published by the U.S Government Accountability Office (GAO) (Ashby, 2008; U.S. Government Accountability Office, 2009); a study by the Washington Lawyers' Committee for Civil Rights and Urban Affairs (2010); and two studies commissioned by DC educational agencies: one for the Office of the State Superintendent of Education, by the 21st Century School Fund, Brookings Institution, and Urban Institute (2008), and one for the Office of the Deputy Mayor for Education by the Development Services Group (2008).

These studies were done for different purposes and used different methods. Some were very broad (e.g., the Council on the Great City Schools and the Washington Lawyers' Committee reports), while others were much narrower (e.g., the Georgetown University Public Policy Institute and Development Services Group reports); some presented new analyses of primary data (e.g., the 21st Century School Fund and Georgetown University reports), while others provided synthesis of existing secondary data (e.g., those of the GAO).

In addition to these published reports, the committee obtained information directly from city agencies and officials, which included publicly available documents and information on websites, as well as information given to the committee by agency and city leaders. City agency information included strategic plans, annual reports, and analytical documents from DC Public Schools (DCPS), the Office of the State Superintendent of Education (OSSE), the Office of the Deputy Mayor of Education (DME), and the Office of Public Education Facilities Modernization (OPEFM).

In May 2010 the committee held a day-long public forum at which community representatives described their experiences with DC public schools and their perspectives on priorities for this evaluation (see Appendix A). Participants included principals and school administrators; teachers; charter school representatives; special education providers; education providers for children and youth; representatives of colleges, universities, and job training programs; students; and parents. The committee also reviewed stories in the local press, including the *Washington Post*, which has published numerous articles on the District's schools and their governance.[1]

In discussing the impressions we have drawn from these sources, we distinguish between information reported by city officials and agencies and independent assessments of circumstances in DC schools or of actions taken by DC officials. The committee was able to amass a considerable body of information, and we believe it provides a useful preliminary picture of what the District is attempting to do and how it is faring. However, the information available was inconsistent; both the published reports and the data and other information available from the city provided much more information about some issues than others.

The District's Data Collection Efforts

This chapter does not offer a systematic evaluation of either what the District has done or how it is measuring itself, but we did find that the Dis-

---

[1] We note that although several provisions in PERAA cover charter schools, traditional public schools have been the primary focus of studies calling for reforms. Time and resource constraints limited the committee's ability to focus on charter schools, but it will be important to include them in the independent evaluation.

trict collects a significant amount of data to monitor its own progress.[2] DCPS staff provided the committee with a list of the databases that are relevant to public education, which is included in Appendix C. Because of limitations in time, resources, and access, we were not able to review these databases in order to assess their quality and utility, though this will be a high and early priority once the evaluation begins. We do have several observations, however, on the basis of the materials we have reviewed.

In a study commissioned by the committee, Turnbull and Arcaira (2009) documented the data gathered by DC and three similar districts (Atlanta, Boston, and Chicago) in six broad areas and found that all four were roughly comparable in their coverage. (Appendix B provides more detail about the study's findings.) For all four districts, there are a number of areas in which data are collected but not made public, however. The study also found that in some areas "the . . . indicators were idiosyncratic, and most of the indicators reported served to highlight positive achievements of the district" (p. 19). For example, DCPS (and other districts) report on outreach efforts as a gauge of community engagement (e.g., the number of school partnership programs that have been established or the number of business volunteers spending time with students), but they do not report on the outcomes of those efforts.

This analysis highlights the fact that districts have many options when it comes to measuring their own progress. Table 6-1 shows some of the outcomes a district might measure (in the left-hand column) and some of the means by which they can be measured (in the right-hand column). This list, while far from comprehensive, suggests the range of what an evaluation should address (looking beyond test scores), as well as the importance of a detailed documentation and analysis of the District's current data collection efforts.

A few points from the literature on performance management will be useful in the analysis of the District's data collection efforts because such systems vary widely by intended purpose. For example, as Childress et al. (2011) found in a study of the performance management system within New York City's Department of Education, such systems can be perceived as punitive or they can be used to build an organizational culture in which excellence is valued and teachers and others feel accountable in a positive way for their efforts.

Professional guidelines for performance management are somewhat general, but several summary discussions that have focused on measurement are worth noting. In a summary of the literature, Behn (2003, p. 588) concluded that public agencies "use performance measurement to (1) evaluate,

---

[2]In considering the District's efforts we include those of DCPS and the other offices concerned with education, including the office of the mayor.

TABLE 6-1 Sample Outcomes and Measures to Evaluate School Systems

Outcomes	Sample Measures
Student Learning and Achievement Gaps	State test scores of cohorts (e.g., average scores for grade 4 in 2007 and 2009)
	State tests and NAEP average scale scores
	Test scores over time (e.g., comparing the growth of students from grade 3 to grade 4 and also comparing students who enter grade 3 from year to year)
	Other assessment scores, e.g., AP, SAT, PSAT
	Course enrollment and completion
	Grade attainment in coursework
	Data sources: State or districts, National Center for Education Statistics (NCES)
Educational Engagement	Student and teacher attendance rates by grade from the district or NAEP background surveys
	Students' self-reports of engagement, including whether schools are safe and supportive places
	Teachers' self-reports of engagement, including whether schools are safe and supportive places
	Data sources: Districts, NCES
Elementary Grade Progression and On-Track High School Credits	Grade progression in elementary grades and credit accumulation, including passing core subjects, for secondary grades
	Data source: Districts
Graduation Rates	Graduation rate, longitudinal and cohort annual data
	Data sources: Districts, NCES
Participation in Postsecondary Education and College Readiness	Percentage of students entering postsecondary institutions, persistence, and completion postgraduation (by survey)
	Data sources: District survey, or district or state program data (e.g., DC scholarships)
Job/Career Readiness (maturity, civic engagement, organizational skills, responsibility, access to and qualifications for labor market opportunities)	Percentage of graduates employed, follow-up survey data on employment status and occupation, social participation, voting rates, use of public welfare, marital status
	Source: District survey of students, survey of employers

continued

TABLE 6-1 Continued

Outcomes	Sample Measures
Physical and Mental Health	Rates of alcohol and drug use, obesity, smoking, unplanned pregnancy
	Mental health or illness, satisfaction/happiness
	Exercise, leisure activities
	Work-related disability
	Sources: Local and state agencies
Contact with Criminal Justice	Rates of victimization and of arrests, incarcerations, and juvenile justice placements
	Sources: Local and state agencies
Parent Involvement and Participation	Parent involvement and participation (in school activities and in organizations such as the PTA; frequency of parent appearances in school, parent involvement in school decision making
	Source: District
Parent Satisfaction	Parent self-reported satisfaction (by survey)
	Enrollment response
	Source: District
Community (increased community participation, buy-in and commitment to education institutions and strategies)	Counts of avenues of accessibility for parents and other residents, and use of data
	Number of parent requests and to whom they are directed (e.g., chancellor, Board of Education, or DC Council)
	Public accountability and transparency
	Source: District
Integrated Data Collection (public modes of access and use, role of the board versus council, public accountability and transparency)	Parent/community accessibility to, understanding of, and use of data
	Independent ratings of data systems and transparency
	Parent and community ratings of access and transparency
	Use rates for data (via web tracking) and other resources
	Review of documented responsibilities, inquiries and responses of government bodies
	Sources: District documents, district web services, surveys

(2) control, (3) budget, (4) motivate, (5) promote, (6) celebrate, (7) learn, and (8) improve." Others (e.g., Hatry, 2007) would add that an important purpose of performance measures is to promote trust in public agencies by transparently tracking results, efficiency, and equity.

Given the numerous potential purposes, Behn (2003, p. 600) cautions that "a public agency should not go looking for their one magic performance measure," but develop an array of measures aligned to the users and purposes. The Office of Management and Budget (2003) generally advises that priorities for performance measures include a focus on quality over quantity, relevance to budget decisions, clarity to the public, feasibility, and collaboration. The trend in the private sector has been away from treating the financial bottom line as the primary performance measure—a trend that could be seen as analogous to the trend in education away from treating test scores as the primary performance measure.

The National Performance Review (1997) study of best practices in performance measurement recommended that any performance measurement initiative have these elements (pp. 2-3):

- strong leadership: clear, consistent, and visible involvement;
- a conceptual framework: clear and cohesive performance measurement framework;
- effective communications: effective communication with employees, process owners, customers, and stakeholders;
- accountability: clearly assigned and well-understood;
- intelligence for decision makers: actionable data;
- rewards: linked compensation, rewards, and recognition;
- no punishments: learning systems with tools, no "gotcha"; and
- transparency: openly shared performance with employees, customers, and stakeholders.

Likierman (2009), in contrast, pointed to a number of "traps" in performance management. Among the common mistakes were making comparisons only against prior performance within an organization, focusing on the past, focusing on the existence of data and not its quality, and "gaming" or otherwise distorting measures. Gaming refers to such practices as selecting measures that may make performance appear better than it is. For example, if school safety is one of the areas the district seeks to address, student reports of their perception of school safety may be a better measure than parents' perceptions.

Pursuing this example, we note that the District's key measure on this point in Schoolstat is parents' perceptions.[3] Across all schools for which

_____
[3] Data from CapStat, see http://capstat.oca.dc.gov/PerformanceIndicators.aspx [accessed July 2009]. SchoolStat and CapStat are discussed later in this chapter.

the district had data, 77 percent of parents in 2008-2009 reported that they were satisfied with safety inside the school. However, 69 percent of students reported feeling safe, a difference of 8 percentage points.[4] In some schools the difference is significantly larger: in Johnson Middle School, for example, 60 percent of students reported that they feel safe but almost 90 percent of parents reported that they are satisfied with safety—a difference of nearly 30 points. The parent report data are also incomplete: for example, Ballou and Anacostia—two high schools that are located in high-crime neighborhoods—had too few parents who responded for researchers to include their data. On this issue, as an alternative, the District might use the number of students who report that their school is "orderly and in control;" for Johnson that number was 31 percent of students.

Decisions about which data to report might also influence the extent to which an indicator is seen as improving. For example, another annual measure used in the District is the number of students whom DCPS referred to nonpublic schools (that is, private schools that specialize in special education). Because of the high cost of nonpublic placements, tracking the rate at which such placements are made seems logical. However, if the goal is to gauge progress toward improving special education for students who need it, other measures would also be needed. For example, random independent assessments of services and updates on the status of individualized education plans (IEPs) at individual schools would provide more information about the services actually being provided.

We cite these examples not as an evaluation of the District's data collection efforts, but as suggestions of the sorts of questions that are likely to be asked in a full-scale evaluation.

THE DCPS EFFECTIVE SCHOOLS FRAMEWORK

DCPS's responses to PERAA are part of a broader plan for improving the schools that was articulated in a six-element "effective schools framework" (District of Columbia Public Schools, 2009a). The framework is relevant to all of the areas of responsibility we discuss in this chapter. It has six elements (District of Columbia Public Schools, 2009a, p. 2).

Element 1: Teaching and Learning All teachers engage in a strategic instructional planning process and deliver high-quality, rigorous, standards-based instruction to ensure continuous growth and high levels of student achievement.

---

[4]Information downloaded from http://dcps.dc.gov/DCPS/Files/downloads/ABOUT%20DCPS/Surveys-08-09/DCPS-Stakeholder-Surveys-District-level-2009.pdf [accessed October 2010].

Element 2: Leadership All school leaders fully understand their role as high-impact instructional leaders and create a coherent organizational structure to support teaching and learning.

Element 3: Job-Embedded Professional Development High-quality professional development is job-embedded, aligned to district and local school goals, data-driven, and differentiated. It supports in-depth development of teachers and leadership and is directly linked to the District's Effective Schools Framework.

Element 4: Resources Resources (funding, staff, materials, and time) are allocated with a specific focus on instructional improvement and increasing student achievement.

Element 5: Safe and Effective Learning Environment Policies, procedures, and practices are in place to support a safe environment characterized by high expectations, mutual respect, and a focus on teaching and learning.

Element 6: Family and Community Engagement Schools make families and community members aware of their important roles in creating effective learners and schools, and invest families and community members in that work.

At the center of this overarching framework is the teaching and learning framework, which describes the specific instructional practices the district has identified as most likely to promote student learning. This second framework is designed to articulate clear expectations for teachers that can be aligned with professional development activities and provide a "common language" for discussion of instructional practice. It provides both objectives (e.g., "effective teachers adopt a classroom behavior management system") and examples of what that behavior looks like (e.g., "successful classroom behavior management systems include norms and rules that are clear, age-appropriate, positively worded, and few in number") (District of Columbia Public Schools, 2009a, pp. 8-9). Thus, the framework is designed both to be useful in providing support to struggling teachers and as an important basis for evaluation.[5]

---

[5]Both the effective schools framework and the teacher and learning framework draw heavily from the work and thinking of Michael Moody, who was special adviser to the chancellor on academics (under Chancellor Michelle Rhee), and his California-based consulting firm, Insight Education Group.

AREAS OF DISTRICT RESPONSIBILITY

Quality of Personnel

The knowledge and skills of teachers, principals, and administrators influence student learning and, as in any organization, the performance of all staff members is important both to outcomes and to the culture and the nature of the working environment. Attracting and retaining high-quality staff for every role—from top leadership to support staff—and supporting them in doing their jobs effectively is a critical school district responsibility.

Teachers

Of all the factors that a school district can influence, the quality of its teachers has perhaps the greatest effect on outcomes for its students (see, e.g., Clotfelter et al., 2007; Kane et al., 2006; Rivikin et al., 2005; Rockoff, 2004; Wenglinsky, 2002). In light of this clear finding, it is noteworthy that districts have persistent difficulty in making sure that students in the highest poverty schools have experienced teachers with preparation in the subject they teach (Lankford et al., 2002; Peske and Haycock, 2006).

Defining teacher effectiveness and identifying the factors that contribute to it have been continuing challenges for researchers, but it is clear that differences among teachers can account for a significant degree of the variation in student outcomes, even within a school. The challenge lies in identifying teacher characteristics that are easy to use as markers for new teachers who are likely to be effective. For example, teacher credentials—such as scores on licensure tests or academic degrees—have not been useful in predicting which teachers will be more effective with students; in contrast, a teacher's years of experience do appear to have some predictive power (Buddin and Zamarro, 2009; Kane et al., 2007).

Other factors that may account for differences among teachers have also been studied. Knowledge of the subject they teach—that is, a body of conceptual and factual knowledge in a particular field—has been identified as a necessary, but not sufficient, foundation for teachers. To foster learning, teachers also draw on understanding of how knowledge develops in a particular field, which means understanding the sorts of difficulties students typically have as their learning progresses and how to build on students' gradually accumulating knowledge and understanding (for summaries of this research, see National Research Council, 2000, 2005a, 2010b). Other knowledge and skills, such as classroom management and the capacity to plan effective lessons, also play a role. Teachers in any district are also likely to be responsible for students with varying degrees of fluency in English and a range of cognitive and physical disabilities: in 2000, 20 percent of all children under 18 in the United States had parents who were recent immigrants (Capps et al., 2005), and 9 percent of the population aged 3 to 21 received special education and related services under the Individuals with Disabilities Education Act (IDEA).

Principals and District Leaders

School and district leadership also affect student learning. A review of qualitative and quantitative research on school leadership found that principals' influence is nearly as important as that of teachers (Louis et al., 2010). The study identified several practices that make school leaders effective: setting goals and direction for teachers; providing intellectual influence, individualized support, and models of best practices for their teachers; and developing and fostering organizational structures and practices (e.g., fostering collaboration) that support teachers in working effectively. A meta-analysis of quantitative research on the characteristics of effective schools, teachers, and leaders found that principals have a measurable effect on student achievement and identified a focus on specific practices aimed at boosting student achievement as one of the factors likely to explain the correlations (Marzano et al., 2005). Others have also studied the importance of principals' leadership in cultivating a culture of shared responsibility for meeting rigorous academic goals (e.g., Bryk et al., 1999; Porter et al., 2008; see also Horng et al., 2009). Recruiting, developing, and retaining high-quality teachers is another way in which effective principals benefit their schools (Béteille et al., 2009; Leithwood and Jantzi, 2000).

The capacity of central office staff is also important. Much of the research on districts' influence on student learning has focused on policy and strategy and on districts' capacity to implement reforms (Duffy et al., 2010; Spillane and Thompson, 1997, 1998). For example, a number of studies have pointed to the importance of such factors as sustained focus on student achievement, clear articulation of goals, informed use of student achievement data and other data to guide planning and instruction, and coordination among staff responsible for curriculum development, assessment, professional development, and other aspects of the system (see, e.g., Louis et al., 2010; Massell, 2000; Shannon and Bylsma, 2004; Waters and Marzano, 2007). Other factors that are often considered include such skills as the capacity to interpret and use student data to guide planning and instruction (Data Quality Campaign, 2009; Massell, 2000).

What Districts Can Do

There are a number of ways districts can influence the quality of their personnel (see, e.g., Chait, 2009; Loeb and Reininger, 2004; Moon, 2007;

Murnane and Steele, 2007; Steele et al., 2010; Stotko et al., 2007). The requirements for new teachers, compensation structures, hiring and recruitment practices, and mentoring for new teachers are tools for attracting and retaining effective new teachers. Professional development and career ladders that provide room for growth and allow newer teachers to learn from those with more experience are tools for improving and updating the practice of current teachers. Similar practices are useful for developing effective principals. Districts can develop structures designed to foster collaboration and develop communities of practice through which teachers and administrators can learn from one another. Some research suggests that particular strategies for management and data use help administrators create successful learning environments in which their staffs are adept at self-assessment (Tozer et al., 2001). The tools may vary, but the primary goals are the same: to attract high-quality teachers to the system, retain them, set high expectations for them, and promote policies and practices that allow them to meet these high expectations (see, e.g., Elmore, 2004; McLaughlin and Talbert, 2006; Rivikin et al., 2005; Wenglinsky, 2000).

Efforts in the District of Columbia

Improving human capital is one of the areas PERAA identified as a focus for improvement and evaluation. Reports have documented the District's long-standing problems in managing its human resources (Council of the Great City Schools, 2004, 2005; DC Committee on Public Education, 1989; District of Columbia Public Schools, 2006b), and the share of educators teaching core classes who are highly qualified has been among the lowest in the nation (55 percent) (Birman et al., 2009).[6]

We look first at what the District has said about its efforts in this area. DCPS describes strategies and performance targets for human capital in its 5-year action plan and annual performance plans (District of Columbia Public Schools, 2010d). In the case of teachers, for example, the action plan calls for the "replacement of poor performers, improved induction . . . professional development, career ladders, compensation, and evaluation" as the major strategies (p. 28).

A major step for DCPS was the adoption of a new performance management system, IMPACT, which was designed to take into account a range of measures of teacher performance and to be used as the basis for recognizing highly effective teachers, strengthening professional development strate-

---

[6]The percentage is based on the District's own definition of qualifications to teach core subjects. (For the purpose of meeting the No Child Left Behind [NCLB] requirements, states and the District are free to define their own standards for qualified teachers, as long as they also meet the NCLB minimum standard.)

gies, and removing ineffective teachers. According to IMPACT guidebooks published by DCPS (District of Columbia Public Schools, 2010f), the new system yields scores for teachers with several components. One major component for a general education teacher is value-added student achievement data, which is 50 percent of the score. Value-added modeling is a statistical method for measuring changes in individual students' achievement from one year to the next to identify the contribution to their achievement made by their teachers (for more on this method, see National Research Council, 2010a). The next major component of a teacher's score is a measure of instructional expertise, which accounts for 35 percent. Instructional expertise is the extent to which the teacher follows the teaching and learning framework (described above). The remainder of the score, 15 percent, covers measures of professionalism, commitment to the school community, and value-added scores (of student achievement) for the school as a whole. The guidebook provides specific descriptions of subscores for these categories, as well as descriptions of what it means to meet expectations for each. For example, to score at the highest level for "leading well-organized, objective-driven lessons" (p. 17) under the teaching and learning framework, a teacher will accomplish such goals as ensuring that students can "explain what they are learning, beyond simply repeating back the stated or posted objective."

It is important to note that measuring teacher effectiveness is a complex endeavor about which there is no established consensus in the education research community. A March 2010 agreement between DCPS and the teachers' union calls for an independent review of IMPACT to see if it meets or exceeds recognized standards for teacher evaluation and to make recommendations for improving it.[7] The results of this review (which is separate from this PERAA-mandated evaluation) are expected in mid-2011.

Evaluation of IMPACT will clearly be a high priority for the next phase of the evaluation called for by PERAA. Prior to IMPACT, the U.S. Government Accountability Office (2009) reported that DCPS could not assess changes in the quality of its teacher workforce because the existing evaluation system did not measure teachers' impact on student achievement—and because "almost all teachers received satisfactory ratings" under the old system (p. 25). A thorough evaluation would examine both the characteristics of IMPACT, in light of research on teacher evaluation, and its effects thus far on the composition of DCPS's teacher and principal workforce.

Another high-profile action was DCPS's dismissal of a large number of central office staff and principals, and later, teachers. At the end of the 2008 school year, about one-fifth of teachers and one-third of principals resigned, retired, or were terminated (U.S. Government Accountability Office,

---

[7] See the Memorandum of Understanding: http://www.wtulocal6.org/custom_images/file/DCPS%20WTU%20MOU%20031910.pdf [accessed March 2011].

2009). Then, in October 2009, DCPS announced the dismissal of 388 staff members, including 229 teachers, and said that the decision was the result of a budget shortfall.[8] By comparison, only 1 of more than 4,000 DCPS teachers had been removed for poor performance in the 2006-2007 school year (U.S. Government Accountability Office, 2009). Changes in the way teachers are employed and managed by DCPS have attracted significant local and national attention. Teacher dismissals have been a flash point in the city, and the fairness of IMPACT has been a frequent topic in letters to the editor of the *Washington Post* and other public forums.

Another important development was DCPS's negotiation of a contract with the Washington DC Teachers' Union, which took effect in July 2010, and which DCPS described as "groundbreaking" (District of Columbia Public Schools, 2010a). DCPS points to the "mutual consent" provision (that both the teacher and the school must agree for a teacher to work in a particular school) and accountability for teachers, based on the new teacher evaluation system, as the most important features of the agreement. The agreement provides teachers with a 21.6 percent increase in base pay over 5 years: that increase will bring DC educators' salaries closer to those of teachers in neighboring districts in Virginia and Maryland. It also allows for voluntary performance pay based on multiple measures, including improvement in student test scores. This provision could add $20,000 to $30,000 to teachers' base salaries, with salaries for high-performing teachers in high-need schools and subjects earning as high as $140,000. The contract also covers professional development for teachers in various areas, including managing classroom behavior and discipline, using achievement data, and working with special-needs students.

The importance of the provision that displaced teachers will no longer be guaranteed another spot in the school system was noted as a key in the agreement (Washington Lawyers' Committee for Civil Rights and Urban Affairs, 2010). Instead, displaced teachers must find administrators willing to take them. If they cannot do so after 60 days, they have three options: a $25,000 buyout, retirement with full benefits if they have 20 or more years of service, or receiving a year with full salary and benefits while they look for another position in the system. The contract does not affect salaries for school principals, although increasing principals' salaries and thus narrowing the gap between those in the District and those in neighboring jurisdictions is a priority for DCPS. Other observers have noted that the contract's provisions included concessions from the union that went sig-

---

[8]For information about this action, see the "Frequently Asked Questions" page of the DCPS website at http://dcps.dc.gov/DCPS/About+DCPS/Press+Releases+and+Announcements/General+Announcements/Frequently+Asked+Questions+Concerning+The+Budget+Shortfall+and+Staffing+Reductions [accessed January 2011].

nificantly beyond what most urban districts have been able to obtain, in return for the prospect of significant increases in compensation (see, e.g., Wingert, 2010).

In its latest annual performance plan (District of Columbia Public Schools, 2010d), DCPS has included measures of the share of teachers who are highly qualified and retention rates for teachers rated highly effective on IMPACT. It has set several goals, including increasing the percentage of teachers who are highly qualified, from 60 percent in 2009 to 85 percent in 2012, and increasing the recruitment of principal candidates who are highly rated.

DCPS officials reported to the committee that they intend to begin tracking additional indicators related to the quality of their personnel. OSSE has also adopted a number of performance measures related to the education workforce and human capital management, such as the percentage of classes in core subjects taught by highly qualified teachers, the percentage of paraprofessionals who have been designated highly qualified, and the percentage of pre-K teachers who meet new qualifications.

Quality of Classroom Teaching and Learning

What occurs in classrooms is at the core of a school district's responsibility to its students. Many factors influence classroom instruction: although this category could encompass much of what districts do, we discuss here the main ingredients of an academic experience that leaves students well prepared for postsecondary education and the workplace.

The Role of Standards

A school district's responsibility begins with primary structures: well-designed and rigorous content and performance standards, and curricula, professional development, and assessments that are aligned with those standards (see Chapter 2). There is a large body of research and analysis on standards—how they function and what their effects have been (see, e.g. Gamoran, 2007; Goertz and Duffy, 2003; Hamilton et al., 2008; Swanson and Stevenson, 2002). Views about standards and their role in education have been constantly evolving. In the 1990s, a number of organizations issued rankings that graded states' standards on such criteria as clarity and rigor, and much attention focused on the use of assessments to measure progress and hold educators accountable. Although states aspire to have rigorous standards, comparisons among standards showed that they vary significantly, and many observers have suggested that states reacted to the improvement targets included in NCLB by diluting their expectations (see, e.g., Porter et al., 2008; Stecher and Vernez, 2010).

More recently, researchers have explored more nuanced views of the role standards can play, examining ways to link content and performance standards to findings from cognitive researchers about the way learning develops.[9] This approach has important implications for the design of curricula, assessments, professional development, and other aspects of education (see National Research Council, 2005b, 2008, and 2010c for more on these issues). It is important in part because of the concern that large-scale assessments—which tend to measure only a small portion of what educators view as important teaching and learning goals—have come to function as *de facto* standards because of the high stakes attached to them (National Research Council, 2010c).

The recent adoption of new common core standards by 36 states was an important development in thinking about standards because the new standards are designed to make expectations for students more consistent across the nation and also to build on exemplary standards from both states and other countries.[10] Since districts ordinarily are covered by—and must comply with—state standards, their own standards have tended to attract less attention. However, some districts have used the common core standards as a reform tool (see Bulkley et al., 2010; Goertz, 2000).

Implementing Coordinated Standards, Curriculum, and Assessments

To have the desired results, standards, curriculum, and assessments have to be implemented effectively and equitably. That implementation means ensuring that every student has access to rigorous courses and other academic programs, such as advanced placement or international baccalaureate courses; catalyst programs; foreign languages; career and technical education programs; athletic programs; and courses in the visual, performing, choral, and instrumental arts. Every school needs to have the resources (books and other materials, computers, internet access, laboratory facilities, etc.) necessary to meet standards and effectively implement the curriculum.

Every school needs teachers who have the knowledge and skills needed to teach the curriculum and guide students in meeting the standards. Addressing the undersupply of effective, qualified teachers in schools that serve low-income neighborhoods is a persistent district problem (which can be considered both in this category and in the category of quality of personnel). What is key is that both the personnel management tools designed to secure excellent staff for these schools (e.g., compensation and hiring strategies) and the strategies for intellectually engaging all teachers

---

[9] See the website of the Berkeley Evaluation and Assessment Research Center for more on this topic, see http://bearcenter.berkeley.edu/ [accessed April 2011].

[10] See http://www.corestandards.org/ [accessed March 2011] for more information.

in the work of implementing rigorous standards (e.g., through professional development, mentoring, and communities of practice) are high priorities.

One strategy that many states and districts are pursuing is the adoption of college-preparatory curriculum standards for all students. A recent study by the Chicago Consortium on School Research (Allensworth et al., 2009) suggests mixed results from this approach. In Chicago, a 1997 policy that eliminated remedial classes and required all high school students to take college-preparatory coursework did reduce inequities in 9th grade coursework, but the failure rates increased, grades declined slightly, test scores did not improve, and students were no more likely to enter college.

Another strategy that has been developed is a composite measure that can indicate whether students are on track to graduate on time. A study of this approach found that students who accumulate at least five semester credits and fail no more than one core course during their freshman year were almost four times as likely to graduate as students who do not do so (Allensworth and Easton, 2007). These measures have been built into an "on-track indicator" adopted by Chicago and other urban districts as part of their overall accountability systems.

Efforts in the District of Columbia

Reports that span more than 20 years (Council of the Great City Schools, 2005; DC Committee on Public Education, 1989, 1995; District of Columbia Public Schools, 2006a, 2006b) have described the urgent need for redesigning teaching, curriculum, and testing with the goal of improving students' academic performance. Even before PERAA, DCPS had adopted new, higher standards (adapted from Massachusetts' state standards). Now, under the terms of the grant DCPS recently received from the federal Race to the Top Initiative,[11] DCPS has committed to adopting the common core standards developed under the leadership of the Council of Chief State School Officers and Achieve, Inc. (see Chapter 2), and, eventually, an assessment system that will align with those standards (currently under development). According to the city's Race to the Top application (Office of the State Superintendent of Education, 2010), both DCPS and public charter schools will use interim assessments that will be aligned with the new state standards.

DCPS reports several efforts to improve the learning experience for students. For example, they report that they have transformed 13 (of 16 in total) high schools into "catalyst" schools that offer in-depth instruction in arts integration, STEM (science, technology, engineering, and mathematics),

---

[11]For a description of the initiative and the winners, see http://www2.ed.gov/programs/racetothetop/index.html [accessed March 2011].

or world cultures. DCPS also reports having expanded its specialized preschools to include Montessori- and Reggio Emilia-inspired programs and has instituted dual-language education at some secondary schools.

An earlier report (Washington Lawyers' Committee for Civil Rights and Urban Affairs, 2005) found that higher-level instruction was mostly limited to the advanced placement (AP) courses offered at comprehensive high schools or the six selective schools that require applications for admission. More recently, the Washington Lawyers' Committee for Civil Rights and Urban Affairs (2010) found that AP courses were offered at all but four high schools and that the new catalyst schools offered additional options. The report notes progress in making advanced coursework accessible to all students, but it also notes that instructional offerings are still limited in many schools, especially in the areas of foreign language, art, and music.

Another study (21st Century School Fund, Brookings Institution, and Urban Institute, 2008) analyzed the academic offerings in DC by examining the District's schools in each of three categories: (1) basic schools, those that offer grade-level coursework and have no special programs; (2) themed academic, career technical, special education, or alternative schools (one to which students are assigned because of chronic behavior or other problems); and (3) adult education programs. The study further analyzed the offerings by the number of each type of school in each of the city's eight wards: see Table 6-2. This information shows a disparity in the distribution of the different types of schools between Wards 7 and 8, which serve high percentages of students living in poverty and Ward 3, which serves the most affluent students.

TABLE 6-2 Number of Public Schools (DCPS and charter) by Educational Program and Ward

School Program Type	Ward 1	2	3	4	5	6	7	8	Total
Basic	11	8	7	20	21	19	25	29	140
Themed Academic	17	7	4	5	9	9	6	2	59
Career Technical	1	0	0	1	1	1	1	0	5
Special Education	1	2	0	2	9	2	0	3	19
Alternative Education	3	0	0	0	3	1	1	1	9
Adult Education	2	0	0	1	1	0	0	1	5
Total Schools [in ward]	36	19	14	33	49	38	40	44	237

NOTE: Several schools were not included in this analysis; see 21st Century School Fund, Brookings Institution, and Urban Institute (2008) for details.
SOURCE: 21st Century School Fund, Brookings Institution, and Urban Institute (2008, p. 42, Table 2-1).

Identifying valid and reliable measures of how well a school district is doing with respect to its fundamental mission is a challenging task. Test scores and enrollment numbers are often used because they are readily available and because many people believe they are very important (as discussed above). Enrollment is a basic measure of the success of a school or school system, particularly in DC, where many families have opted for public charter or independent schools, applied to traditional schools that are "out of boundary," or moved to suburban school districts. In 2010, DCPS announced its first increase in enrollment in 39 years (District of Columbia Public Schools, 2010b). More specifically, enrollment had increased at schools in all eight wards; a number of schools had seen major increases in enrollment; and early childhood education was growing rapidly, with the most recent annual increase of 481 preschool and prekindergarten. A 2008 study (21st Century School Fund, Brookings Institution, and Urban Institute, 2008) found that the District's current system of choice does not meet many families' demands for quality schools (21st Century School Fund, Brookings Institution, and Urban Institute, 2008). The study concluded that the schools in greatest demand are not located close to where most students live and that many families seeking high-quality schools look outside their boundaries. The same study also found high mobility in the city's public schools (as we discuss in Chapter 3), with many students exiting early (changing schools before the final grade). The study concludes that the District should do more to support families and students in establishing long-term commitments with schools and schools in maintaining long-term presences in their communities.

Other factors affect DC families' confidence in their schools. As one study found (21st Century School Fund, Brookings Institution, and Urban Institute, 2008), parents identified curriculum and programs as a top priority for their children's schools, but were also concerned about school safety, the location of the school, and the quality of the teachers. In a study of the DC Opportunity Scholarship Program (a federally-funded voucher program that provides about 1,700 low-income DC students up to $7,500 a year for tuition at a private school), parents were asked how they measured their children's success (Stewart et al., 2007). The parents cited their children's academic development as critical, though they reported measuring academic progress "by the level of enthusiasm the students express about school and their improved attitudes towards learning" (p. vii) rather than by grades or test scores.

DCPS has adopted or is considering a mix of different measures of the overall quality of schools that include test scores, course offerings, student engagement, student safety, and postsecondary student outcomes. These measures include (personal communications, DCPS staff, July 2010 and February 2011):

- performance on DC Comprehensive Assessment System (CAS) in reading and math, including percentage scoring at each level, median performance levels, and annual growth for individual students;
- 4-year and 6-year graduation rates;
- share of students who have earned at least one passing score on an Advanced Placement (AP) or International Baccalaureate (IB) exam;
- Student engagement score (derived from student responses to a district-wide survey);
- retention rate of effective teachers;
- share of first-year 9th grade students who are promoted to the 10th grade;
- average daily attendance rate;
- suspensions and expulsions;
- student re-enrollment;
- number of serious incidents at schools (e.g., behavior infractions or violence);
- share of 8th graders who pass Algebra 1 with a C or higher grade and pass the end-of-course exam;
- Share of students identified as ready for 4-year colleges based on their grade point averages and results of the preliminary SAT (PSAT); and
- Scores in school safety, community satisfaction, and parent engagement (all derived from parent, teacher, student and staff responses to a districtwide survey).

These sorts of data could be used to examine results for subgroups of students and neighborhoods.

Serving Vulnerable Children and Youth

Districts are responsible for meeting the needs of every student, and many children and young people require special services and supports to succeed in school and in other ways. In this category we include students with disabilities; students who are not yet fluent in English; students whose lives have been disrupted by such stresses as family dysfunction, poverty, frequent moves, and violence or crime; and young people who fail to thrive academically and are at risk for school failure and dropping out—or have already dropped out of school or are incarcerated. Attention to the needs of these students encompasses many aspects of schooling, as well as the missions of other city agencies.

Beyond the School System

Coordination among city agencies concerned with child welfare, juvenile justice, public health, housing, and other social services has become a focus in many cities as these agencies recognize the overlap in their responsibilities (see, e.g., National Research Council and Institute of Medicine, 2007). Many of the children and youth at risk for school failure have multiple challenges—including chronic health problems, mental health or substance use problems, dysfunctional family situations, or homelessness—and thus require a range of services and supports, typically provided by different agencies. Each agency is better able to help if staff are aware of all the relevant circumstances and can readily communicate with the others who have relationships with the young people and their families. Challenges to effective coordination include preserving confidentiality while sharing important information and coordinating data systems, but many jurisdictions have explored solutions (see National Research Council and Institute of Medicine, 2007).

Beginning with the youngest children, disparities in the characteristics that predict academic success are evident as early as 9 months of age, and children from low-income families and children whose mothers have the least formal education are at the greatest risk for later difficulty in school (Halle et al., 2009; National Research Council and Institute of Medicine, 2001). Many districts and states have focused on providing preschool options for children aged 3 to 5, but the existence of disparities among infants under age 1 indicates that other supports are needed to ensure that all children are ready to learn when they enter kindergarten.

Academic achievement gaps only widen as children progress through school, and risk factors that affect individuals, schools, and communities play a role. Strategies for supporting students with multiple risk factors are an important district responsibility. Such strategies might begin with ensuring that students in every school have access to challenging coursework and the resources and support they need to succeed. They would also encompass coordination with social service and health agencies and the juvenile justice system to identify students with particular needs and connect them with sources of assistance.

Students with Disabilities and English Language Learners

Students with disabilities, including mild to severe physical, emotional, and cognitive impairment, require a wide range of supports, the provision of which is covered under the Individuals with Disabilities Education Act. Districts are expected to provide these services in the least restrictive possible setting, which has increasingly meant educating them in regular classrooms, with teachers and special educators providing supplementary supports. Districts face a challenge in accurately identifying students' disabilities and matching students' needs with appropriate accommodations and supports. States and districts vary widely in their criteria for identifying disabilities and the measures with which they address them (National Research Council, 2002, 2004).

Similar issues affect students who are learning English (National Research Council, 2004; National Research Council and Institute of Medicine, 1998). These students come from very diverse backgrounds—some districts are educating students representing many linguistic backgrounds, but even among native Spanish speakers, the largest group, prior educational preparation and academic skills vary widely. Districts face the challenge of continuing to build these students' skills and knowledge in every subject while they are improving their facility with academic English.

Efforts in the District of Columbia

Special Education Many studies have documented problems with the District's capacity to serve and support special education students (Council of the Great City Schools, 2005; DC Committee on Public Education, 1989; District of Columbia Public Schools, 2006a, 2006b): see Box 6-1. The achievement gap between special education students and others has grown since 2006; the most recent data show that the gap on DC CAS is 5 percentage points for reading and 11 percentage points for math (Office of the State Superintendent of Education, 2010, p. 48). The gap may be accounted for by a variety of factors, including efforts by DC to educate a greater proportion of special education students within the system, rather than placing them in private schools, but the need for attention to special education in DC is clear.

Since PERAA, DCPS reports that OSSE has made changes in procedural aspects of the special education system (District of Columbia Public Schools, 2010h; Simmons, 2010). These include providing more "related services" as called for by IDEA,[12] developing individualized education plans (IEPs) in a timely manner, resolving disputes more quickly, identifying developmental delays and disabilities among children aged 3 to 5, recouping payments from Medicaid, and monitoring and supporting students in nonpublic placements.

Other Vulnerable Youth The Office of the Deputy Mayor for Education, OSSE, and DCPS also report efforts to improve educational and other

---

[12] "Related services" are defined by IDEA as services needed to address the individual needs of students with disabilities so that they may benefit from their educational program. Examples of related services include occupational and physical therapy, school health services, and special transportation assistance.

BOX 6-1
Special Education in the District

It is difficult to overstate the extent of the problems the DC public school system has had in identifying and educating students with special education and related needs (Parrish et al., 2007; DC Appleseed Center, 2003; Washington Lawyers' Committee, 2010). Problems with special education have had negative ripple effects throughout the public education system. A recent study of special education financing in DC concluded (Parrish et al., 2007, p. 1):

> [. . .] a radical re-direction in current policies and practices in the District is imperative. While the financial commitment to special education in the District is substantial, a great deal of this money is being spent on relatively few students in [non-public schools] whose special education needs in terms of disability categories do not appear to set them apart, many of whom—it could be argued—are being served contrary to the least restrictive environment (LRE) requirements of the federal Individuals with Disabilities Education Act (IDEA). In addition, special education transportation consumes a considerable portion of the overall budget.

The district has one of the highest per-pupil expenditure rates in the nation (National Center for Education Statistics, 2008). In comparison with other school districts, more students, 17.5 percent, are identified as needing special education than the national average, 13.8. More of DC's identified students are placed in restrictive placements, meaning in public or private schools exclusively for special education students: about 25 percent in comparison with 5 percent station average nationally.

It is not clear to what extent this disparity in expenditure reflects greater needs in the city's population in comparison with those of other states, but private settings place a large cost burden on the school system. Almost 20 percent of the city's special education students are in private schools, for which the District pays about $57,700 annually per student (in fiscal 2008), and transportation costs add another $19,000 to this figure. These tuition expenditures represent 17 percent of DCPS' total budget, and the funding for special education transportation represents 9 percent of DCPS' budget. Together, these functions account for more than 25 percent of the budgeted allocations for DC public schools.

Because of its failure to comply with federal special education regulations, DC has been designated a "high risk grantee" by the U.S. Department of Education, and in June 2009 it became the first jurisdiction to have 20 percent of its federal special education funding withheld. The school system is also currently under two federal consent decrees. The Petties Consent requires that DCPS make timely special education tuition payments to special education schools, residential facilities, and private providers of related services, as well as to provide requisite transportation for these services. (The court also appointed an independent special master to monitor compliance with the consent decree and to oversee payment issues.) The Blackman Jones decree is also based on multiple violations of federal regulation and requires DC to provide due process hearings within 45 days of hearing requests and to maintain a community-based service center for parents of special education students and maintain an accurate reliable data system.

services for vulnerable youth. While the needs are clear (21st Century School Fund, Urban Institute, and Brookings Institution, 2010; Washington Lawyers' Committee for Civil Rights and Urban Affairs, 2010), the results of new programs, such as DC START, Second Step®, LifeSkills® Training, and the services and supports under the city's new strategic education and youth development plan (described in Chapter 4) are not yet clear. DCPS has also established the Youth Engagement Academy for students who are not doing well in traditional school environments and who can benefit from smaller settings with added supports and alternative approaches to teaching and learning. It has also revised its attendance and truancy policies with the goal of increasing attendance (DCPS staff, personal communication, July 2010).

DCPS reports that it provides a variety of resources for vulnerable students, including alternative programs and schools in every ward (District of Columbia Public Schools, 2010e). For example, DCPS reports that 16 elementary schools are using a schoolwide applications model to provide academic, health, and social services; youth and community development; and community engagement. The goal is for the school to be open daily to the community, including evenings and weekends.[13]

In 11 middle schools, DCPS is also piloting the full-service school program, which is designed to promote academic success as well as social, emotional, and behavioral well-being. At the high school level, DCPS offers alternative programs in comprehensive high schools that are designed to retain students who are not succeeding in traditional high school settings by providing them with more student-centered supports and instruction, as well as a broader array of career and technical programs. A number of academies and programs are provided for students who have been suspended or have dropped out (or are at high risk of doing so), are incarcerated, or have been detained by the juvenile justice system and are wards of the state.

In addition to these special programs and academies, DCPS has a high school credit recovery program in which students who have fallen behind can catch up by taking after-school credit recover courses and perhaps graduate on time (within 4 years); free tutoring supports for students in Title I schools that have failed to meet Adequate Yearly Progress (AYP) for 3 consecutive years; and visiting instructional services for students whose education is interrupted because of a temporary physical disability or health impairment.

DCPS's Office of Youth Engagement coordinates a variety of education and other service providers with the goal of registering, enrolling, and sup-

---

[13]For more information about the community schools movement, see http://www.communityschools.org/ [accessed December 2010].

porting regular school attendance; these include a student placement team who engage students and find placements for them; a homeless children and youth program that ensures that homeless children continue with their schooling and that their basic educational rights are protected; a 12-week Saturday Scholars academic intervention program that runs from January to April.

According to the report from the 21st Century School Fund, Brookings Institution, and Urban Institute (2008), the city faces a big challenge in serving its vulnerable youth, particularly students in Wards 1, 7, and 8, who have the highest level of risk factors. However, the Washington Lawyers' Committee for Civil Rights and Urban Affairs (2010) finds that under the provisions of PERAA, DCPS and OSSE have improved coordination among the city agencies that serve vulnerable youth in some way. For example, the city has resolved several class action lawsuits related to the provision of special education services, and it has improved transportation services for special education students. Although the costs of both transportation and tuition for serving special education students in private settings remain very high, the report found that DCPS had been able to move 155 of these students from private settings to public schools by 2010.

Family and Community Engagement

Relationships between public schools and the communities and families they serve are intuitively recognized as important. The importance of local governance of schools has long been a guiding principle in the United States, but expectations for these relationships go much deeper. In contemporary academic terms, this idea is discussed in terms of education's contribution to "social capital," the idea that social networks within communities play a critical role in helping individuals and their communities thrive (Buckley and Schneider, 2007; Putnam, 2000). Research has supported the view that engagement with school protects young people from negative influences in disadvantaged neighborhoods and supports their academic success. Strong ties to local schools build parental and community support for schools, and schools can be a community resource—a tool for building parenting skills and civic engagement for recent immigrants and disaffected communities (Battistich and Horn, 1997; Battistich et al., 1995; Blum, 2005; Bryk and Schneider, 2002; Epstein and Dauber, 1991; Jeynes, 2003, 2007; Lee and Bowen, 2006; Warren, 2005). A recent study of governance changes in New York City's public schools (Henig et al., 2011) has noted that if parents and the broader community do not have a strong voice in the establishment of priorities for policy and reform, they may not support changes.

Approaches to Engagement

Effective community engagement can be a particular challenge in urban districts that serve large shares of low-income families (Schultz, 2006). Districts must learn effective ways of communicating with families who may be highly mobile, have language and literacy barriers, and have few connections to the internet or electronic communications. Schools in highly challenged neighborhoods may need extra support if they are to engage families (including connecting the parents themselves with needed programs and services) and build effective long-term relationships with them.

Strategies for those connections include the development of after-school and weekend programs in schools to serve and attract children and youth, their families, and other community residents. Such programs include sports and recreational programs, language classes, and other kinds of supports that meet community needs and provide young people with extra adult role models and mentors (see, e.g., Dryfoos and Maguire, 2002; Dynarski et al., 2004; National Research Council and Institute of Medicine, 2003). Other strategies include structures for engaging parents in their children's education; public forums, questionnaires, and other tools for gauging opinion and identifying concerns; clear and open channels for communication of individual concerns; the use of communication tools—both computer based and accessible to those without web access—to inform and engage families and community members; and professional development for staff to build communication skills and understanding of diverse cultural traditions represented in the school and district community.

Efforts in the District of Columbia

DCPS has made student, parent, and community engagement one of its six overarching goals (District of Columbia Public Schools, 2009a) and has an Office of Family and Public Engagement (OFPE) specifically dedicated to these activities. Like all districts, DC is responsible for meeting federal requirements that school districts that receive Title I funds craft parental involvement policies jointly with parents. The federal regulations are designed to coordinate parental involvement policies across a host of other programs (e.g., Head Start, Reading First, Early Reading First, Even Start, Parents as Teachers, Home Instruction Program for Preschool Youngsters, and limited English proficiency programs) and also to identify barriers to parent involvement, especially barriers to parents who are economically disadvantaged, disabled, have limited English proficiency, have limited literacy, or belong to a racial or ethnic minority group.

DCPS outlined goals for improving family and community engagement in its 5-year action plan (District of Columbia Public Schools, 2009b).

Among the issues DCPS hoped to address were the fact that many parents have felt unwelcome at their children's schools and that the presence and effectiveness of parent groups varied considerably from one school to another, with schools in more affluent neighborhoods enjoying more parent support. DCPS also reported that it had no record of which community groups were working in which schools and no system for matching offers of help from community groups with schools that could most benefit. The 5-year action plan outlines specific strategies for engaging students in their own academic success, empowering parents and families to act as partners with students and schools and better advocate for their children's educational interests, and improving ties with the broader community.

The city reports that it has established parent resource centers in Wards 1, 7, and 8. DCPS hosts monthly chancellor's forums, other citywide community meetings, and smaller living room meetings, and has convened a Chancellor's High School Student Cabinet and a group of parent advisers. DCPS also reports that is has made changes in response to input it has received (District of Columbia Public Schools, 2009b). For example, an official reported to the committee that DCPS had revised its out-of-boundary school application process in response to requests from families.

In addition to community- and school-based meetings, DCPS has developed its web-based and digital communications. The agency's website won the 2010 Best of the Web in the K-12 District Education Website category from the Center for Digital Education, in recognition of innovative use of technology to meet the needs of students, parents, and educators.[14] Among other resources, the DCPS website includes a profile for every school in the system that provides information on enrollment, test scores, student demographics, academic and extracurricular programs, and parent engagement. The agency reports that between the 2008 and 2009 school years, page-views on the site increased by 42 percent and the average time viewers spent on the site increased 31 percent (District of Columbia Public Schools, 2010c).

DCPS regularly fields several stakeholder surveys to collect opinions from students, parents, teachers, administrations, and staff about perceptions of school safety, school quality, and other issues (District of Columbia Public Schools, 2010g). The latest findings from the student survey reveal, on the whole, flat or more positive scores since 2007. It should be noted, however, that opinions such as those collected through stakeholder surveys are often a lagging, rather than a leading, indicator of change (Wooden, 2010). DCPS also uses other measures of family and community engagement (District of Columbia Public Schools, 2010c). Measures that either

---

[14]For more information on the award, see http://www.convergemag.com/awards/education-achievement/DEAA-BOW-Awards-Announced.html [accessed January 2010].

appear in the agency's annual performance reports to the city or are being used or considered for internal management purposes include (personal communication, February 2011):[15]

- share of parents satisfied with schools' academic programs and opportunities for parent engagement;
- school performance on the community engagement performance of the Quality School Review (QSR);
- share of families who attend parent-teacher conferences;
- number of community forums attended by the chancellor;
- retention rate of highly effective teachers;
- share of community that is satisfied with the direction schools are taking; and
- number of users of DCPS website.

Nevertheless, community engagement seems to be an ongoing challenge for the District. A number of organizations—including parent groups and the local philanthropic community—report having felt shut out from DCPS' reform efforts in the wake of PERAA (McCartney, 2009; U.S. Government Accountability Office, 2009), and DCPS leaders have commented publicly that they understand the need to better engage the public about the many changes they are making. This position can be contrasted with a telling remark by the former chancellor (to the Aspen Institute): "cooperation, collaboration and consensus-building are way overrated" (see Turque, 2009). Given the climate, the abolition of the Office of the Ombudsman for Public Education, mandated by PERAA, will be important to examine.

Operations, Management, and Facilities

School districts are highly complex systems that require effective management of school buildings, vehicles, and many noninstructional business operations, including food and nutrition services, safety and security, information technology, and procurement. These underlying systems make it possible for school systems to function, and when they do not work smoothly, it is an immediate and powerful signal of an ineffective system. For example, many observers focus on school facilities. Problems with the aging stock of K-12 facilities across the country have been well documented by the U.S. Government Accounting Office (1995, 1996). Media coverage of dilapidated and overcrowded schools has highlighted the problem, though many districts are building new schools and renovating old ones.

---

[15]The Public Charter School Board (PCSB) is also reporting some limited data on community involvement and engagement (District of Columbia Public Charter School Board, 2010).

It is critical to note that researchers have documented correlations between the attributes of facilities and student outcomes, finding that both students and teachers benefit from having clean air, good light, and quiet, comfortable, and safe learning environments (Schneider, 2002). It would not be necessary, however, even if it were possible, to document empirical connections between each aspect of management and operations and student achievement to recognize that these functions are critical supports for the daily life of a school system.

Measuring Performance

A variety of measures are used to assess the safety and security of school facilities and other management and operations functions. For example, detailed measures with checklists have been developed to evaluate school grounds, buildings and facilities (including portable classrooms and restrooms), communications systems, building access control and surveillance, utility systems, mechanical systems, and emergency power (Schneider, 2002). There are also guides for mitigating various hazards including acts of violence or terrorism and natural disasters.

The Council of the Great City Schools (a national organization representing the largest urban public school systems) has examined districts' responsibilities for operations and management and identified key performance measures as well as strategies for collecting and reporting data about these functions (Council of the Great City Schools, 2009). The performance measures they recommend are intended to support better resource allocation, management decisions, and policy making.

Efforts in the District of Columbia

DCPS reports that it has taken a number of steps to modernize its schools. A report from the Washington Lawyers' Committee for Civil and Urban Affairs (2010) confirms this, noting that a 2001 master plan for modernizing the schools and addressing urgent problems was starved for funding, but that the governance change under PERAA has yielded "significant results" (p. 29). As described in Chapter 4, the new Office of Public Education Facilities Modernization (OPEFM) has used its independent procurement and personnel authority, as well as funding from a dedicated Public School Capital Improvement Fund administered by the District's chief financial officer, to make improvements in many DCPS school facilities. An initial, immediate focus was to ensure that all schools had working heating and cooling systems and to reduce the backlog of facility repair work orders from about 25,000 to just over 5,000.

Following those initial steps, OPEFM initiated a phased modernization program. The office focused on improving classrooms in elementary and middles schools (e.g., lighting, air quality, technology improvements, and furniture) in the first phase; then on other core spaces, such as cafeterias, gymnasiums, and school grounds; and finally on systems components, such as mechanical, electrical, plumbing, and security systems. For high schools, the plan calls for addressing all of these elements at the same time, with a preference for rehabilitating existing structures over new construction. According to the Washington Lawyers Committee report (2010), by the summer of 2009, the first phase had been completed at four schools and full modernization had been completed at five schools. Another five schools were in the process of being fully modernized, and still others schools are in the design or construction phases.

Some observers have suggested that capital investments have been disproportionately distributed—that they reflect the basic geographic and racial inequities in the city. For example, the 21st Century School Fund (2010), an independent advocacy organization focused on the infrastructure of DC schools, has argued that Wards 2 and 3, the most affluent sections of the city, have received the most funding for school improvements. However, DCPS (2010e) reports that its modernization efforts are focused on the most at-risk areas of the city, including Ward 8, where it has spent $133 million, the second largest amount spent in a single ward. A *Washington Post* analysis of spending patterns concluded that the mayor did not "favor particular wards" (Stewart, 2010). The Washington Lawyers' Committee for Civil and Urban Affairs report (2010, p. 37) agrees with that finding:

> comparisons of short-term capital expenditures by ward in an effort to demonstrate a failure to serve neediest students are, at best, misleading. They ignore longer term expenditures, do not take into account factors such as overcrowding in some schools and over-capacity at others, and ignore the fact that some schools are attended by numerous students living outside the ward in which the school is located.

OPEFM tracks a number of performance measures related to school construction, maintenance, and operations, such as the number of modernization projects under way that are on time and on budget, the number square feet that have been modernized, the number of open work orders, and the average number of days it takes to complete a new work order (Office of Public Education Facilities Modernization, 2010).

The District uses its citywide performance measurement system, CapStat, to track performance in many areas.[16] Under this system, each

---

[16] For information on CapStat, see http://capstat.oca.dc.gov/performanceindicators.aspx [accessed December 2010].

agency, including OSSE and DCPS, has developed performance measures that it tracks and reports on regularly. In addition to using these in their annual performance plans and reports, agency heads must report on their progress and outline steps for improvement at regular meetings. Some of these performance measures are reported publicly and others are not. DCPS has a wide range of measures that it is currently using or considering tracking for management purposes (personal communication, Office of the State Superintendent of Education, July 2010):

- share of data systems improving data quality annually until 96 percent accuracy is achieved;
- share of data systems hitting data usage rate targets;
- share of customers satisfied with central office services;
- number of monthly financial reports that are timely and accurate;
- share of invoices paid within 30 days;
- dollar reduction in central office expenditures;
- share of teachers that report having the necessary textbook and instructional materials;
- share of faculty and staff satisfied with school facilities; and
- share of central office staff that feels aligned to the DCPS mission.

CONCLUSION

We emphasize again that both this chapter and Chapter 5 report first impressions, based on the information available to the committee. It would be premature to draw general conclusions about the effectiveness of DC public school reform under PERAA from these impressions. The city and DCPS have implemented many changes. Evaluating whether the new and altered systems are operating as intended and whether the city's implementation of reforms is yielding desired outcomes will also require much more than a review of a limited number of published reports or testimony from officials, teachers, parents, and students. Moreover, reforms of this magnitude can not be expected to take full effect in just a few years. Thus, it will be important to continue monitoring the system through an ongoing formal evaluation.

With that caveat, a few points are nevertheless evident now:

- The city and DCPS have made a good-faith effort to implement PERAA.
- Publicly available, aggregate data suggest that there has been modest improvement in student test scores, but they do not support any conclusions about the effectiveness of PERAA in improving student learning. To draw any conclusions about this will require

a longer period of observation and access to longitudinal test score data for individual students, population groups, and schools.
- The city has developed strategies for pursuing improvement in the basic areas of district responsibility, but more complete information will be need to evaluate them. Ongoing data collection and analysis are needed to assess whether these strategies were well chosen, as well as how they are functioning and what their effects have been.

The city has some tools in place for measuring its own progress, but not enough information is publicly available to support firm conclusions about the system's progress under PERAA.

REFERENCES

Allensworth, A., and Easton, J.Q. (2007). *What Matters for Staying On-Track and Graduating in Chicago Public Schools*. Chicago: Consortium on Chicago School Research. Available: http://ccsr.uchicago.edu/content/publications.php?pub_id=116 [accessed April 2011].

Allensworth, E., Nomi, T., Montgomery, N., and Lee, V.E. (2009). College preparatory curriculum for all: Academic consequences of requiring algebra and English I for ninth graders in Chicago. *Educational Evaluation and Policy Analysis, 31*(4), 367-391.

Ashby, C.M. (2008). *District of Columbia Public Schools: While Early Reform Efforts Tackle Critical Management Issues, a District-Wide Strategic Education Plan Would Help Guide Long-Term Efforts*. Testimony before the Subcommittee on Oversight of Government Management, the Federal Workforce, and the District of Columbia, Committee on Homeland Security and Governmental Affairs, U.S. Senate. GAO-08-549T. Washington, DC: U.S. Government Accountability Office.

Ashby, C.M., and Franzel, J.M. (2007). *District of Columbia Opportunity Scholarship Program: Additional Policies and Procedures Would Improve Internal Controls and Program Operations. Report to Congressional Requesters*. GAO-08-9. Washington, DC: U.S. Government Accountability Office.

Battistich, V., and Horn, A. (1997). The relationship between students' sense of their school as a community and their involvement in problem behaviors. *Journal of Public Health 87*(12), 1997-2001.

Battistich, V., Solomon, D., Kim, D., Watson, M., and Schaps, E. (1995). Schools as communities, poverty levels of student populations, and students' attitudes, motives, and performance: A multilevel analysis. *American Educational Research Journal, 32*, 627-358.

Behn, R.D. (2003). Why measure performance? Different purposes require different measures. *Public Administration Review, 63*(5), 586-606.

Béteille, T., Kalogrides, D., and Loeb, S. (2009). *Effective Schools: Managing the Recruitment, Development, and Retention of High-Quality Teachers*. Working Paper #37. Washington, DC: Urban Institute.

Birman, B.F., Boyle, A., Le Floch, K.C., Elledge, A., Holtzman, D., Song, M., et al. (2009). *State and Local Implementation of the No Child Left Behind Act. Volume VII—Teacher Quality under NCLB: Final Report*. Washington, DC: U.S. Department of Education.

Blum, R.W. (2005). *School Connectedness: Improving the Lives of Students*. Baltimore, MD: Johns Hopkins Bloomberg School of Public Health.

Bryk, A.S., and Schneider, B. (2002). *Trust in Schools: A Core Resource for Improvement. A Volume in the American Sociological Association's Rose Series in Sociology.* New York: Russell Sage Foundation.

Bryk, A., Camburn, E., and Louis, K.S. (1999). Professional community in Chicago elementary schools: Facilitating factors and organizational consequences. *Educational Administration Quarterly, 35*(5), 751-781.

Buckley, J., and Schneider, M. (2007). *Charter Schools: Hope or Hype?* Princeton, NJ: Princeton University Press.

Buddin, R., and Zamarro, G. (2009). *Teacher Qualifications and Student Achievement in Urban Elementary Schools.* Santa Monica, CA: RAND Corporation.

Bulkley, K.E., Christman, J.B., Goertz, M.E., and Lawrence, N.R. (2010). Building with benchmarks: The role of the District in Philadelphia's benchmark assessment system. *Peabody Journal of Education, 85*(2), 186-204.

Capps, R., Fix, M., Murray, J., Ost, J., Passel, J.S., and Herwantoro, S. (2005). *The New Demography of America's Schools: Immigration and the No Child Left Behind Act.* Washington, DC: Urban Institute.

Chait, R. (2009). *Ensuring Effective Teachers for All Students: Six State Strategies for Attracting and Retaining Effective Teachers in High-Poverty and High-Minority Schools.* Washington DC: Center for American Progress.

Childress, S., Higgins, M., Ishimaru, A., and Takahashi, S. (2011). *Managing for Results at the New York City Department of Education.* Washington, DC: American Institutes for Research.

Clotfelter, C.T., Ladd, H.F., and Vigdor, J.L. (2007). *How and Why Do Teacher Credentials Matter for Student Achievement?* Working Paper #2, revised. Washington, DC: Urban Institute.

Council of the Great City Schools. (2004). *Restoring Excellence to the District of Columbia Public Schools. Report of the Strategic Support Team of the Council of the Great City Schools.* Washington, DC: Author.

Council of the Great City Schools. (2005). *Financing Excellence in the District of Columbia Public Schools.* Washington, DC: Author.

Council of the Great City Schools. (2007). *Restoring Excellence in the District of Columbia Public Schools Redux.* Washington, DC: Author.

Council of the Great City Schools. (2009). *Managing for Results in America's Great City Schools: A Report of the Performance Measurement and Benchmarking Project.* Washington, DC: Author.

Data Quality Campaign. (2009). *The Next Step: Using Longitudinal Data Systems to Improve Student Success.* Washington, DC: Author.

DC Appleseed Center and Piper Rudnick. (2003). *A Time for Action: The Need to Repair the System for Resolving Special Education Disputes in the District of Columbia.* Available: http://www.dcappleseed.org/library/Special_Ed_Rprt.pdf [accessed March 2011].

DC Committee on Public Education. (1989). *Our Children, Our Future. Revitalizing the District of Columbia Public Schools.* Washington, DC: Author.

DC Committee on Public Education. (1995). *Our Children Are Still Waiting: A Report to the Citizens of Washington, DC.* Washington, DC: Author.

Development Services Group. (2008). *FY 2008 Annual Evaluation Report: To the Interagency Collaboration and Services Integration Commission.* Washington, DC: Author.

District of Columbia Public Charter School Board. (2010). *FY 2011 Performance Plan.* Available: http://capstat.oca.dc.gov/Pdf.aspx?pdf=http://capstat.oca.dc.gov/docs/fy11/PCSB.pdf [accessed December 2010].

District of Columbia Public Schools. (2006a). *All Students Succeeding: A Master Education Plan for a System of Great Schools: Executive Summary.* Available: http://www.dc.gov/downloads/ABOUT%20DCPS/Strategic%20Documents/MEP/MEP_Exec_Sum_English.pdf [accessed December 2010].

District of Columbia Public Schools. (2006b). *Business Plan for Strategic Reform—Board Summary.* Available: http://www.dcwatch.com/schools/ps010723.htm [accessed November 2010].

District of Columbia Public Schools. (2009a). *DCPS Effective Schools Framework.* Available: http://dcps.dc.gov/DCPS/About+DCPS/Strategic+Documents/Effective+Schools+Framework [accessed March 2011].

District of Columbia Public Schools. (2009b). *Working Draft: Making Student Achievement the Focus: A Five-Year Action Plan for District of Columbia Public Schools.* Available: http://dc.gov/downloads/SCHOOLS/Strategic%20Documents/Five%20Year%20Plan/DCPS-TMO-STRATEGIC%20DOCUMENTS-FIVE%20YEAR%20ACTION%20PLAN-APR-2009.pdf [accessed March 2011].

District of Columbia Public Schools. (2010a). *Chancellor's Notes: The Power of a Teacher—Groundbreaking New Contract Takes Effect.* Available: http://dcps.dc.gov/DCPS/About+DCPS/Chancellor%E2%80%99s+Corner/Chancellor%E2%80%99s+Notes/Chancellor%E2%80%99s+Notes:+The+Power+of+a+Teacher+-+Groundbreaking+New+Contract+Takes+Effect+-+July+9,+2010 [accessed December 2010].

District of Columbia Public Schools. (2010b). *DCPS Enrollment Up for the First Time in 39 Years.* Available: http://dcps.dc.gov/DCPS/About+DCPS/Press+Releases+and+Announcements/Press+Releases/DCPS+Enrollment+Up+for+the+First+Time+in+39+Years [accessed December 2010].

District of Columbia Public Schools. (2010c). *DCPS website wins best-in-nation award: Center for Digital Education and Converge Online names DCPS as winner in the K-12 district education website category.* Press release, September 8. Available: http://dcps.dc.gov/DCPS/About+DCPS/Press+Releases+and+Announcements/Press+Releases/DCPS+Website+Wins+Best-in-Nation+Award [accessed December 2010].

District of Columbia Public Schools. (2010d). *FY2011 Performance Plan.* Washington, DC: Government of the District of Columbia. Available: http://capstat.oca.dc.gov/Pdf.aspx?pdf=http://capstat.oca.dc.gov/docs/fy11/DCPS.pdf [accessed March 2011].

District of Columbia Public Schools. (2010e). *How Students Are Supported.* Available: http://dcps.dc.gov/DCPS/In+the+Classroom/How+Students+Are+Supported [accessed December 2010].

District of Columbia Public Schools. (2010f). *IMPACT Guidebooks.* Available: http://dcps.dc.gov/DCPS/In+the+Classroom/Ensuring+Teacher+Success/IMPACT+%28Performance+Assessment%29/IMPACT+Guidebooks/IMPACT+Guidebooks [accessed December 2010].

District of Columbia Public Schools. (2010g). *Satisfaction Stakeholder Surveys.* Available: http://dcps.dc.gov/DCPS/About+DCPS/Satisfaction+Stakeholder+Surveys [accessed December 2010].

District of Columbia Public Schools. (2010h). *Special education progress and commitment to continue: 2009-2010 school year.* Press release, July 21. Available: http://dcps.dc.gov/DCPS/About+DCPS/Press+Releases+and+Announcements/General+Announcements/Special+Education+Progress+and+Commitment+to+Continue [accessed December 2010].

Dryfoos, J., and Maguire, S. (2002). *Inside Full-Service Community Schools.* Thousand Oaks, CA: Corwin Press.

Duffy, H., Brown, J., O'Day, J., and Hannan, S. (2010). *Building Capacity for Accelerated Reform: The Fresno-Long Beach Learning Partnership as a Leadership Strategy.* Washington, DC: American Institutes for Research.

Dynarski, M., James-Burdumy, S., Moore, M., Rosenburg, L., Deke, J., and Mansfield, W. (2004). *When Schools Stay Open Late: The National Evaluation of the 21st Century Community Learning Centers Program, New Findings.* Washington, DC: U.S. Department of Education, National Center for Education Evaluation and Regional Assistance.

Elmore, R.F. (2004). *School Reform from Inside Out: Policy, Practice and Performance.* Cambridge, MA: Harvard Education Press.

Epstein, J.L., and Dauber, S.L. (1991). School programs and teacher practices of parent involvement in inner-city elementary and middle schools. *Elementary School Journal, 91*(3), 289-305.

Gamoran, A.E. (2007). *Standards-Based Reform and the Poverty Gap: Lessons for No Child Left Behind.* Washington, DC: Brookings Institution Press.

Goertz, M.E. (2000). *Local Accountability: The Role of the District and School in Monitoring Policy, Practice and Achievement.* Philadelphia, PA: Consortium for Policy Research in Education.

Goertz, M., and Duffy, M. (2003). Mapping the landscape of high-stakes testing and accountability programs. *Theory into Practice, 42*(1), 4-11.

Halle, T., Forry, N., Hair, E., Perper, K., Wandner, L., Wessel, J., et al. (2009). *Disparities in Early Learning and Development: Lessons from the Early Childhood Longitudinal Study—Birth Cohort (ECLS-B).* Washington, DC: Child Trends.

Hamilton, L.S., Stecher, B.M., and Yuan, K. (2008). *Standards-Based Reform in the United States: History, Research, and Future Directions.* Washington, DC: Center on Education Policy.

Hatry, H.P. (2007). *Performance Measurement: Getting Results, Second Edition.* Washington, DC: Urban Institute Press.

Henig, J.R., Gold, E., Orr, M., Silander, M., and Simon, E. (2011). *Parent and Community Engagement in New York City and the Sustainability Challenge for Urban Education Reform.* Washington, DC: American Institutes for Research.

Horng, E.L., Klasik, D., and Loeb, S. (2009). *Principal Time-Use and School Effectiveness.* Working Paper #34. Washington, DC: Urban Institute Press.

Jeynes, W.H. (2003). A meta-analysis: The effects of parental involvement on minority children's academic achievement. *Education and Urban Society, 35*(2), 202-218.

Jeynes, W.H. (2007). The relationship between parental involvement and urban secondary school student academic achievement: A meta-analysis. *Urban Education, 42*(1), 82-110.

Kane, T.J., Rockoff, J.E., and Staiger, D.O. (2006). *What Does Certification Tell Us About Teacher Effectiveness? Evidence from New York City.* Cambridge, MA: National Bureau of Economic Research.

Kane, T.J., Rockoff, J.E., and Staiger, D.O. (2007). Photo finish: Certification doesn't guarantee a winner. *Education Next, 7*(1), 60-67.

Lankford, H., Loeb, S., and Wyckoff, J. (2002). Teacher sorting and the plight of urban schools: A descriptive analysis. *Educational Evaluation and Policy Analysis, 24*(1), 37-62.

Lee, J.-S., and Bowen, N.K. (2006). Parent involvement, cultural capital, and the achievement gap among elementary school children. *American Educational Research Journal, 43*(2), 193-218.

Leithwood, K., and Jantzi, D. (2000). The effects of transformational leadership on organizational conditions and student engagement with school. *Journal of Educational Administration, 38*(2), 112-126.

Likierman, A. (2009). The five traps of performance measurement. *Harvard Business Review, 87*(10), 96-101.

Loeb, S., and Reininger, M. (2004). *Public Policy and Teacher Labor Markets. What We Know and Why It Matters.* East Lansing, MI: Education Policy Center.

Louis, K.S., Leithwood, K., Wahlstrom, K.L., and Anderson, S.E. (2010). *Learning from Leadership: Investigating the Links to Improved Student Learning, Final Report of Research to the Wallace Foundation*. New York: Wallace Foundation.

Marzano, R.J., Waters, T., and McNulty, B.A. (2005). *School Leadership That Works: From Research to Results*. Alexandria, VA: Association for Supervision and Curriculum Development.

Massell, D. (2000). *The District Role in Building Capacity: Four Strategies*. CPRE Policy Briefs. Philadelphia, PA: Consortium for Policy Research in Education.

McCartney, R. (2009). Schools pay when Rhee snubs donors. *Washington Post*, October 14. Available: http://www.washingtonpost.com/wp-dyn/content/article/2009/10/14/AR2009101403564.html [accessed October 2010].

McLaughlin, M.W., and Talbert, J.E. (2006). *Building School-Based Teacher Learning Communities: Professional Strategies to Improve Student Achievement (Series on School Reform)*. New York: Teachers College Press.

Moon, B. (2007). Research *Analysis: Attracting, Developing and Retaining Effective Teachers: A Global Overview of Current Policies and Practices*. Paris, France: United Nations Educational, Scientific and Cultural Organization.

Murnane, R.J., and Steele, J.L. (2007). What is the problem? The challenge of providing effective teachers for all children. *Future of Children*, 17(1), 15-43.

National Center for Education Statistics. (2008). *Total Students, Revenues, Current Expenditures, and Current Expenditures per Pupil for the 100 Largest Public Elementary and Secondary School Districts in the United States, by School District: Fiscal Year 2008*. Available: http://nces.ed.gov/pubs2010/revexpdist08/tables/table_07.asp [accessed December 2010].

National Performance Review. (1997). *Serving the American Public: Best Practices in Performance Measures: Benchmarking Study Report*. Washington, DC: Author.

National Research Council. (2000). *Testing English-Language Learners in U.S. Schools: Report and Workshop Summary*. Committee on Educational Excellence and Testing Equity. K. Hakuta and A. Beatty (Eds.). Board on Testing and Assessment. Division of Behavioral and Social Sciences and Education. Washington, DC: National Academy Press.

National Research Council. (2002). *Minority Students in Special and Gifted Education*. Committee on Minority Representation in Special Education. M.S. Donovan and C.T. Cross (Eds.). Division of Behavioral and Social Sciences and Education. Washington, DC: National Academy Press.

National Research Council. (2004). *Keeping Score for All: The Effects of Inclusion and Accommodation Policies on Large-Scale Educational Assessment*. J.A. Koenig and L.F. Bachman (Eds.). Committee on Participation of English Language Learners and Students with Disabilities in NAEP and Other Large-Scale Assessments. Board on Testing and Assessment. Division of Behavioral and Social Sciences and Education. Washington, DC: The National Academies Press.

National Research Council. (2005a). *How Students Learn: History, Mathematics, and Science in the Classroom*. Committee on How People Learn, A Targeted Report for Teachers. M.S. Donovan and J.D. Bransford (Eds.). Center for Studies on Behavior and Development. Division of Behavioral and Social Sciences and Education. Washington, DC: The National Academies Press.

National Research Council. (2005b). *Systems for State Science Assessment*. M.R. Wilson and M.W. Bertenthal (Eds.). Committee on Test Design for K-12 Science Achievement. Board on Testing and Assessment. Division of Behavioral and Social Sciences and Education. Washington, DC: The National Academies Press.

National Research Council. (2008). *Common Standards for K-12 Education?: Considering the Evidence: Summary of a Workshop Series.* A. Beatty (Ed.). Committee on State Standards in Education: A Workshop Series. Center for Education. Division of Behavioral and Social Sciences and Education. Washington, DC: The National Academies Press.

National Research Council. (2010a). *Getting Value Out of Value-Added: Report of a Workshop.* H. Braun, N. Chudowsky, and J. Koenig (Eds.). Committee on Value-Added Methodology for Instructional Improvement, Program Evaluation, and Accountability. Center for Education. Division of Behavioral and Social Sciences and Education. Washington, DC: The National Academies Press.

National Research Council. (2010b). *Preparing Teachers: Building Evidence for Sound Policy.* Committee on the Study of Teacher Preparation Programs in the United States. Center for Education. Division of Behavioral and Social Sciences and Education. Washington, DC: The National Academies Press.

National Research Council. (2010c). *State Assessment Systems: Exploring Best Practices and Innovations: Summary of Two Workshops.* A. Beatty (Ed.). Committee on Best Practices for State Assessment Systems: Improving Assessment While Revisiting Standards. Board on Testing and Assessment. Division of Behavioral and Social Sciences and Education. Washington, DC: The National Academies Press.

National Research Council and Institute of Medicine. (1998). *Educating Language-Minority Children.* Committee on Developing a Research Agenda on the Education of Limited English-Proficient and Bilingual Students. D. August and K. Hakuta (Eds.). Washington, DC: National Academy Press.

National Research Council and Institute of Medicine. (2001). *Early Childhood Development and Learning: New Knowledge for Policy.* Committee on Integrating the Science of Early Childhood Development. J.P. Shonkoff and D.A. Phillips (Eds.). Board on Children, Youth, and Families. Division of Behavioral and Social Sciences and Education. Washington, DC: National Academy Press.

National Research Council and Institute of Medicine. (2003). *Engaging Schools: Fostering High School Students' Motivation to Learn.* Committee on Increasing High School Students' Engagement and Motivation to Learn. Board on Children, Youth and Families. Division of Behavioral and Social Sciences and Education. Washington, DC: The National Academies Press.

National Research Council and Institute of Medicine. (2007). *Challenges in Adolescent Health Care: Workshop Report.* Committee on Adolescent Health Care Services and Models of Care for Treatment, Prevention, and Healthy Development. Board on Children, Youth and Families. Division of Behavioral and Social Sciences and Education. Washington, DC: The National Academies Press.

Office of Management and Budget. (2003). *Performance Measurement Challenges and Strategies.* Washington, DC: Author. Available: http://georgewbush-whitehouse.archives.gov/omb/performance/challenges_strategies.html [accessed April 2011].

Office of Public Education Facilities Modernization. (2010). *FY 2011 Performance Plan.* Available: http://capstat.oca.dc.gov/Pdf.aspx?pdf=http://capstat.oca.dc.gov/docs/fy11/OPEFM.pdf [accessed December 2010].

Office of the State Superintendent of Education. (2010, June 1). *DC's Application for Race to the Top.* Available: http://osse.dc.gov/seo/frames.asp?doc=/seo/lib/seo/cos/race_to_the_top/dc_rttt_section_vi_application.pdf [accessed October 2010].

Parrish, T., Harr, J.J., Poirier, J.M., Madsen, S., and Yonker, S. (2007). *Special Education Financing Study for the District of Columbia.* Washington, DC: American Institutes for Research.

The Parthenon Group. (2006). *Fact-Base for DCPS Reform.* Boston: Author.

Peske, H.G., and Haycock, K. (2006). *Teaching Inequality, How Poor and Minority Students Are Shortchanged on Teacher Quality: A Report and Recommendations by the Education Trust*. Washington, DC: Education Trust.

Porter, A., Goldring, E., Elliott, S., Murphy, J., Polikoff, M., and Cravens, X. (2008). *Setting Performance Standards for the VAL-ED: Assessment of Principal Leadership*. Available: http://www.eric.ed.gov/PDFS/ED505799.pdf [accessed March 2011].

Putnam, R.D. (2000). *Bowling Alone: The Collapse and Revival of American Community*. New York: Simon & Schuster.

Rivikin, S.G., Hanushek, E.A., and Kain, J.F. (2005). Teachers, schools, and academic achievement. *Econometrica, 73*(2), 417-458.

Rockoff, J.E. (2004). The impact of individual teachers on student achievement: Evidence from panel data. *American Economic Review, 94*(2), 247-252.

Schneider, M. (2002). *Do School Facilities Affect Academic Outcomes?* Washington, DC: National Clearinghouse for Educational Facilities.

Schutz, A. (2006). Home is a prison in the global city: The tragic failure of school-based community engagement strategies. *Review of Educational Research, 76*(4), 691-743.

Shannon, G.S., and Bylsma, P. (2004). *Characteristics of Improved School Districts: Themes from Research*. Olympia, WA: Office of Superintendent of Public Instruction.

Simmons, D. (2010). Special education atop DC's to-do list: City must curb costs, fulfill needs. *Washington Times*, October 18. Available: http://www.washingtontimes.com/news/2010/oct/18/special-education-atop-dc-to-do-list/print/ [accessed October 2010].

Spillane, J.P., and Thompson, C.L. (1997). Reconstructing conceptions of local capacity: The local education agency's capacity for ambitious instructional reform. *Educational Evaluation and Policy Analysis, 19*(2), 185-203.

Spillane, J.P., and Thompson, C.L. (1998). Looking at local districts' capacity for ambitious reform. *Consortium for Policy Research in Education Policy Bulletin*. Available: http://www.cpre.org/images/stories/cpre_pdfs/pb-05.pdf [accessed April 2011].

Stecher, B.M., and Vernez, G. (2010). *What Can We Learn from the Implementation of No Child Left Behind? Research Brief*. Santa Monica, CA: RAND Corporation.

Steele, J.L., Hamilton, L., and Stecher, B. (2010). *Incorporating Student Performance Measures into Teacher Evaluation Systems*. Washington, DC: Center for American Progress.

Stewart, N. (2010). Spreading D.C's money around: Recent data on projects indicate Fenty doesn't favor particular wards. *Washington Post*, June 6.

Stewart, T., Wolf, P.J., Cornman, S.Q., and McKenzie-Thompson, K. (2007). *Satisfied, Optimistic, Yet Concerned: Parent Voices on the Third Year of the DC Opportunity Scholarship Program. School Choice Demonstration Project Report 0702*. Fayetteville: University of Arkansas.

Stotko, E.M., Ingram, R., and Beaty-O'Ferrall, M.E. (2007). Promising strategies for attracting and retaining successful urban teachers. *Urban Education, 42*(1), 30-51.

Sullivan, M.D., Campbell, D.B., and Kisida, B. (2008). *The Muzzled Dog That Didn't Bark: Charters and the Behavioral Response of D.C. Public Schools*. Fayetteville: University of Arkansas.

Swanson, C.B., and Stevenson, D.L. (2002). Standards-based reform in practice: Evidence on state policy and classroom instruction from the NAEP state assessments. *Educational Evaluation and Policy Analysis, 24*(1), 1-27.

Tozer, S., Violas, P.C., and Senese, G. (2001). *School & Society: Historical & Contemporary Perspectives*: Columbus, OH: McGraw-Hill.

Turnbull, B., and Arcaira, E. (2009). *Education Indicators for Urban School Districts*. Washington, DC: Policy Studies Associates.

Turque, B. (2009). Education reform long troubled in District: Personalities, politics thorny, new tumult reflected in pace of Rhee's changes. *Washington Post*, October 31. Available: http://www.washingtonpost.com/wp-dyn/content/article/2009/10/31/AR2009103102357.html [accessed November 2010].

21st Century School Fund. (2010). *21CSF Data Shop: Financials*. Available: http://www.21csf.org/csf-home/datashop.asp [accessed October 2010].

21st Century School Fund, Brookings Institution, and Urban Institute. (2008). *Quality Schools, Healthy Neighborhoods, and the Future of DC: Policy Report*. Washington, DC: Author. Available: http://www.21csf.org/csf-home/publications/QualitySchoolsResearchReport/QualitySchoolsPolicyReport9-18-08.pdf [accessed March 2011].

21st Century School Fund, Urban Institute, and Brookings Institution. (2010). *DC Public Schools Enrollment Projections 2010-2011*. Washington, DC: Author. Available: http://www.dccouncil.us/media/2010%20Budget/Attachment%20m.%202010%20Enrollment%20Projections.pdf [accessed March 2011].

U.S. Government Accounting Office. (1995). *School Facilities: America's Schools Not Designed or Equipped for 21st Century. Report to Congressional Requesters*. Washington, DC: Author.

U.S. Government Accounting Office. (1996). *School Facilities: America's Schools Report Differing Conditions. Report to Congressional Requesters*. Washington, DC: Author.

U.S. Government Accountability Office. (2005a). *Charter Schools: Oversight Practices in the District of Columbia: Report to Congressional Committees*. Washington, DC: Author.

U.S. Government Accountability Office. (2005b). *D.C. Charter Schools: Strengthening Monitoring and Process When Schools Close Could Improve Accountability and Ease Student Transitions Report to Congressional Committees*. Washington, DC: Author.

U.S. Government Accountability Office. (2009). *District of Columbia Public Schools: Important Steps Taken to Continue Reform Efforts, but Enhanced Planning Could Improve Implementation and Sustainability*. Washington, DC: Author.

Warren, M.R. (2005). Communities and schools: A new view of urban education reform. *Harvard Educational Review, 75*(2), 133-173.

Washington Lawyers' Committee for Civil Rights and Urban Affairs. (2005). *Separate and Unequal: The State of the District of Columbia Public Schools Fifty Years After Brown and Bolling*. Washington, DC: Author.

Washington Lawyers' Committee for Civil Rights and Urban Affairs. (2010). *The State of the District of Columbia Public Schools 2010: A Five-Year Update*. Available: http://www.washlaw.org/pdf/DC%20Public%20Schools-5%20Year%20Update%20-%20Final.pdf [accessed March 2011].

Waters, J.T., and Marzano, R.J. (2007). School district leadership that works: The effect of superintendent leadership on student achievement. *ERS Spectrum, 25*(2), 1-12. Available: http://www.mcrel.org/pdf/leadershiporganizationdevelopment/4005RR_Superintendent_leadership.pdf [accessed March 2011].

Wenglinsky, H. (2000). *How Teaching Matters: Bringing the Classroom Back into Discussions of Teacher Quality*. Princeton, NJ: Educational Testing Service.

Wenglinsky, H. (2002). The link between teacher classroom practices and student academic performance. *Education Policy Analysis Archives, 10*(12), 1-30. Available: http://epaa.asu.edu/ojs/article/view/291/417 [accessed March 2011].

Wingert, P. (2010). Breaking the teachers' union monopoly. *Newsweek*, June 4. Available: http://www.newsweek.com/blogs/the-gaggle/2010/06/04/breaking-the-teacher-unions-monopoly-as-new-details-emerge-dc-school-contract-huge-win-for-reformers.html [accessed October 2010].

Wooden, R. (2010). *Using Opinion Research and Engagement to Advance Educational Improvement.* PowerPoint presentation to the Committee on the Independent Evaluation of DC Public Schools, March 8, National Research Council, Keck Center, Washington, DC.

7

From Impressions to Evidence: A Program for Evaluation

We have described some of what DC has done to implement the Public Education Reform Amendment Act (PERAA) of 2007 and provided a first look at what has happened since the reform law was passed. However, because these first impressions do not support firm conclusions about the effects of the reform initiative or about the overall health and stability of the school system, they should be treated as only the beginning of the process of collecting reliable evidence to guide decisions about the city's schools. There are no quick answers: education reform itself is a long-term process, and the evaluation of its outcomes also has to be seen in the long term. Thus, our primary recommendation to the city takes the form of a program for ongoing evaluation.

Recommendation 1 We recommend that the District of Columbia establish an evaluation program that includes long-term monitoring and public reporting of key indicators as well as a portfolio of in-depth studies of high-priority issues. The indicator system should provide long-term trend data to track how well programs and structures of the city's public schools are working, the quality and implementation of key strategies to improve education, the conditions for student learning, and the capacity of the system to attain valued outcomes. The in-depth studies should build on indicator data. Both types of analysis should answer questions about each of the primary aspects of public education for which the District is responsible: personnel (teachers, principals, and others); classroom teaching and learning; vulnerable children and youth; family and community engagement; and operations, management, and facilities.

The committee believes that a school district should be judged ultimately by the extent to which it provides all of its students—regardless of their backgrounds, family circumstances, or neighborhoods—the knowledge and skills they need to progress successfully through each stage of their schooling and graduate prepared for productive participation in their communities. Our goal is an evaluation program that will document the actions taken by decision makers (city leaders and school officials), the way those actions influence a broad range of behaviors among students, teachers, and school administrators, and the relationships those actions have to a broad range of important outcomes for students. The program should not only provide answers about what has already happened under PERAA, but also support decisions about how to continue to improve public education in DC.

This chapter begins with a description of the committee's framework for evaluation. We then discuss in detail the way in which ongoing indicators and in-depth studies can be integrated in practice and how the most important priorities for the District of Columbia can be addressed in this framework. The chapter closes with a discussion of the practical challenges of establishing and managing the program we recommend. Our evaluation program addresses the school system of the District of Columbia; as we discuss in Chapter 4, the responsibility for public education is shared among several offices because of the city's unique political status and structure.

A FRAMEWORK FOR EVALUATION

The committee's framework for evaluation covers both the implementation and effects of PERAA and, more generally, the condition of education in the District. Although the immediate goal for the District is to answer questions about PERAA, we also see an opportunity to build an ongoing program of analyses that will be useful to the District regardless of future changes in governance or policy. Although our proposed framework was developed for the District of Columbia, it can be used in any school district. It is designed to be adaptable to changing priorities and circumstances as well as to the varying availability of resources to support evaluation, in DC and in any school district.

Figure 7-1 depicts our proposed evaluation framework, which begins with the goals the District has set for itself, as shown in the horizontal box that appears at the top of the figure. The logic of this framework reflects a point that may be obvious but is worth underscoring: passing a law does not automatically result in increased student learning, reduced achievement

131

A "jolt" to: increase accountability, efficiency, clarity of roles and division of labor; facilitate action; improve coordination across agencies; accelerate pace of educational improvement; focus on teaching/learning; improve conditions for student learning and outcomes for students.

Elements of Reform

1. Structures & Roles: Established and working as intended?

2. Strategies: Are strategies evidence-informed, of sufficient scope and quality, and implemented well?

3. Conditions: Are conditions for student learning improving overall and across diverse schools and students?

4. Outcomes: Are valued outcomes being attained overall and across diverse schools and students?

Examples of District's Steps for Achieving PERAA Goals

New Structures and Roles

Mayoral Control

New roles:
- Chancellor
- State Superintendent
- State Board of Ed.
- Facilities Management
- Interagency Collaboration and Services Integration Commission
- Ombudsman

New Strategies

- Personnel recruitment, evaluation, retention, support
- Rigorous standards, curriculum, assessments
- Operations, management and facilities
- Integrated services (over time, across agencies)
- Preschool, postsecondary nonacademic support
- Community/Family engagement

Better Conditions

- Effective teachers, principals
- Rigorous, differentiated teaching and learning
- Clean and safe schools; adequate facilities
- Timely receipt of quality supplies and services
- Preschool and postsecondary readiness
- Coherent support services
- Supported communities, satisfied families

Better Outcomes

- Reduced absenteeism
- Increased student learning
- Reduced achievement gaps
- Improved graduation rates
- Increased participation in postsecondary education
- Improved access to and qualifications for labor market opportunities
- Increased community participation, buy-in and commitment to education
- Strengthened institutions

Contextual Factors

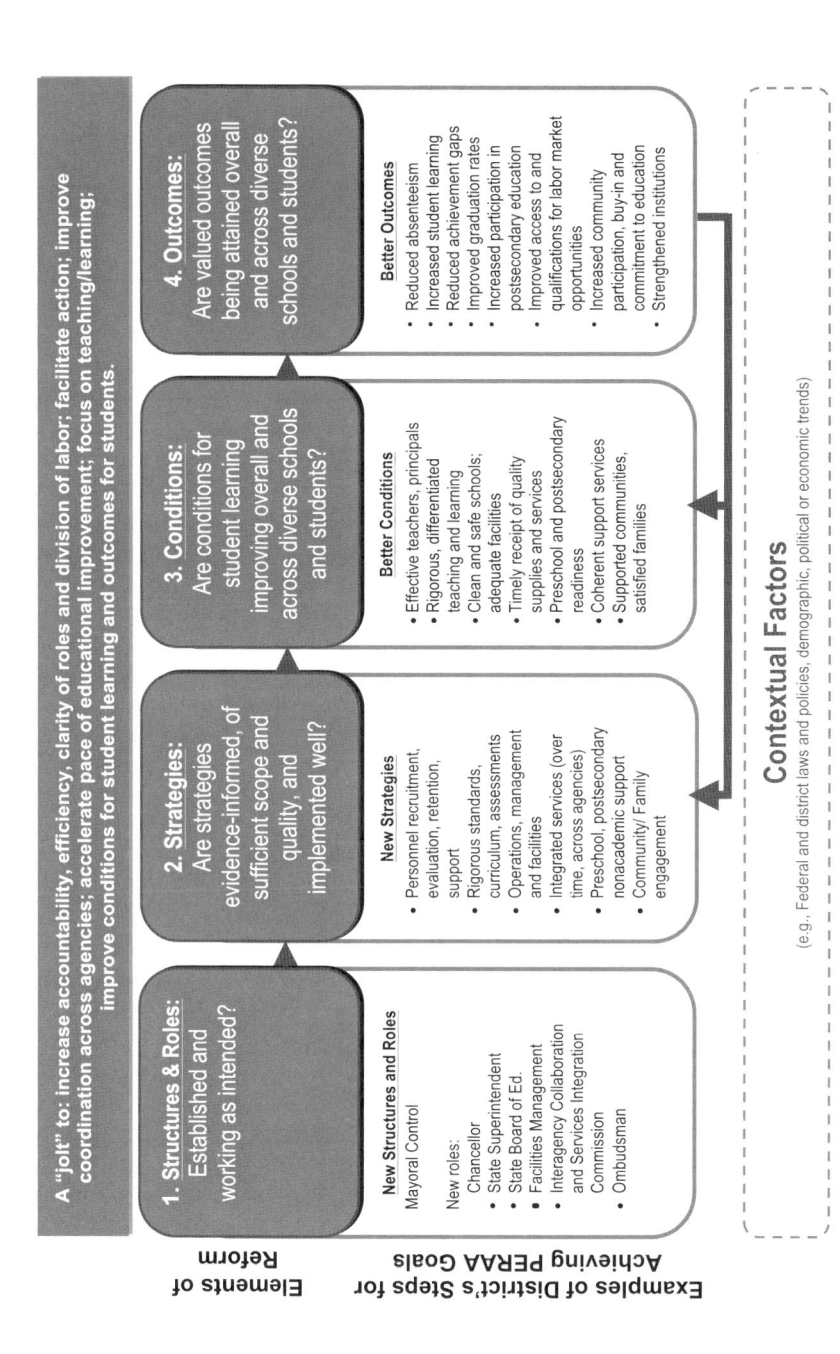

(e.g., Federal and district laws and policies, demographic, political or economic trends)

FIGURE 7-1 A framework for evaluating DC public education under the Public Education Reform Amendment Act.

gaps, increased graduation rates, or other valued outcomes. For these outcomes to occur in DC, the new structures and relationships that PERAA mandated must be established and working as intended; school system leaders must identify and adopt strategies likely to be effective; those strategies must be understood and well implemented; and the conditions for student learning—for example the quality of school staff and instruction—must improve. These prerequisites—or phases of reform—are represented in the first three vertical boxes in Figure 7-1. The fourth box represents a sample of ultimate outcomes for the system (e.g., strengthened institutions) and for students (including academic ones, such as increased learning and participation in postsecondary education, and nonacademic ones, such as reduced absenteeism).

The purpose of the framework design is to ensure that the evaluation encompasses all of the primary elements that could contribute to the outcomes. The framework simplifies the realities of urban school districts in order to help evaluators and the entire community make sense of a complex reality and to ensure that a full range of data are collected to answer the most important questions. As noted above, it is designed to accommodate the city's changing priorities and concerns over time.

The evaluation is envisioned neither as a one-time study nor as just the annual collection of certain data, but, rather, as a continuing process of data collection and analysis. As the District's public school system responds to new information and makes changes, the evaluation agenda should also evolve. The arrows beneath the model represent the potential responsiveness of strategies and conditions to changes in outcomes.

The framework also reflects the fact that contextual factors, such as changing demographic, political, cultural, and financial circumstances, exert constant influence and must be taken into account; they are represented in the box underneath the model. (For example, budget shortfalls may force a district to cut back on services that have significant effects on students and families.)

Element 1: Structures and Roles
Are they established and working as intended?

A principal goal of PERAA was to establish clearer functions and lines of authority, on the theory that a leaner, less complicated structure would lead to better coordination and more efficient operations, which would in turn promote improvements in teaching and learning. To assess this element, evaluators should document that the new offices were in fact established with clear roles and responsibilities, that they are operating as intended in the legislation, and that the changes were sufficient to eliminate major problems and create the momentum for ongoing improvement. If the District makes additional changes to those structures (e.g., as it has done by deciding not to have an ombudsman), perhaps even in response to the evaluation, those changes, in turn, should be assessed. (Chapters 4 and 6 describe what had been done by the time this report was being written, but a formal evaluation would entail review of multiple perspectives, close analysis of numerous documents, interviews with individuals throughout the system, and other data collection that were not part of the committee's task.)

Element 2: Strategies
Are they evidence-informed, of sufficient scope and quality, and implemented well?

Establishing new structures and relationships is not the same as developing approaches to improve the system; to produce the intended outcomes for students, the offices created by PERAA would have to initiate strategies that effectively address critical needs facing the schools. Thus, a second focus of the evaluation program will be to identify and describe how education leaders have set out to accomplish the stated reform goals, in the context of the new functions and lines of authority.

Specifically, evaluators will need to focus on whether DC's education officials are doing what they said they would do and how well they are doing it. We are guided by the abundant research on school reform indicating that education strategies can founder if they are not based in research and practice or if a promising practice is not implemented well (e.g., Aladjem and Borman, 2006; McLaughlin, 1990; Ruiz-Primo, 2006). Studies of the fidelity with which reforms are implemented reveal important differences in the way they are viewed and understood (Hedges and Schneider, 2005). Effective implementation means understanding the rationale and key features of a program or strategy, and achieving a balance between adherence to these features and adaptation to the unique features of a school, a district, or the students. Thus, the evaluation program should assess the extent to which the research and practice evidence supports the choice of specific strategies and determine whether those strategies are being faithfully and effectively implemented.

Element 3: Conditions for Student Learning
Are conditions improving overall and across diverse schools and students?

For strategies to improve student outcomes, such as academic achievement or high school graduation rates, or to reduce gaps in achievement among student subgroups, another step is needed—the new structures and strategies, once in place, have to lead to improved conditions for student learning. Many conditions are related to student learning:

- core conditions, such as having effective teachers and principals;
- the articulation of clear content and performance standards aligned with curriculum and instruction;
- school climate (e.g., safety, a focus on academic goals and a constructive working environment for teachers);
- the availability of art and music instruction, physical education, and other extracurricular opportunities; and
- clean, safe, and properly equipped facilities.

Changes in conditions are a critical intermediate step between the implementation of strategies and the achievement of outcomes. Improved conditions for learning are the critical means by which reforms influence student outcomes, and monitoring them is an integral aspect of the proposed evaluation program. The monitoring should be done in individual classrooms and schools, but it will also be important to look at distributions of conditions across the entire system and how they vary by neighborhood, type of school, and subgroups of students. Which specific conditions a district should monitor, and how, are important questions; we discuss below the process of setting specific evaluation priorities and our recommendations to the District.

Element 4: Outcomes
Are valued outcomes being attained overall and for diverse schools and students?

Improvements to particular conditions for learning are valuable because they may lead to improvements in outcomes for the system and for students. Although test scores and high school completion or dropout rates are often considered the only or most important outcome, there are many other important outcomes. Grade retention, college entrance and completion, civic participation, and successful entry into the labor market provide fuller information about students' trajectories. The development of technical and vocational skills is also important. As with achievement data, it will be important to examine how equitably outcomes are being achieved. Some of these other outcomes may be included in the information system the District is already collecting or developing, but many—particularly post-K-12 outcomes, such as the need for remediation for college freshmen and on-time college graduation—will require new data systems. (See Chapter 4 for information about the District's data collection.)

The Evaluation Goal

The proposed evaluation program will serve two interrelated purposes: to determine whether the provisions of the legislated reform have been implemented as intended and to evaluate whether the short- and long-term goals of the reform are being achieved. Thus, the framework mirrors our earlier distinction among PERAA's *intent*, how it has been *implemented*, and its short- and long-term *effects*. Treating these three components separately could seem to imply that they occur in a linear fashion, and can be examined in order. In practice, of course, this is not the case, and evaluation activities cannot be organized quite so neatly. For example, comprehensive study of a strategy (e.g., the teacher evaluation system) would need to include examination of the conditions it was designed to create (e.g., presence of better teachers, higher teacher satisfaction), and, ultimately, student outcomes (e.g., whether teachers who receive high ratings have a measurable effect on students' test scores).

Moreover, although the framework is a simple depiction of the primary components of a reform, the basic questions to be asked under each of the four elements will, in practice, need to be answered using many different study designs, data collection methods, and types of analysis. Thus, the evaluation framework is intended to address the kinds of questions usually posed by policy makers, system administrators, and the community at large, and answering these questions requires a combination of tools.

A Combination of Ongoing Indicators and In-Depth Studies

One primary function of evaluation is to collect data to monitor the basic status of students, staff, resources, and facilities. Some of this information is collected as part of the internal management that the system itself undertakes (and assessing the quality of that internal management is also a function of the evaluation); other information that is needed may not be. Another function is to probe more deeply into specific questions, which may require not only supplemental data collection, but also more sophisticated analysis than is usually a part of regular data collection.

Ongoing Indicators

Indicators are measures that are used to track progress toward objectives or monitor the health of a system. In education, for example, school districts typically collect average scores on a standardized reading assessment for each grade to monitor how well students are meeting basic benchmarks as they progress in reading. Other commonly used indicators include high school graduation rates, rates of truancy, ratios of teachers to students, and per-pupil expenditures, as well as measures of less quantifiable factors, such as teachers' and students' attitudes. Indicators—literally signals of the state of whatever is being measured—can cover outcomes, the presence or state of particular conditions, or the effectiveness of management approaches. Outcome indicators might be used to make overall evaluations, while management indicators would be used to fine-tune the operation of the system. Indicators are generally collected on a regular basis and in a way that allows for comparisons over time. Thus, indicators can be useful for documenting trends (positive or negative) over time; documenting trends within relevant subgroups (through disaggregated data); drawing attention to significant changes (typically sharp increases or decreases), which may indicate areas of concern or success; flagging relationships among indicators (e.g., a correlation between measures of a strategy's implementation and an outcome); developing hypotheses for further study (e.g., through observations of the co-occurrence of two or more phenomena); and providing early warnings of problems (e.g., students who struggle to meet benchmarks in elementary school are more likely to struggle or drop out during high school).

As we discussed in Chapter 6, the District currently does collect much of this data in SchoolStat, the District's management indicator system that is part of CapStat, a citywide performance monitoring system. The first steps in the committee's proposed evaluation program will be to examine thoroughly the data already collected regularly and to assess the quality of the measures and whether they yield the information needed for evaluation purposes.

In-Depth Studies

Ongoing indicators provide a general picture of a system and identify patterns that warrant further investigation, but in-depth studies are needed to provide finer resolution. We use the term "in-depth studies" to include any additional undertaking, such as analysis of existing data or collection of new data using focus groups, observations, or surveys. Such studies could be designed to describe practices, examine relationships, or determine the effectiveness of particular practices. They might shed light on the causes of the findings from indicator data, explore potential reasons for disappointing outcomes, provide information to help improve existing strategies, or help explain why some strategies appear to be working better in some schools than in others. They might require significant resources and intrusion into classrooms or be comparatively simple and inexpensive. They are important because they are the means by which evaluators can answer policy makers' questions about the effects of policies, practices, and reforms.

The design of an in-depth study and its data collection methods depends in large part on the questions being asked. Some studies seek answers to descriptive questions about what is happening in schools (for example, what is being taught in certain grades or subjects). Descriptive studies can also examine relationships, asking whether there are differences across schools, for example, or across different groups of teachers or students. Some studies seek answers to explanatory questions, such as how particular student outcomes occurred. A third type of question aims to attribute an outcome to a particular policy or practice, asking, "Did this particular policy or practice cause student outcomes to improve?"

For example, implementation studies examine how well (that is, how consistently, effectively, and efficiently) a district has put into action the improvement strategies it has chosen. Such studies might assess the implementation of new roles and structures (Element 1 in our framework) or strategies for improving education (Element 2), as well as relationships to education conditions (Element 3) and system and student outcomes (Element 4). Implementation studies do not generally provide evidence of causality—that is, they do not provide evidence that a particular strategy led to a particular outcome. To obtain information on causality requires an impact study and generally involves more sophisticated and costly data collection activities and study designs (e.g., randomized trials) to determine the impact of a specific intervention.

Whatever questions they ask, in-depth studies can and should be designed rigorously to provide complete and accurate information. For descriptive studies, for example, if a researcher wishes to generalize to a larger population, rigor would include selecting study respondents who will produce unbiased information through stratified random samples and using data collection methods that ensure high response rates.

Studies that address causal questions have to be designed especially carefully to rule out alternative explanations of outcomes. This can be done through randomly assigning subjects (schools, teachers, or students) to different conditions or through other designs that eliminate alternative explanations of the outcomes when random assignment is not possible (e.g., regression discontinuity studies). For a full discussion of the relationship between evaluation questions and study designs, see National Research Council (2002).

The two components of the evaluation program—ongoing indicators and in-depth studies—interact with one another. Ongoing indicators may identify an area of focus for a special study, and special studies may point to new indicators that need to be added to the ongoing monitoring program. Both indicators and in-depth studies are expected to evolve, as different needs and issues emerge for the District. Although the evaluation program we propose will be independent, this evolution would be shaped to a significant degree by the concerns and priorities of DCPS and the broader community.

Reporting

The way in which the results of both monitoring and in-depth studies are conveyed to stakeholders is critical to the value of the evaluation system. Reporting of student achievement results and some other kinds of information is a requirement of the No Child Left Behind (NCLB) Act, with which most districts are in compliance, and many go beyond those requirements (Turnbull and Arcaira, 2009). The District already reports many sorts of information to the public. However, the primary information is not currently consolidated in a single report.

Recommendation 2 The Office of the Mayor of the District of Columbia should produce an annual report to the city on the status of the public schools, drawing on information produced by DCPS and other education agencies and by the independent evaluation program that includes

- summary and analysis of trends in regularly collected indicators,
- summary of key points from in-depth studies of target issues, and
- an appendix with complete data and analysis.

These data and analyses should be supplemented by an online data resource in a format that is easily navigated by users and can be updated more frequently. The annual report should be concise and easy for policy makers, program managers, and the public to use. This reporting would also be supplemented by the reports generated by the evaluators.

AN EXAMPLE OF INTEGRATING EVALUATION ACTIVITIES: IMPROVING TEACHER QUALITY

The committee's proposed evaluation framework and the discussion above provide an overview of the primary elements of evaluation and the kinds of anlyses it would include, but they do not indicate in detail how these pieces would be integrated and how priorities for topics and studies will be established. For some areas, particularly operations and management, the relationship is fairly straightforward. For example, DC might monitor the efficiency of core operations using such measures as the average number of days it takes for a procurement process to be completed. If delays in the procurement of, say, textbooks, are a clear problem, the evaluators might conduct case studies to determine the cause of these delays. Monitoring the effectiveness of operations and using focused analysis to diagnose problems in this area is comparatively simple, but many evaluation questions are more complex.

Improving teacher quality is a primary strategy that DC has adopted as part of its implementation of PERAA, and it is arguably one of the most important responsibilities of any school district. Because it will therefore inevitably be a primary part of any evaluation of DC schools and because it is a very challenging area to evaluate, we examine this topic in detail as an illustration of how our evaluation framework would work.

Strategies

The key question is whether the District is taking effective steps to hire and keep good teachers (as well as principals and administrators)—and to make sure that all schools have them. Improving the quality of DCPS's teachers was a key element of the strategy of former chancellor Michelle Rhee: see Box 7-1.

As we discuss in Chapter 6, the research on teacher quality suggests that it is the product of many district and school strategies, including efforts to

- recruit and retain effective teachers and ensure that they are equitably distributed across schools;
- evaluate teachers' effectiveness;
- provide professional support and development to all teachers, as well as targeted support for teachers who need it; and
- foster working conditions that support trust and collaboration among teachers.

More specifically, procedures that allow a district to make early offers to the teacher they wish to hire, for example, may make a significant difference in the quality of new teachers (Levin and Quinn, 2003; Liu et al., 2008, 2010; Murnane, 1991). Mentoring and support for new teachers during their first few years in the classroom may help a district retain the most promising novices, although recent evidence raises questions about the role of induction in retaining novice teachers overall (Glazerman et al., 2010a; Ingersoll and Kralik, 2004; Ingersoll and Smith, 2004). Working conditions in schools can strongly influence teachers' decisions about whether to stay in particular schools. For example, teachers often value the support of a professional learning community more than salaries, and new teachers report that rules and practices in their schools affect their decisions about whether to stay in the field (Berry et al., 2008; Inman and Marlow, 2004; Johnson, 2004; McLaughlin, 1993; Mervis, 2010). Administrator leadership and support also appear to be important for teacher retention (Ladd, 2009). A teacher evaluation system that is perceived as rewarding highly effective teachers and providing learning opportunities (and, if necessary,

> **BOX 7-1**
> **DCPS Strategies to Improve Teacher Quality: Example**
>
> A central goal of Chancellor Rhee's reform strategy was to improve the effectiveness of DCPS teachers through performance-based accountability. A primary element of her approach was the establishment of a new evaluation system (IMPACT). Fifty percent of a teacher's score comes from student achievement data, 40 percent from observations of teaching practice, and 10 percent from student outcomes for the school as a whole and teachers' contributions to the school community. A new contract negotiated with the teachers union tied teacher salaries to teacher performance as measured by IMPACT, as discussed in Chapter 4.
>
> To determine the likely effectiveness of the strategy, the evaluation should answer two key questions:
>
> 1. How sound and well conceived is the strategy?
> 2. How well implemented is the strategy?
>
> Evaluating this strategy would first involve documenting any evidence from research and practice for the chosen strategy and for competing theories that might have been the basis for a different strategy. For example, some research may document the importance of objective measures of teacher quality, while other work may emphasize the importance of trust among teachers to improving educational outcomes. In that case, evaluators would need to ask whether performance-based accountability is at odds with the need to build trusting relationships with other staff and whether both are likely to be needed to achieve valued outcomes.
>
> To answer the question on implementation, an evaluation might examine, for example, whether the strategy to evaluate teacher performance was reliable and understandable to participants. If the methods of linking student performance to teacher outcomes are not technically sound, if the observations of teachers are performed by individuals without the requisite expertise, or if the system is not adequately explained to the teachers, teachers might question the legitimacy of the system, which could undermine its effectiveness.

the basis for removing) for ineffective teachers also can contribute to the quality of the teaching force, according to some analysts (Gordon et al., 2006; Kane et al., 2006).

This knowledge base provides the basis for thinking about ongoing indicators that can be used to monitor the District's strategies for fostering teacher quality and in-depth studies that would supplement the indicators.

Ongoing Indicators

A robust set of indicators will provide information on whether the quality of teachers improves over time and whether high-quality teachers are equitably distributed across schools. That is, the indicators would include measures of the characteristics of the teachers themselves and of the systems used to improve the quality of the teacher workforce.

There are several possible measures of teacher quality that could be used. The percentage of DC teachers who are "highly qualified" as defined by NCLB is easy to obtain. However, this definition has been criticized. Researchers have found that the vast majority of teachers appear to meet the criteria—94 percent nationwide in 2006-2007, according to one study—and also that states differ substantially in how they measure teacher quality for the purpose of meeting NCLB requirements (Birman et al., 2009; see also Berry, 2002; Lu et al., 2007; Miller and Davison, 2006). At present, it provides at least a starting point on which to build, especially in DC, which has the lowest percentage of classes taught by a teacher defined as highly qualified under NCLB in the nation (in comparison with states, not school districts) (Birman et al., 2009). The basic requirements are that teachers have a bachelor's degree and be fully licensed by a state, and be able to "prove that they know each subject they teach"; many states have added additional requirements (U.S. Department of Education, 2004, p. 2).[1] The NCLB definition might be viewed at present as necessary but not sufficient, because it sets a low bar and allows states substantial discretion in setting their own bars. Researchers are engaged in pursuing other means of measuring teacher quality (Birman et al., 2009).

The purpose of seeking high teacher quality is to improve student outcomes. However, there is currently limited evidence that teachers with master's degrees or state certification do produce higher student outcomes than other teachers (Goldhaber and Brewer, 1996; Rockoff, 2004).[2] Measures for which there is empirical evidence of a modest relationship to student outcomes include years of experience and certification by the National Board for Professional Teaching Standards (NBPTS), and holding a degree in mathematics (for math teachers) (Huang and Moon, 2009; Kane et al., 2006; National Research Council, 2008; Rice, 2010; Wayne and Youngs, 2003). Measures of teacher effectiveness, including using student achievement data to determine teachers' "value added" and rigorous instruments for observ-

---

[1] DC's definition, which elaborates several ways in which teachers can demonstrate mastery of core subjects, can be found at http://newsroom.dc.gov/show.aspx?agency=sboe&section=2&release=13083&year=2008&month=3&file=file.aspx%2frelease%2f13083%2fFinal_HQT_resolution.pdf [accessed December 2010].

[2] One reason that the evidence about the benefits of these qualifications is not strong may be that the categories are extremely broad. That is, programs that award master's degrees to teachers vary so much in their requirements, admissions standards, and quality that any benefits conferred by excellent programs would be obscured in the data by the lack of benefits conferred by other programs. Similarly, states' requirements for licensure vary and are not generally high: for a full discussion of these issues, see National Research Council (2010).

ing teachers, also hold promise for understanding and improving teacher quality. However, many technical issues related to use of these methods for making individual personnel decisions have not yet been resolved (Baker et al., 2010; Bill & Melinda Gates Foundation, 2010; Glazerman et al., 2010b; Kupermintz et al., 2001; McCaffrey et al., 2004; Rothstein, 2011).

It may also be useful to track how long effective teachers stay in the system (i.e., their retention rates) and what schools and neighborhoods they serve. In general, schools in high-poverty neighborhoods have greater difficulty than other schools in attracting and retaining the highest quality teachers (Hirsch, 2001; Rice, 2010). For these kinds of measures, data from administrative records (e.g., teacher qualifications and other characteristics) are another important resource, as are the results of teacher evaluations (Stanton and Matsko, 2010).

The District already is collecting many of these indicators, and, as we note above, a comprehensive examination of the existing data collection activities is a first task of the evaluation program. We also note that indicators of teacher effectiveness that rely on student achievement or teacher observations will need to be reconsidered as knowledge about the characteristics of the measures improves. Indeed, in-depth studies should include internal analyses of the validity of measures of teacher quality, and those measures should be improved as needed.[3]

Ongoing indicators related to teacher quality that can produce the kinds of information the District needs fall into two categories: those that measure characteristics of the teachers themselves and those that measure teacher recruitment, retention, and support for teachers.

Teacher Quality

A range of measures would be valuable as indicators of teacher quality, including

- number and percentage of highly qualified teachers under NCLB, on a districtwide basis and by school characteristics, such as the socioeconomic status of the students;
- number and percentage of teachers with experience teaching at the grade level and subject of current teaching assignment, on a districtwide basis and by school characteristics, such as the socioeconomic status of the students;

---

[3]The validity of a measure is a way of describing the extent to which it accurately measures what it is intended to measure and supports accurate inferences about the question the measure was designed to answer. In the context of teacher quality, there is debate over the extent to which available measures actually capture characteristics that make a teacher effective.

- number and percentage of teachers who score at each performance level (using a valid evaluation tool that includes measures of student learning), on a districtwide basis and by school characteristics, such as the socioeconomic status of the students;
- number and percentage of teachers with relevant background characteristics, such as college grade point average, and scores on certification tests, such as PRAXIS, on a districtwide basis and by school characteristics, such as the socioeconomic status of the students; and
- number and percentage of teachers with NBPTS certification, on a districtwide basis and by school characteristics, such as the socioeconomic status of the students.

Recruitment, Retention, and Professional Support

Similarly, a range of measures would be valuable as indicators of teacher recruitment, retention, and professional support:

- number and percentage of high-quality (by district definition) teachers retained, on a districtwide basis and by school characteristics, such as the socioeconomic status of the students;
- timely and efficient recruitment process, as measured by the percentage of offers to prospective teachers and principals before the end of the school year;
- percentage of novice teachers who receive mentoring or other induction supports such as reduced teaching load, common planning time, orientation seminars, or release time to observe other teachers;
- percentage of teachers who participate in high-quality professional learning opportunities, that is, those that are sustained, content-focused, and involve participation with colleagues;
- percentage of teachers who participate in high-quality professional learning opportunities for high-need subjects and populations; and
- percentage of teachers who report positive working conditions and professional learning environment in their schools.

In-Depth Studies

The indicators detailed above would provide necessary baseline information about teachers' characteristics and the conditions in which they work, as well as about the effectiveness of the DCPS's strategies for raising the overall level of teacher quality. But making good use of this information would require further study, particularly in two areas.

First, which measures of teacher quality provide the most accurate and useful information? Studies of the validity and reliability of using student outcome data and teacher observations to measure teacher effectiveness, as is currently done in the District under IMPACT, will be a valuable contribution to the evolving research in this area.[4] Studies of other teacher quality measures, such as NBPTS certification, possession of advanced degrees, scores on teacher assessments, and novice status will also be valuable as the District continues to refine its means of identifying the most effective teachers. Researchers have examined these measures in other contexts, and it will be useful to explore the applicability of their findings to the DC context.

Second, what strategies are working to attract effective teachers to the District and retain them? What can be concluded about why good teachers do or do not stay in DC schools and whether they leave teaching or just leave DC schools? Answering these questions entails study of the effectiveness of the city's primary strategies for hiring and retaining high-quality teachers and supporting their professional development. Such in-depth studies could include

- evaluation of recruitment practices, including interviews with applicants who accepted and declined offers regarding their experiences with the recruitment process;
- evaluations of the quality of mentoring and coaching for novice teachers to determine the skills of coaches and the perceived usefulness for novice teachers;
- study of changes teachers make in their practice in response to evaluations that use student achievement and observations to assess teacher effectiveness;
- follow-up studies of teachers who left the school system to determine whether they moved to a neighboring district and why they moved;
- study of the costs and benefits of different approaches to professional development (e.g., coaching or academic courses); and
- study of the features of the work environment for teachers, perhaps involving surveys and focus groups of teachers, observations to compare high- and low-performing schools, and benchmark schools outside the system.

---

[4]Many organizations are currently supporting research on teacher quality, including the Bill & Melinda Gates Foundation (see http://www.gatesfoundation.org/highschools/Documents/met-framing-paper.pdf [accessed January 2011]); Mathematica Policy Research, Inc. (see http://www.mathematica-mpr.com/Newsroom/Releases/2010/Education_wins_12_10.asp [accessed January 2011]); the American Institutes for Research (see http://www.air.org/expertise/index/?fa=view&id=95 [accessed March 2011]); and RAND Corporation (see http://www.rand.org/topics/teachers-and-teaching.html [accessed March 2011]).

With a combination of the ongoing indicators and focused in-depth studies discussed above, it would be possible to examine relationships across the elements of reform in our proposed framework. For example, such evaluations could examine whether the strategies the DCPS has chosen to recruit and retain effective teachers (Element 2 in our framework) are strategies for which there is empirical and practical evidence; whether those strategies are related to conditions for learning in the way that was intended (Element 3); and whether any changed conditions are related to improved outcomes for students (Element 4).

A combination of ongoing indicators and in-depth studies can also be used to assess the evidence base for specific approaches the DCPS is using to attract and keep effective teachers in schools in the highest poverty areas—which would include assessing the measures of quality on which they relied; whether the numbers of highly effective teacher in those schools did increase; and whether educational experiences improved in any measurable way in those schools. The last link is to determine whether those improvements resulted in higher achievement or other valued outcomes for the students in those schools.

DETERMINING PRIORITIES FOR EVALUATION

In a world without time and resource constraints a full evaluation program would supply information about every aspect of what school districts do. In reality, though, priorities are needed, and the District will need to develop the portfolio of data collection and analysis that will best meet its needs and answer its most pressing questions and support policy and practice decisions. Developing a comprehensive set of indicators and an evaluation agenda is a long-term endeavor. What are the highest priorities for the District of Columbia? What areas should be the first priority for the evaluation program? These questions ultimately should be answered by city and education leaders and the broader community they serve, but we offer some structures for those decisions.

First, we stress that the identification of specific indicators and studies with which the actual evaluation will begin should be based on (1) a systematic analysis of the indicators already available and (2) systematic analysis of the data available regarding important issues for the city's schools, combined with a process of exploration and priority-setting that would involve both city and school leaders and other stakeholders, such as teachers, parents, and other interested city residents. We expect that once a stable set of long-term indicators, combining those already collected by the District and other new measures, is in place, a series of in-depth studies will address a range of specific issues over time.

Our framework is intended above all to facilitate an evaluation that, however lean resources may require it to be, nevertheless addresses the most important aspects of a school system. That is, it must address the elements of reform (the selection of strategies, their implementation, the conditions they create, and their outcomes), and it must also address the primary substantive responsibilities a district has. We discuss in Chapter 6 five broad categories of responsibility for a school district: we believe any evaluation program must address each of these categories if it is to provide a comprehensive overview of the state of the District's schools. These two mandates can be compared to the warp and woof in a piece of fabric, as shown in Figure 7-2: the elements of reform and the broad evaluation questions pertaining to them are depicted in the vertical boxes; the substantive areas of responsibility are depicted with shaded horizontal bands. A comprehensive evaluation program would include indicators and studies to address critical evaluation questions about each of the elements of reform (depicted in Figure 7-1, above) and about a school district's substantive areas of responsibility.

Of course, it is not necessary or possible to address all possible questions related to each of these areas at once; rather, we emphasize that no one of these areas should be neglected in the long-term evaluation program.

Primary Responsibilities to Be Evaluated

As we discuss in Chapter 6, a school district's responsibilities to students, families, and the community cover:

- personnel (teachers, principals, central office);
- classroom teaching and learning;
- vulnerable children and youth;
- family and community engagement; and
- operations, management, and facilities.

Each of these categories encompasses many specific responsibilities and thus entails many possible evaluation questions.

Our evaluation framework is designed to ensure that there is balance in the detailed program of indicators and in-depth studies. Examples of the sorts of questions one might ask for each of these areas are shown in Table 7-1. These examples do not have special importance: we offer them simply to illustrate the distinctions among questions that address the strategies the District has selected, the conditions for learning they are designed to affect, and the outcomes that changes in those conditions might have with respect to each of the areas of responsibility.

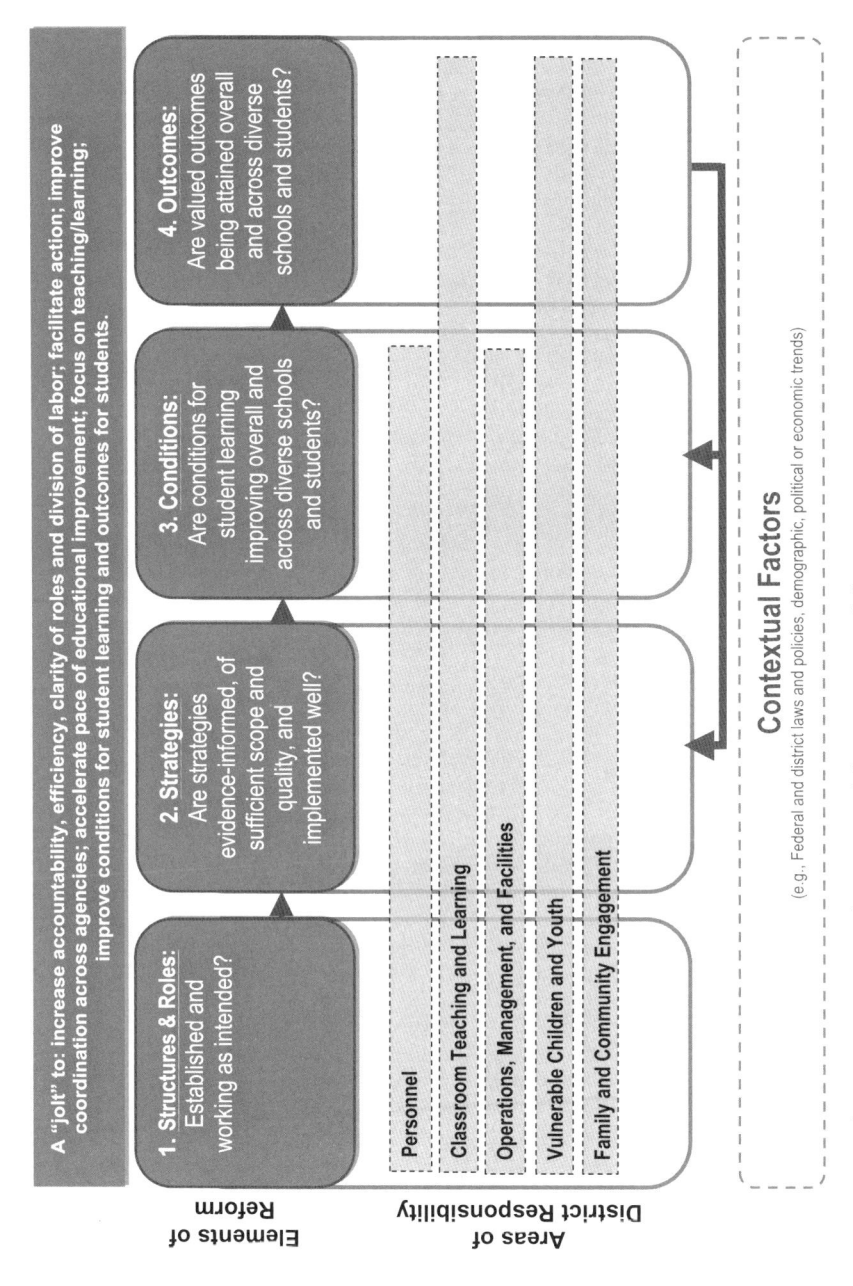

FIGURE 7-2 Evaluation priorities in key areas of district responsibility.

TABLE 7-1 Evaluation Questions for DC: Examples

Category of Responsibility and Possible Focus	Questions on Structures and Strategies	Questions on Conditions	Questions on Outcomes
Personnel: Principal Quality	What methods are used to evaluate principals? Does the method discriminate among effective and ineffective principals in a valid and reliable way, given DCPS objectives? Does it work equally well for principals at all levels (elementary, middle, and secondary)?	Is the number of principals who are rated as effective increasing, and are they equitably distributed?	Are students in the schools that have principals rated as highly effective under the new system improving in their academic performance, in comparison with students in schools that do not have such principals?
Classroom Teaching and Learning: Alignment Between Curriculum and Professional Development	Do professional development plans and activities address the learning goals that are articulated in the curriculum?	Do teachers who have received professional development demonstrate increased use of the content knowledge and practices that target curricular goals?	Do the students of teachers who have received professional development demonstrate greater mastery of curricular goals?
Vulnerable Children: Special Education	To what extent does DCPS identify and serve students with disabilities in an appropriate, timely, and cost-effective manner (consistent with the core provisions of the Individuals with Disabilities Education Act)?	To what extent are special education students served in the least restrictive settings and receiving educational and related services that are appropriate and evidence based?	To what extent are students with disabilities, especially those with learning disabilities and behavioral disorders, meeting the goals identified in their individual education plans (IEPs), and are IEP goals high enough to narrow the achievement gap between students who do and do not have disabilities?

TABLE 7-1 Continued

Category of Responsibility and Possible Focus	Questions on Structures and Strategies	Questions on Conditions	Questions on Outcomes
Family and Community Engagement: Communication	To what extent does DCPS have structures in place that allow parents, legal custodians, and other community residents to voice their concerns, seek remedies to problems, and make general recommendations to the school system?	To what extent do parents and others throughout DC use these structures regularly? Does the use vary across neighborhoods, grade levels, etc.?	To what extent do parents and others report that they are heard and valued? Do parents report greater involvement and satisfaction with their children's education over time? Does this involvement vary across neighborhoods and schools?
Operations, Management, and Facilities: Technology	To what extent are structures in place to coordinate technology in the schools, such as internet access and computer hardware and software, and to ensure that those resources are equitably distributed?	To what extent do schools in all wards and neighborhoods have sufficient up-to-date and properly maintained computer systems, as measured by the ratio of students to computer stations?	Are students meeting benchmarks in the academic standards that include technical skills, such as internet searching and graphic functions?

Criteria for Setting Priorities

The examples in Table 7-1 are only a few of the many empirical questions that can be asked, and District leaders, in collaboration with the evaluators, will need to make choices. Policy makers will seek information to help them determine whether to continue or abandon a policy or practice. Program managers will want to know how to improve operations or services. Practitioners will be interested in specific techniques that they might use to achieve program goals, and members of the public will ask a range of questions not only about the school system but also about issues such as the wise use of tax revenue and the level of local participation in decisions (Weiss, 1998).

Analysis of costs and benefits will be a key part of the process of identifying the easiest problems to tackle. All things being equal, it makes sense to address first problems that might be solved easily or at relatively low cost, while laying the foundation for more difficult issues. For example, a problem with the distribution of textbooks or transportation is likely to be quick and easy to solve, in comparison with, say, the challenge of improving teacher quality.

High priority should be given to core problems facing practitioners and decision makers and the strategies that have been undertaken to address them (Roderick et al., 2009). Core problems often will be identified through the analysis of student performance indicators. Significant changes in student outcomes will always warrant the attention of evaluators, as will poor outcomes for specific grade levels, or for subgroups of the student population or for schools in particular neighborhoods.

Evaluating the reform strategies undertaken to address core problems also should be a major priority. For DCPS, a primary reform strategy has been upgrading the qualifications and effectiveness of human resources and strategies to improve teacher quality, so this is one obvious evaluation priority. But other strategies should also be included in the evaluation program.

Another obvious priority would be conditions that have historically been significant sources of problems for DC. One example, as we discuss in Chapter 6, is special education, which has been a big drain on the DCPS budget without providing adequately for students' needs. Areas of success, whether identified in DC or through external research, should also be included in the evaluation program, so that they can be replicated, if possible.[5] Another area for inclusion is problems for which external research suggests likely solutions.

These criteria are starting points: they should be used to stimulate public conversation among stakeholders. These conversations should lead to refinements and revisions of the way in which each of the broad categories in our evaluation framework will be considered and the specific questions that are important to answer. We emphasize that these conversations, and the process of establishing priorities for the evaluation program, should be much more than public relations exercises. The evaluation studies should be firmly grounded in the strongest scientific standards for data collection and analysis, but the information collected will be used for many purposes. It can be assumed that all stakeholders share the goal of applying information to improve the schools in technically sound ways, but the evaluation studies must be responsive to the different questions asked by different

---

[5]The U.S. Department of Education's Doing What Works web page is one resource for information about research-based practices, see http://dww.ed.gov/ [accessed January 2011].

groups. A delicate balance will be needed between the competing pressures of budget, practicality, scientific purity, and political exigencies. An independent funding and management structure should ensure not only that evaluation activities are conducted according to the highest professional standards, but also that they continuously produce information that meets the needs of those working in the school system, city leaders, and the public. Stability and independence will be essential to an effective evaluation program, and the precise means of ensuring both will need to be determined by the local institutions and entities that become involved.

ESTABLISHING LONG-TERM EVALUATION CAPACITY

Building and maintaining a set of high-quality indicators, designing in-depth studies that address pressing issues, and organizing the presentation and dissemination of findings so that all stakeholders can use them will require deliberate and skillful management. We have argued that periodic attempts to evaluate the effects of PERAA and the status of the public schools will provide neither the breadth nor depth of information needed. The scale and scope of the evaluation program we recommend calls for a gradual increase in both data collection and analysis activities over a period of years.

The technical and professional challenges of building and maintaining the infrastructure needed for an indicator system capable of supporting direct analysis of large-scale datasets as well as periodic studies of key issues and topics include

- establishing procedures for ensuring that researchers and stakeholders collaborate in research agenda setting and planning activities;
- establishing agreements with schools and other entities for accessing data and drawing study samples;
- negotiating agreements about the ownership and use of data;
- setting procedures for the review and reporting of research findings to stakeholders such as program managers, practitioners, policy makers, the public, and the media;
- identifying principal investigators and consultants with the expertise to carry out specific analyses and in-depth studies; and
- creating research advisory structures, both to ensure rigorous designs and to review methodological and reporting strategies.

The usefulness of any school district's evaluation program hinges on its credibility. To be trusted and valued, the evaluation program must focus on issues the community and education leaders view as important. To guard against the natural tendency of any organization to seek data that support existing programs, it must also be independent. Both the questions asked and the interpretation of the information collected need to reflect the highest levels of impartiality.

There are few examples of research organization and management that have addressed such an array of challenges. Thus, if it is to implement an evaluation program that addresses these challenges and meets the goals we have described, the District will need both to benefit from experiences in other cities and to capitalize on local institutions and expertise to craft a sustainable structure.

Evaluation Programs: Resources and Examples

Districts and states have paid increasing attention to collecting data and using it to guide planning and decision making, partly in response to NCLB, which includes many requirements for assessing and reporting on student achievement and other questions. Most states and school districts are in compliance, and the U.S. Department of Education has awarded grants to districts for the purpose of improving the quality of their data collection and analysis (Stecher and Vernez, 2010). The Data Quality Campaign, a foundation-funded partnership of numerous nonprofit education organizations, has taken the lead in advocating for and supporting jurisdictions in the use of data to improve student achievement.[6] In a study of data collection in four districts (DCPS, Atlanta, Boston, and Chicago) commissioned for this project, Turnbull and Arcaira (2009) found that all had expanded on the data requirements of NCLB. For example, she found that all four have begun monitoring "leading" indicators, which allow them to identify potential problems at an early stage and to collect more detailed information about school climate and other areas using qualitative data, such as survey responses.

The Consortium on Chicago School Research (CCSR) performs many of the research functions that are important for school districts, and it is an early example of a structure for providing independent information to support a district's efforts to improve. This consortium, which includes researchers from the University of Chicago, the school district, and other organizations, was formed in 1990 to study reform efforts in the city's public schools, following legislation that decentralized their governance.[7]

CCSR maintains a data archive that includes student test scores, administrative records, and grade and transcript files, as well as other data such as census and crime information and qualitative information from annual

---

[6]For more information, see http://www.dataqualitycampaign.org/ [accessed November 2010].
[7]For information about CCSR, see http://ccsr.uchicago.edu/content/index.php [accessed November 2010].

surveys of principals, teachers, and students. (CCSR also collects teacher assignments, samples of student work, interview and classroom observation records, and longitudinal case studies of schools.) CCSR has produced a significant library of studies and special reports, which, although they are specific to Chicago, have been influential nationally. CCSR has also been noted for its success in engaging the community (Turnbull and Arcaira, 2009).

New York City and Baltimore also have comparable research structures in place—though each has its own features: see Boxes 7-2 and 7-3 for further information on these evaluation and research structures.

BOX 7-2
Baltimore Education Research Consortium

Founded in 2007, the Baltimore Education Research Consortium (BERC) is a partnership between Baltimore City Public Schools (BCPS) and education researchers at Johns Hopkins University and Morgan State University (see http://baltimore-berc.org/ [accessed November 2010]). BERC's activities are authorized by an executive committee of nine voting members representing the university, BCPS, and other community partners. The consortium is funded by a number of private foundations, including the Open Society Institute and the Bill & Melinda Gates Foundation. BERC conducts research on education policies and provides data to assist BCPS in making policy decisions. Although the consortium is independent of BCPS, it works with the district to develop a research agenda and welcomes comments from BCPS leaders prior to releasing any studies.

BOX 7-3
Research Alliance for New York City Schools

In 2008, New York University launched the Research Alliance for New York City Schools (RANYCS) (New York University, 2010) to provide valid and reliable to the New York City Department of Education. RANYCS is independent of the department: its operations, financing, and research agenda are guided by a governing board, whose members include leaders of local civic organizations, foundations, as well as the chancellor of the schools and the president of New York University. The governing board outlines the general topics for the research agenda, and RANYCS develops a more specific research agenda in consultation with community leaders, practitioners, researchers, and the Department of Education.

A number of independent organizations have also developed approaches to assist districts in planning data collection and analyzing and using the results.[8] The Broad Foundation uses an array of data to identify districts that have made significant progress in raising achievement and closing achievement gaps. The Council of the Great City Schools conducts detailed reviews of individual districts, at their request, analyzing quantitative and qualitative data and making tailored recommendations for improvement. The Central Office Review for Results and Equity, housed at the Annenberg Institute, also conducts reviews of individual districts, using data to assess how well they meet its criteria for effective district functioning:

- communicating big ideas,
- service orientation,
- data orientation,
- increasing capacity,
- brokering partnerships,
- advocating for and supporting underserved students, and
- addressing inequities.

Another model is the Strategic Education Research Partnership (SERP) (which began as an investigation of the potential for research to inform improvements in educational practice) (National Research Council, 1999; National Research Council and Institute of Medicine, 2003).[9] Although SERP was not a research enterprise of the sort we recommend, it offers useful principles: see Box 7-4. SERP paid explicit attention to the importance of collaboration between researchers and practitioners in the development of research questions, and it also placed a premium on identifying the strategic use of research findings in schools and classrooms.

It is difficult to generalize about what school districts do, and few models exist for the comprehensive approach to evaluation we believe is necessary. Researchers in Canada conducted a study of methods for measuring districts' progress in reforming themselves in the United Kingdom, Canada, the United States, Hong Kong, and New Zealand (Office of Learning and Teaching, Department of Education and Training, 2005). They found that although districts have many goals for their reform efforts, most rely heavily on measures of student achievement, primarily measures of "student performance on tests of literacy and numeracy, perhaps with science and social studies included in the mix" (p. 42). They note problems with the

---

[8]See Turnbull and Arcaira (2009) and the following websites: http://www.broadeducation.org/, http://www.cgcs.org/, and http://www.annenberginstitute.org/wedo/CORRE.php [accessed March 2011].

[9]For information about SERP, see http://www.serpinstitute.org/ [accessed November 2010].

> **BOX 7-4**
> **Strategic Education Research Partnership**
>
> The Strategic Education Research Partnership (SERP) currently has relationships with Boston, San Francisco, and a group of four smaller, inner-ring suburban districts that are part of the Minority Student Achievement Network: Arlington, Virginia; Evanston, Illinois; Madison, Wisconsin; and Shaker Heights, Ohio. SERP represents a decentralized approach, with management decisions coming at the site level.
>
> The priorities at each of the sites differ, but all programs follow a set of SERP principles:
>
> 1. programs are to address the most urgent problems identified by the school district;
> 2. an interdisciplinary team of researchers, developers, and practitioners are recruited by SERP;
> 3. multiple approaches are taken simultaneously to solve the problem(s) identified by the school district;
> 4. researchers and practitioners are involved throughout the entirety of a project; and
> 5. all projects are evaluated rigorously.
>
> The products produced by SERP thus far include assessments, instructional programs, pedagogical tools, and online professional development. Other school districts are using the organization's findings to pursue their own projects. SERP is funded by a number of private foundations, individual donations, and federal agencies.

use of student test scores to monitor districts' progress with broad reform goals, including limitations to the inferences that can be drawn from tests in a few subject domains, methodological concerns about how to include demographic data in analysis, and the difficulty of establishing causal links between specific practices or reform and information about student outcomes.

There is probably no one model that can readily be adopted in the District. The key to success for both the CCSR and SERP, for example, has been the organic way in which they came to exist and to evolve over time. These examples will be useful for DC to consider as it develops a specific structure for its own evaluation program. We hope that the city will collaborate with a variety of local organizations to establish a structure that will meet its needs, and will draw on analysis of the experiences of other districts, such as interviews with key figures in those districts, about how to manage and evaluate their reforms. Specifically, we believe that DC will need to engage local universities, philanthropic organizations, and other institutions to develop and sustain an infrastructure for ongoing research and evaluation of its public schools that

- is independent of school and city leaders,
- is responsive to the needs and challenges of all stakeholders (including the leaders), and
- generates research that meets the highest standards for technical quality.

We believe that collaboration will be key to meeting these objectives.

The Committee's Goal

School districts across the country have embarked on different paths in an effort to provide their students with an excellent and equitable education. Some, like the District of Columbia, have chosen dramatic "jolts" to the system that emphasize governance and performance measurement changes, while others have proceeded more incrementally toward the goal of bringing about significant change. Whatever the basic approach, there are numerous strategies by which the basic goals and reforms are implemented. For example, the District of Columbia's strategy included the establishment of the office of chancellor of education with authority to develop ways to meet the goals laid out in PERAA. The individual first hired to fill that position chose to focus on improving human capital, but another chancellor might have chosen a different combination of strategies to meet the same goals, under the same or similar structural arrangements.

Our analysis of the origins, goals, and implementation of the DC reforms led to our recommendation for a comprehensive and sustainable program of evaluation. We note that many other districts have experimented with major reforms that require systematic evaluation. Just as there is no one model that can readily be adopted in the District, it is unlikely that the specific program adopted by DC will be instantly transferable to other school districts. Our hope, though, is for an evaluation program that is independent of school and city leaders, while remaining responsive to the needs and challenges of all stakeholders, that can generate research that meets the highest standards for technical quality. The independent program will necessarily involve collaboration with DCPS, OSSE, and other agencies because they will continue to conduct their own internal management and performance tracking functions. Their data will be useful to the evaluation program, just as new data and analysis provided by the evaluation will be useful to them.

Our evaluation framework is aimed at providing both the breadth and depth of information that will assist policy makers and community members to assess whether PERAA and the education reform effort are achieving their goals and stimulating ongoing improvements. The evaluation program should be primarily focused on supplying timely and relevant information about the system, rather than definitive pronouncements on whether particular reforms are working or not. Objective evidence derived from multiple sources of data can be a tool for monitoring progress and guiding continuous improvement, and it is our hope that this model will be of use to districts around the country.

REFERENCES

Aladjem, D.K., and Borman, K.M. (2006). *Examining Comprehensive School Reform*. Washington, DC: Urban Institute Press.

Baker, E.L., Bartson, P.E., Darling-Hammond, L., Haertel, E.H., Ladd, H.F., and Linn, R.L. (2010). *Problems with the Use of Student Test Scores to Evaluate Teachers*. Washington, DC: Economic Policy Institute.

Berry, B. (2002). *What It Means to Be a Highly Qualified Teacher*. Chapel Hill, NC: Southeast Center for Teaching Quality.

Berry, B., Smylie, M., and Fuller, E. (2008). *Understanding Teacher Working Conditions: A Review and Look to the Future*. Chapel Hill, NC: Center for Teaching Quality.

Bill & Melinda Gates Foundation. (2010). *Working with Teachers to Develop Fair and Reliable Measures of Effective Teaching*. Seattle, WA: Author.

Birman, B.F., Boyle, A., Le Floch, K.C., Elledge, A., Holtzman, D., Song, M., et al. (2009). *State and Local Implementation of the No Child Left Behind Act. Volume VIII—Teacher Quality Under NCLB Final Report*. Jessup, MD: U.S. Department of Education.

Glazerman, S., Isenberg, E., Dolfin, S., Bleeker, M., Johnson, A., Grider, M., Jacobus, M., and Ali, M. (2010a). *Impacts of Comprehensive Teacher Induction: Final Results from a Randomized Controlled Study*. Jessup, MD: U.S. Department of Education.

Glazerman, S., Loeb, S., Goldhaber, D., Staiger, D., Raudenbush, S., and Whitehurst, G. (2010b). *Evaluating Teachers: The Important Role of Value-Added*. Washington, DC: Brookings Institution.

Goldhaber, D.D., and Brewer, D.J. (1996). Why don't schools and teachers seem to matter? Assessing the impact of unobservables on educational productivity. *Journal of Human Resources*, 32(3), 505-520.

Gordon, R., Kane, T.J., and Staiger, D.O. (2006). *Identifying Effective Teachers Using Performance on the Job*. The Hamilton Project Policy Brief No. 2006-01. Washington, DC: Brookings Institution.

Hedges, L., and Schneider, B. (2005). *The Social Organization of Schooling*. New York: Russell Sage Foundation.

Hirsch, E. (2001). *Teacher Recruitment: Staffing Classrooms with Quality Teachers*. Denver, CO: State Higher Education Executive Officers.

Huang, F.L., and Moon, T.R. (2009). Is experience the best teacher? A multilevel analysis of teacher characteristics and student achievement in low performing schools. *Educational Assessment, Evaluation and Accountability*, 21(3), 209-234.

Ingersoll, R.M., and Kralik, J.M. (2004). *The Impact of Mentoring on Teacher Retention: What the Research Says*. Denver, CO: Education Commission of the States. Available: http://www.ecs.org/clearinghouse/50/36/5036.pdf [accessed March 2011].

Ingersoll, R.M., and Smith, T.M. (2004). Do teacher induction and mentoring matter? *NASSP Bulletin, 88*(638), 28-40.

Inman, D., and Marlow, L. (2004). Teacher retention: Why do beginning teachers remain in the profession? *Education, 124*(4), 605.

Johnson, S.M. (2004). *Finders and Keepers: Helping New Teachers Survive and Thrive in Our Schools.* Indianapolis, IN: Jossey-Bass.

Kane, T.J., Rockoff, J.E., and Staiger, D.O. (2006). What does certification tell us about teacher effectiveness? Evidence from New York City. *Economics of Education Review, 27*(6), 615-631.

Kupermintz, H., Shepard, L., and Linn, R. (2001). *Teacher Effects as a Measure of Teacher Effectiveness: Construct Validity Considerations in TVAAS (Tennessee Value-Added Assessment System).* Los Angeles: University of California.

Ladd, H.F. (2009). *Teachers' Perceptions of Their Working Conditions: How Predictive of Policy-Relevant Outcomes?* Working Paper #33. Washington, DC: Urban Institute.

Levin, J., and Quinn, M. (2003). *Missed Opportunities: How We Keep High-Quality Teachers Out of Urban Classrooms.* New York: The New Teacher Project.

Liu, E., Rosenstein, J.G., Swan, A.E., and Khalil, D. (2008). When districts encounter teacher shortages: The challenges of recruiting and retaining mathematics teachers in urban districts. *Leadership and Policy in Schools, 7*(3), 296-323.

Liu, E., Rosenstein, J.G., Swan, A.E., and Khalil, D. (2010). *Urban Districts' Strategies for Responding to Mathematics Teacher Shortages.* New Brunswick, NJ: Rutgers, The State University of New Jersey.

Lu, X., Shen, J., and Poppink, S. (2007). Are teachers highly qualified? A national study of secondary public school teachers using SASS 1999-2000. *Leadership and Policy in Schools, 6*(2), 129-152.

McCaffrey, D.F., Koretz, D.M., Lockwood, J.R., and Hamilton, L.S. (2004). *Evaluating Value-Added Models for Teacher Accountability.* Pittsburgh, PA: RAND Education.

McLaughlin, M. (1990). The Rand change agent study revisited: Macro perspectives and micro realities. *Educational Researcher, 19*(9), 11-16.

McLaughlin, M. (1993). *Teachers' Work: Individuals, Colleagues, and Contexts.* New York: Teachers College Press.

Mervis, J. (2010). What's in a number? *Science, 330*(6004), 580-581.

Miller, K.W., and Davison, D.M. (2006). What makes a secondary school science and/or mathematics teacher highly qualified? *Science Educator, 15*(1), 56-59.

Murnane, R.J. (1991). *Who Will Teach? Policies That Matter.* Cambridge, MA: Harvard University Press.

National Research Council. (1999). *High Stakes: Testing for Tracking, Promotion, and Graduation.* J.P. Heubert and R.M. Hauser (Eds.). Committee on Appropriate Test Use. Board on Testing and Assessment. Division of Behavioral and Social Sciences and Education. Washington, DC: National Academy Press.

National Research Council. (2002). *Scientific Research in Education.* Committee on Scientific Principles for Education Research. R.J. Shavelson and L. Towne (Eds.). Center for Education. Division of Behavioral and Social Sciences and Education. Washington, DC: National Academy Press.

National Research Council. (2008). *Assessing Accomplished Teaching: Advanced-Level Certification Programs.* M.D. Hakel, J.A. Koenig, and S.W. Elliott (Eds.). Committee on Evaluation of Teacher Certification by the National Board for Professional Teaching Standards. Board on Testing and Assessment. Division of Behavioral and Social Sciences and Education. Washington, DC: The National Academies Press.

National Research Council. (2010). *Preparing Teachers: Building Evidence for Sound Policy*. Committee on the Study of Teacher Preparation Programs in the United States. Division of Behavioral and Social Sciences and Education. Washington, DC: The National Academies Press.

National Research Council and Institute of Medicine. (2003). *Engaging Schools: Fostering High School Students' Motivation to Learn*. Committee on Increasing High School Students' Engagement and Motivation to Learn. Board on Children, Youth, and Families. Division of Behavioral and Social Sciences and Education. Washington, DC: The National Academies Press.

New York University. (2010).*The Research Alliance for New York City Schools, NYU Steinhardt*. Available: http://steinhardt.nyu.edu/research_alliance/ [accessed November 2010].

Office of Learning and Teaching, Department of Education and Training. (2005). *An Environmental Scan of Tools and Strategies That Measure Progress in School Reform*. Available: http://www.education.vic.gov.au/edulibrary/public/publ/research/publ/Scan_of_Tools_Measuring_Progress_in_School_Reform_2005-rpt.pdf [accessed March 2011].

Rice, J.K. (2010). *The Impact of Teacher Experience: Examining the Evidence and Policy Implications*. Brief No. 11. Washington, DC: Urban Institute.

Rockoff, J.E. (2004). The impact of individual teachers on student achievement: Evidence from panel data. *American Economic Review,* 94(2), 247-252.

Roderick, M., Easton, J.Q., and Sebring, P.B. (2009). *A New Model for the Role of Research in Supporting Urban School Reform*. Chicago, IL: Consortium on Chicago School Research.

Rothstein, J. (2011). *Review of Learning About Teaching: Initial Findings from the Measures of Effective Teaching Project*. Boulder, CO: National Education Policy Center.

Ruiz-Primo, M.A. (2006). *A Multi-Method and Multi-Source Approach for Studying Fidelity of Implementation*. CSE Report 677. Los Angeles, CA: National Center for Research on Evaluation, Standards, and Student Testing.

Stanton, L.B., and Matsko, K.K. (2010). Using data to support human capital development in school districts: Measures to track the effectiveness of teachers and principals. In R.E. Curtis and J. Wurtzel (Eds.), *Teaching Talent: A Visionary Framework for Human Capital in Education*. Cambridge, MA: Harvard Education Press.

Stecher, B.M., and Vernez, G. (2010). *Reauthorizing No Child Left Behind: Facts and Recommendations*. Pittsburgh, PA: RAND Corporation.

Turnbull, B., and Arcaira, E. (2009). *Education Indicators for Urban School Districts*. Washington, DC: Policy Studies Associates.

U.S. Department of Education. (2004). *Fact Sheet: New No Child Left Behind Flexibility, Highly Qualified Teachers*. Available: http://www2.ed.gov/nclb/methods/teachers/hqtflexibility.pdf [accessed November 2010].

Wayne, A.J., and Youngs, P. (2003). Teacher characteristics and student achievement gains. *Review of Educational Research,* 73(1), 89-122.

Weiss, C.H. (1998). *Evaluation: Methods for Studying Programs and Policies* (2nd ed.). Upper Saddle River, NJ: Prentice Hall.

Appendix A

Public Community Forum Agenda and Summary

Keck 100
500 Fifth Street NW, Washington, DC
Committee to Conduct an Independent Evaluation of DC Public Schools
Division of Behavioral and Social Sciences and Education
National Research Council

AGENDA

Sunday May 23, 2010

9:00 *Welcome and Introductions, Committee Cochairs*
Christopher Edley, Dean, Berkeley School of Law, University of California
Robert Hauser, Vilas Research Professor, University of Wisconsin, Madison

9:05-9:45 *Principals/School Administrators*
(40 min) **Carolyn Cobbs,** Principal, Ludlow-Taylor Elementary School
Dwan Jordon, Principal, Sousa Middle School

9:50-10:30   *Teachers*
(40 min)   **Erich Martel,** Social Studies, Woodrow Wilson Senior High
                 School; Executive Board, Washington Teachers' Union
              Marni Baron, Chairperson, Washington Teachers' Union,
                 IMPACT Evaluation Task Force
              Tynika Young, Academy Coordinator, Rising Academy,
                 Ballou Senior High School

10:35-11:15   *Charters*
(40 min)   **Jennifer Niles,** Founder and Head of School, E.L. Haynes
                 Charter
              Darren Woodruff, DC Public Charter Schools Board
              Naomi Rubin DeVeaux, Director, School Quality, Friends of
                 Choice in Urban Schools

11:20-12:00   *Special Education Providers*
(40 min)   **Rick Henning,** Rock Creek Academy
              Lauren Onkeles, Children's Law Center

12:00-12:30   *Break for lunch (on your own)*

12:30-1:10   *Other Education Providers for Children and Youth*
(40 min)   **Ellen London,** Interim President and CEO, DC Children &
                 Youth Investment Trust Corporation
              Lucretia Murphy, Executive Director, See Forever Foundation/
                 Maya Angelou Schools

1:15-2:10   *Colleges/Universities and Job Training*
(55 min)   **Jeffrey Barton,** Center Director, Potomac Job Corps Center
              Sarah Irvine Belson, American University School of
                 Education
              John Parham, Director, School Programs, College Success
                 Foundation-District of Columbia
              Allen Sessoms, University of the District of Columbia

2:15-3:00   *Students*
(45 min)   **Shanell Brown,** Anacostia High School
              Sakinah Muhammad, Cesar Chavez Public Charter School
                 for Public Policy, Capitol Hill Campus
              Nicoisa Young, graduate of Cesar Chavez Public Charter
                 School
              Darius Duvall, 2009 graduate of Booker T. Washington
                 Public Charter School

APPENDIX A 163

3:20-4:05   *Parents*
(45 min)   **Cathy Reilly,** Senior High Alliance of Parents, Principals and Educators
            Iris Toyer, Parents United for DC Public Schools
            Gwendolyn Griffin, President, DC Congress of PTAs
            Tijwanna Phillips, parent of a student at Janney, one at McKinley, and one graduate of McKinley
            Danitra Dorsey-Daniels, PTA President, Ballou High School

4:10-5:00   *Other Community Representatives*
(50 min)   **Margaret Singleton,** Vice President and Executive Director, DC Chamber of Commerce Foundation
            Erika Landberg, Program Director, DC Voice
            John Hill, Chief Executive Officer, Federal City Council

SUMMARY OF PUBLIC COMMUNITY FORUM

On Sunday, May 23, 2010, the Committee to Conduct an Independent Evaluation of DC Public Schools held a day-long public forum. The committee invited various stakeholders within the District of Columbia Public Schools (DCPS) and the community to share their experiences and perspectives about DCPS and the evaluation. Members of the public and the press were also invited. The committee heard from nine different panels: (1) principals and school administrators, (2) teachers, (3) charter school representatives, (4) special education providers, (5) education providers for children and youth, (6) colleges/ universities and job training, (7) students, (8) parents, and (9) community representatives.

An elementary school and middle school principal discussed measures each principal used to determine whether their schools were successful. Both cited the importance of tracking student achievement, maintaining school decorum, and creating an engaging professional community among staff members as good indicators of success. The teacher panel included a high school teacher, an instructional coach for high schools, and a chairperson for the Washington Teachers' Union. The panelists discussed the implementation of IMPACT, the new program to evaluate teachers within DCPS, and compared it to the previous teacher evaluation system. The teachers also offered various suggestions for the committee when examining areas of DCPS.

Next the committee heard from representatives of DC charter schools. Panelists included board members of the DC Public Charter School Board, a charter school founder, and a representative from the nonprofit FOCUS. The board members discussed the system they used to monitor and evaluate charters and how they distinguished between the high- and low-performing charter schools. The panel also listed some of the major operational differences between DCPS and charter schools.

A Children's Law Center attorney and a private special education school founder shared their experiences with the committee about the status of special education in the District.

The committee also heard from representatives of other education providers for children and youth. Representatives from the DC Children & Youth Investment Trust Corporation and the See Forever Foundation discussed the significance of wraparound services and other before and after school programs to support students attending DCPS. The panelists stated that the programs are pivotal in improving student behavior in schools and classrooms.

Representatives of local colleges, universities, and job training programs discussed how DCPS high school graduates compare to high school graduates from across the nation. The committee heard from American University, University of the District of Columbia, Potomac Job Corps Center, and the College Success Foundation-District of Columbia. Next, four charter high school students spoke about their experiences as students. The students discussed the importance of quality teachers, and the role they play in encouraging and engaging students. Suggestions for improving DCPS included teaching with more hands-on activities and offering a broader range of elective courses. Students also cited the need to create alternative training programs in high schools for students who may not want to pursue college immediately after graduation.

The committee also heard from parents who discussed the need to increase community engagement and open more streams of communication to ensure the reform effort is sustainable and successful. Some parents expressed concern about school funding and whether funding is equitable. Lastly, the committee heard from other community organizations such as DC Voice, Federal City Council, and the DC Chamber of Commerce Foundation. The representatives discussed an interest in improving and developing DCPS because students eventually become the pool for the workforce and members of the DC community.

Appendix B

Student Achievement and Attainment Indicators Collected by DC and Three Other Districts

TABLE B-1 Student Achievement and Attainment Indicators Collected by DC and Three Other Districts

Processes and Indicators	Atlanta	Boston	Chicago	DC
Student Achievement and Attainment				
Grade Level Performance on State Mandated Tests (G3–G11) *(math, reading/English language arts, & science)*	✓	✓	✓	✓
Achievement Gap Among Subgroups *(by racial/ethnic group, linguistic background, poverty, & disability status)*	○	✓	✓	✓
Adequate Yearly Progress Status *(for district and individual schools)*	✓	✓	✓	✓
Comparative Performance on State Tests and Other Exams *(NAEP & TUDA)*	✓	✓	○	✓
Progress Over Time/Growth	✓	✓	✓	✓
Participation in Advanced Courses *(Advanced Placement or International Baccalaureate participation)*	✓	✓	✓	○
Progress to Graduation Measures *(promotion rates or "on-track" to graduate measures)*	✓	✓	✓	✓
Graduation Rates	✓	✓	✓	
College Readiness Measures *(PSAT, SAT, & ACT)*	✓	✓	✓	✓
Postsecondary Outcomes *(college enrollment rates or employment rates)*	✓		○	
Teaching and Curriculum				
Teacher quality indicators	✓		✓	
Alignment among standards, curriculum, and instruction	✓	✓	✓	✓
Recruitment and professional development programs and investments	✓		✓	
Student and parent perspectives on curriculum and instruction				○

167

School and District Climate			
Demographic information	✓		
Measures of professional culture		✓	✓
Student perceptions of climate	✓🔍 ✓🔍	✓🔍	✓🔍
Parent and community perceptions of climate	✓	✓🔍 ✓	✓🔍
School and class size	✓	✓	✓🔍 ✓
Family and Community Engagement			
Communication and outreach efforts	✓	✓🔍 🔍	✓
Family and community participation and involvement	✓	🔍 🔍	✓
Resources			
Revenues disaggregated by source	✓	✓	✓
Spending patterns	✓	✓ ✓	✓
Per pupil expenditure	✓	✓	✓
Financial audits	✓	✓	✓
Central Office Operations			
Facilities, transportation, food services, etc.	✓	✓	✓
Central Office service feedback	🔍	✓	✓

NOTE: Check marks denote indicators for which data are gathered and reported. Magnifying glasses denote indicators for which data are gathered but not publicly reported.
SOURCE: Information compiled from Turnbull and Arcaira (2009).

Appendix C

Education Data for the District of Columbia

The data available for use in an evaluation of District of Columbia (DC) Public Schools include both that collected by the city itself (by various offices, including DC Public Schools [DCPS], the Office of the State Superintendent of Education [OSSE], and the Office of the Chief Financial Officer [OCFO]), and data collected by National Center for Education Statistics (NCES) of the U.S. Department of Education.

DISTRICT OF COLUMBIA DATA SOURCES

The District of Columbia has a number of data systems related to schools. DCPS provided the committee with a list of current databases housed within DCPS, OSSE, and the OCFO, and a list of evaluations or studies currently under way or recently completed (see tables below, as of March 2011). The DCPS systems include all of the basic student attendance, achievement, attainment, and tracking systems (e.g., DC STARS, ThinkLink Online), reading interventions (e.g., Read 180), human capital management systems (e.g., IMPACT), and management, operations, and finances systems (e.g., Transportation Management System). OSSE's sources of data include the State Longitudinal Education Data (SLED) warehouse (not yet operational) and a tracking system for individualized education plans (IEPs) required under IDEA. The OCFO data systems include the procurement and accounting systems. The evaluations include on-time studies, such as the City Year Evaluation, as well as ongoing assessments, such as the stakeholder surveys for which DC reports data every year at the school and district levels (see http://dc.gov/DCPS/About+DCPS/Satisfaction+Stakeholder+Surveys [accessed March 2011]).

We were not able to review all of these data systems, but have a few comments. A report recently released by the Council of the Great City Schools (2010),[1] for example, listed as its first finding about DC that there were "significant challenges to data quality" and "there was a lack of universal practice and oversight by the district in creating data comparable across DCPS schools and ensuring accurate information within the system. For example, there was no central control over student ID creation and no validations (automatic or hand-checked) to the system to guard against duplication."

The DC data and accountability chief made a presentation to the Committee, in which she acknowledged that, although the office had made significant progress in improving data collection efforts, much more needs to be done. She cited as an example of problems she found on taking office the formerly standard practice in DC's student tracking system of counting students as present unless otherwise noted by the school, which led to greatly overstated attendance rates.

Quality issues have also been raised with other DCPS databases. For example, in 2007, independent monitors of DC's special education system said of the special education data that "Most [case analyses] require tracking down the student at a school that differs from the one listed as the attending school in [the data system] . . . [the system] does not meet standard system requirements of . . . data quality control[.] . . . There are several hundred 'lost students.' . . . No one is really sure where they are at any one time." In 2009, the District also terminated its contractor on the building of their State Longitudinal Data System for default.

These preliminary findings do not in any way suggest that all of the district data are of poor quality or unsuitable for use in a thorough evaluation. They do suggest that, as would be done at the beginning of any research study, the evaluation begin with careful consideration of the quality of the data available to support investigation of the specific research questions and methods envisioned.

Table C-1, below, is the list of data sources related to education that DCPS staff provided to the committee. These include data collected by each of the relevant city agencies.

DCPS also provided information about data being collected by the National Center for the Analysis of Longitudinal Data in Education

---

[1]Smerdon, B., and Evan, A. (2010). *The Senior Urban Education Research Series, Volume 1: Lessons for Establishing a Foundation for Data Use in DC Public Schools*. Washington, DC: Council of the Great City Schools. See http://www.cgcs.org/publications/DC_FellowReport2010.pdf [accessed March 2011].

Research (CALDER), through a memorandum of understanding with DC and supported by the U.S. Department of Education. This project links data from the multiyear enrollment automated database (MEAD), assessment data, student residential information, and school files. Tables C-2 and C-3 list the sorts of information being collected through this project.

DATA FROM THE NATIONAL CENTER FOR EDUCATION STATISTICS

The federal data collections within NCES of the U.S. Department of Education that include information about DC's schools and students are the Common Core of Data (CCD), the Schools and Staffing Survey (SASS), the National Assessment of Educational Progress (NAEP), and the Trial Urban District Assessment (TUDA). Below is a summary of the measures included in each.

Common Core of Data (CCD)

The CCD survey annually collects data about all public elementary and secondary schools, all local education agencies, and all state education agencies throughout the United States. CCD contains three categories of information: general descriptive information on schools and school districts; data on students and staff; and fiscal data. The general descriptive information includes name, address, phone number, and type of locale; the data on students and staff include selected demographic characteristics; and the fiscal data cover revenues and current expenditures. Most of the data are compiled by state education agencies and sent to the Department of Education. The CCD data are comparable across all states. Data are also collected for DCPS, and, since 2004, for charter schools operating in DC.

Specific data include the number of students by grade level; fulltime staff by major employment category; high school graduates and completers in the previous year; average daily attendance; school district revenues by source (local, state, federal); and expenditures by function (instruction, support services, and noninstruction) and subfunction (school administration, etc).

Then Acting Commissioner of NCES, Stuart Kerachsky, made a presentation to the committee about these data. He noted that collecting data for DC is more challenging than doing so for other jurisdictions for several reasons. Both the quality and the timeliness of the DC data have not been comparable to those of other states. For example, the District's data exhibit a high percentage of missing data, especially for staff categories. In addition, the average tenure of the fiscal data coordinator in DC is markedly shorter than the average for states, which hampers continuity. Finally, new

TABLE C-1 List of Education-Related Data Systems Provided by DCPS

DISTRICT OF COLUMBIA PUBLIC SCHOOLS

DCPS Data Systems Inventory

#	Title	Owner (Agency)	Description
1	Genesis Earth	DCPS	Head Start workflow management
2	Work Sampling Online	DCPS	Head Start comprehensive child assessment tool
3	DCPS Administrator	DCPS	Used to process principal and assistant principal applications
4	Gov Delivery	OCTO	Used to send bulk emails to parents, etc.
5	Imagine Learning	DCPS	Reading intervention program for certain English language learner 3rd through 5th grade students. Used as learning aid directly by students
6	Early Steps and Stages Tracker	OSSE	Early Stages IDEA Part C tracking. Tracks students identified as possibly having special needs (birth - 2yr)
7	Early Stages Tracking, Monitoring, and Reporting	DCPS	Early Stages IDEA Part B tracking. Tracks students identified as possibly having special needs (2yr - 4yr 9mo)
8	DC STARS	DCPS	Student Information System (SIS)
9	Blackman-Jones Database	DCPS	Tracks Blackman-Jones statistics for consent decree reporting and case management
10	CAASS	DCPS	Student access control system. Tracks students as they enter school buildings, currently used for school security
11	DCPS Public Website	DCPS	Public website for DCPS
12	SEDS (Easy IEP)	OSSE	Individualized Education Program (IEP) management system
13	FileNet	OCTO	Document imaging system
14	PD Planner	DCPS	Online catalog and activity management system for professional development offerings for DCPS educators and employees
15	PASS	OCTO	Procurement management system
16	SOAR	OCFO	System of accounting and reporting (financial mgmt system) - General ledger, accounts payable, budget, fixed assets, accounts receivable, cash management, inventory management

17	PeopleSoft	OCTO	Human resources management system
18	WinSnap/WebSmart	DCPS	Food services management and point of sale system
19	FSS (Full Service Schools) Dashboard (beta)	DCPS	Allows principals to view current state of different measures of their school, combining information from different data sources in one place
20	IQ	OCTO	Districtwide correspondence management
21	Out-of-Boundary Lottery	DCPS	Lottery system to randomly select enrollment for out-of-boundary students
22	DCPS PS/PK and Out-of-Boundary Database	DCPS	Manages postlottery activities (results, managing waitlist, etc.) for the DCPS Pre-School / Pre-K / Head Start and Out-of-Boundary Lottery
23	Capital Gains	DCPS	Allows teachers to enter data on student performance for Capital Gains Program
24	DCPS CFO Budget V2	DCPS	Allows principals to work with CFO analysts to develop coming year budget
25	DCPS CFO Budgeting	DCPS	Tracks actual vs budgeted spending for Central Office divisions
26	IMPACT	DCPS	Manages school-based staff assessments
27	DCPS UELIP Application	DCPS	Allows people (DCPS and non-DCPS) to apply for UELIP Internship Program
28	Comp Ed Database V2	DCPS	Houses data about compensatory education providers, program, and services for use in comp ed determinations
29	Labor Management and Employee Relations	DCPS	Tracks grievances, adverse actions, etc. for DCPS employees
30	Performance Assessments	DCPS	Central Office employee performance evaluations
31	Probationary ET-15 Portal	OSSE	Tracks final disposition of teachers on probation
32	SST Tracker	DCPS	Pilot application used in a limited number of schools. Provides basic tracking of students referred to Student Support Team
33	Textbook Request System	DCPS	Allows principals to make textbook requests
34	Destiny	DCPS	Textbook tracking system
35	DCPS Summer School Application	DCPS	Allows people (DCPS and non-DCPS) to apply for summer school positions
36	TCTL Application	DCPS	Allows people to apply for TCTL Summer Program
37	Nonpublic and Charter School Assessments: School Year 2009-2010	DCPS	Used by both nonpublic and charter schools to track the ordering and completion of special needs assessments
38	DCPS Provider Management Application	DCPS	Monitors, reports on, and updates related service provider information
39	DCPS Accommodations and IEP Changes	DCPS	Used to manage DCPS' Read Aloud and DC CAS alt process for state testing (DC CAS)
40	Read 180	DCPS	Online reading intervention program designed to accelerate the learning of students who are reading below grade level

continued

173

TABLE C-1 Continued

#	Title	Owner (Agency)	Description
41	EBIS	OCTO	A web-based application that maps residential addresses to school boundaries
42	Transportation Management System	DCPS	Used to submit transportation requests for students who have transportation as a related service in their IEP
43	Trapeze	OSSE	Routes students for transportation
44	Extrata	DCPS	Part of system and used to scan, classify, and index human resource documents that belong in an employee's personnel folder
45	IGP-Individual Graduation Plan	DCPS	Online system that allows students to view electronic portfolio of educational, career, and achievement information
46	Connect Ed	DCPS	Automated calling system used to confirm student absences and for principals to send messages home to parents
47	Dibels	DCPS	Package of services that includes handheld Palm devices installed with software that allows teachers to assess students on DIBELS (Dynamic Indicators of Basic Early Literacy Skills) and sync data with online monitoring system
48	Burst	DCPS	Reading intervention system related to Dibels (see above)
49	SLED	OSSE	State Longitudinal Education Data warehouse
50	ELIS	DCPS	Serves as system of record for individuals who seek licensure in the District of Columbia. Tracks educator preparation (e.g., degrees earned, degree major, etc.), teaching testing info, teacher license info, etc.
51	ThinkLink Online	DCPS	Discovery Education's online data system for capturing DCPS Benchmark Assessment Data (DC BAS) student-level data. This system contains assessment data, teacher reports, sample items, and teacher resources
52	Security Incident Tracker	DCPS	Tracks security incidents occurring at schools
53	Schools DataLINK	DCPS	System of record for school-level data for which the Student Information System (DC STARS) is not the system of record. Provides aggregate-level information
54	Nonpublic Unit Tracker	DCPS	Tracks information about students in nonpublic schools that DCPS oversees for special education purposes

SOURCE: Personal communication from DCPS, March 2011.

TABLE C-2 Information on DC Schools Being Organized by CALDER

	MEAD	Assessment	Residential	School
Students	Traditional + Charter	Traditional + Charter	Traditional + Charter	Traditional + Charter
Years	2001/2–2008/9	Spr2005-Spr2009	2003/4–2008/9	2003/4–2008/9
Data Elements	USIs Student characteristics: Gender Ethnicity English proficiency Special ed. Date of birth School attended Grade	Reading & math scores Student characteristics: Gender Ethnicity English proficiency Special ed. Date of birth School attended Grade Full name	Student address School attended Grade Full name Date of birth	School addresses Grades served

SOURCE: Jane Hannaway presentation to committee, prepared by the National Center for Analysis of Longitudinal Data in Education Research (CALDER).

TABLE C-3 Links That Can Be Established Using the DC Data, By Year

	School Years								
	01-02	02-03	03-04	04-05	05-06	06-07	07-08	08-09	09-10 (expected)
Test scores	N	N	N	Y	Y	Y	Y	Y	Y
Gender	Y	N	N	Y	N	Y	Y	N	Y
Ethnicity	N	N	N	N	N	Y	Y	Y	Y
Special Ed.	N	Y	Y	N	Y	Y	Y	Y	Y
English Prof.	N	Y	Y	N	Y	Y	Y	Y	Y
Grade	Y	Y	Y	Y	Y	Y	Y	Y	Y
School Att.	Y	Y	Y	Y	Y	Y	Y	Y	Y
Address	N	N	Y	Y	Y	Y	Y	Y	Y

SOURCE: Jane Hannaway presentation to committee, prepared by the National Center for Analysis of Longitudinal Data in Education Research (CALDER).

strategies have been needed each year to make the data comparable to those for other states and prior years, for example, to account for changing classifications of charter schools.

Schools and Staffing Survey (SASS)

The SASS is an integrated sample survey comprised of four questionnaires targeting public and private schools, school districts, and principals and teachers. Data collection at the state level began in 1987-1988 and again in 1990-1991, 1993-1994, 1999-2000, 2003-2004, and 2007-2008, resulting in public release and restricted-use datasets. The next SASS collection is scheduled for the 2011-2012 and 2015-2016 school years.

One year following each administration of the SASS survey, a follow-up questionnaire is administered to the initial group of teachers to determine the numbers of those who have left their positions or have moved on to other positions. For the first time in 2007-2008, this follow-up questionnaire, known as the Teacher Followup Survey (TFS), was also used to monitor the movement of first-year teachers. In addition, the year after SASS 2007-2008, a state-level Principal Follow-up Survey (PFS) was conducted on all principals interviewed in SASS.

The SASS 2007-2008 collection includes 104 DC traditional public schools, their principals and school libraries at the state level, as well as an additional sample of public charter schools from 16 districts (many DC charter schools are their own districts). Finally, a sample of three to eight teachers per school based on school enrollment is also included.

The SASS provides data on

- **Districts,** including enrollment, teachers, principals, count of newly-hired teachers, teacher schedules and salaries, types of benefits offered to teachers, number of newly-hired principals, principal salary schedule, number of contract days for teachers and principals per year, existence of a collective bargaining agreement or other type of agreement, school choice policies, high school graduation requirements, presence of incentives to recruit or retain teachers, poor performance dismissals or contract nonrenewals, high school graduation policy;
- **Schools,** including staffing counts, Title I teacher count, grade levels offered, student enrollment by race/ethnicity, IEP and LEP students, migrant students, school year length, programs/services offered, public school designation as charter or traditional;
- **Library Media Centers,** including services, policies, expenditures in previous year, types of holdings and equipment, assistive technology availability;

- **Principals,** including demographics, salary, hours worked per week, number of instructional hours students receive per week at grades 3 and 8 for core academic subjects, attitudes and school climate, policies on school safety; and
- **Teachers,** including demographics, salary, workload, preparation, certification, teaching assignment, grades taught, number of students taught (average class size can be calculated), professional development, attitudes on school climate.

National Assessment of Student Progress and Trial Urban District Assessment

The National Assessment of Educational Progress (NAEP) collects academic achievement data and related background information. Table C-4 shows the DC data available from NAEP.

The Trial Urban District Assessment (TUDA) is designed to explore the feasibility of using NAEP to report on the performance of public school students at the district level, for those districts selected to be a part of TUDA (see Table C-5). As authorized by federal law, NAEP has administered the mathematics, reading, science, and writing assessments to samples of students in selected urban districts public schools.

TABLE C-4 Available NAEP Data

Subject	National Only Results	National and State Results	Participating Urban District Results
Arts	✓	—	—
Civics	✓	—	—
Economics	✓	—	—
Geography	✓	—	—
Long-Term Trend	✓	—	—
Mathematics	—	✓	✓
Reading	—	✓	✓
Science	—	✓	✓
U.S. History	✓	—	—
Writing	—	✓	✓

NOTE: Unshaded rows are areas for which DC data are available.
SOURCE: Nation's Report Card, available: http://nationsreportcard.gov/about.asp [accessed December 2010].

TABLE C-5 District Assessment Participation

	2002 Reading and Writing	2003 Reading and Mathematics	2005 Reading, Science, and Mathematics	2007 Reading, Mathematics, and Writing	2009 Reading, Mathematics, and Science
Atlanta Public Schools	✓	✓	✓	✓	✓
Austin Independent School District		✓	✓	✓	✓
Baltimore City Public Schools					✓
Boston School District		✓			✓
Charlotte-Mecklenburg Schools		✓	✓	✓	✓
Chicago Public Schools	✓	✓	✓	✓	✓
Cleveland Metropolitan School District		✓	✓	✓	✓
Detroit Public Schools					✓
District of Columbia Public Schools	✓	✓	✓	✓	✓
Fresno Unified School District					✓
Houston Independent School District	✓	✓	✓	✓	✓
Jefferson County Public Schools (KY)		✓		✓	✓
Los Angeles Unified School District	✓	✓	✓	✓	✓
Miami-Dade County Public Schools					✓
Milwaukee Public Schools					✓
New York City Public Schools	✓	✓	✓	✓	✓
San Diego Unified School District		✓	✓	✓	✓
School District of Philadelphia					✓

NOTES: Beginning in 2009, if the results for charter schools are not included in the school district's Adequate Yearly Progress (AYP) report to the U.S. Department of Education under the Elementary and Secondary Education Act, they are excluded from that district's TUDA results. See more information on the comparability of the 2009 NAEP design. Due to an insufficient sample size, the District of Columbia did not participate in the science assessment in 2005 and 2009 and the writing assessment in 2007.

SOURCES: U.S. Department of Education, Institute of Education Sciences, National Center for Education Statistics, National Assessment of Educational Progress (NAEP), various years, 2002-2009 assessments. Nation's Report Card, TUDA, available: http://nationsreportcard.gov/tuda.asp [accessed December 2010].

NAEP and TUDA provide scale scores and achievement level data, along with background information and allow for trend analyses within states and districts, and comparisons with others. NAEP and TUDA also survey school administrators regarding information about the school and teachers regarding their educational background, experiences, and instructional practices. Every 4 years a high school transcript study is conducted.

In 2009, charter school results were included in the state-level NAEP assessment but were not included in the district-level TUDA results for DC. In that year, the math sample for DC 4th grade included approximately 1,900 students in NAEP and 1,400 in TUDA; for 8th grade approximately 1,800 students in NAEP and 900 in TUDA. State-level (NAEP) and district-level (TUDA) math and reading assessments will be next administered for DC in 2011, 2013, and 2015 (schedule subject to change, see table). The schedule for NAEP and TUDA administrations is shown in Table C-6.

TABLE C-6 Schedule of NAEP and TUDA Assessments, 2005-2017

Year	National	State/TUDA	Long-Term Trend
2005	reading mathematics science high school transcript study	reading (4, 8) mathematics (4, 8) science (4, 8)	
2006	U.S. history civics economics (12)		
2007	reading (4, 8) mathematics (4, 8) writing (8, 12)	reading (4, 8) mathematics (4, 8) writing (8)	
2008	arts (8)		reading mathematics
2009	reading[a] mathematics[b] science[a] high school transcript study	reading (4, 8, 12)[a,c] mathematics (4, 8, 12)[c] science (4, 8)[a]	
2010	U.S. history civics geography		

TABLE C-6 Continued

Year	National	State/TUDA	Long-Term Trend
2011	reading (4, 8) mathematics (4, 8) science (8) writing (8,12)[a]	reading (4, 8) mathematics (4, 8) science (8, state only)	
2012	economics (12)		reading mathematics
2013	reading mathematics science high school transcript study	reading (4, 8) mathematics (4, 8) science (4, 8)	
2014	U.S. history[a] civics[a] geography technology and engineering literacy[a] (grades TBD)		
2015	reading (4, 8) mathematics (4, 8) writing	reading (4, 8) mathematics (4, 8) writing (4, 8)	
2016	arts (8)		reading mathematics
2017	reading mathematics science high school transcript study	reading (4, 8) mathematics (4, 8) science (4, 8)	

Last Updated March 10, 2010.

[a]Updated or new framework is planned for implementation in this subject. In the case of subjects for which frameworks are already adopted, the Board will decide whether a new or updated framework is needed for this assessment year.

[b]New framework for grade 12 mathematics only, in 2009.

[c]For 2009, there is a pilot study of state-level results, for which 11 states volunteered.

NOTES: At the national level, grades tested are 4, 8, and 12 unless otherwise indicated, except that long-term trend assessments sample students at ages 9, 13, and 17. The Governing Board intends to conduct assessments at grade 12 in world history and foreign language during the assessment period 2018-2011.

SOURCE: See http://nces.ed.gov/nationsreportcard/about/assessmentsched.asp [accessed March 2010].

Appendix D

Biographical Sketches of Committee Members

Christopher Edley, Jr. (*Cochair*) is dean and professor of law at the University of California, Berkeley, School of Law and faculty codirector of the Chief Justice Earl Warren Institute on Race, Ethnicity and Diversity, a multidisciplinary think tank. Previously, he was a professor at Harvard Law School, where he was founding codirector of The Harvard Civil Rights Project. His areas of special interest are administrative law, education policy, and race. His public service includes a 6-year term as a member of the U.S. Commission on Civil Rights, an assistant director of the White House domestic policy staff during the Carter Administration, and associate director of the Office of Management and Budget during the Clinton Administration. He also served as a special counsel to President Clinton and as a senior adviser on the President's race initiative. He has also served on a national nonpartisan commission created to conduct an independent review of the No Child Left Behind Act. He is a trustee of the Russell Sage Foundation and of the Century Foundation, and a fellow of the National Academy of Public Administration, the Council of Foreign Relations, the American Law Institute, and the American Academy of Arts and Sciences. He received a B.A. in mathematics and economics from Swarthmore College and a J.D. and a master of public policy degree from Harvard's Law School and JFK School of Government, respectively.

Robert M. Hauser (*Cochair*) is executive director of the Division of Behavioral and Social Sciences and Education at the National Research Council (NRC). He is also Vilas Research Professor, Emeritus, at the University of Wisconsin, Madison, where he has directed the Center for Demography and Ecology and the Institute for Research on Poverty. He has worked on the Wisconsin Longitudinal Study since 1969 and directed it since 1980. His current research interests include trends in educational progression and social mobility in the United States among racial and ethnic groups, the uses of educational assessment as a policy tool, the effects of families on social and economic inequality, changes in socioeconomic standing, health, and well-being across the life course. He has contributed to statistical methods for discrete multivariate analysis and structural equation models and to methods for the measurement of social and economic standing. He is a member of the National Academy of Sciences and the American Philosophical Society, and he is a fellow of the American Academy of Arts and Sciences, the American Statistical Association, and the American Association for the Advancement of Science. At the NRC, he has served on the Committee on National Statistics, the Division of Behavioral and Social Sciences and Education, the Board on Testing and Assessment and numerous NRC research panels. He recently served on the secretary of education's task force on the measurement of high school dropout rates. He has a B.A. in economics from the University of Chicago and M.A. and Ph.D. degrees in sociology from the University of Michigan.

Beatrice F. Birman is a managing research scientist in the Education, Human Development and Workforce Program of the American Institutes for Research. Previously, she served as assistant director of education and employment issues for the U.S. Government Accountability Office, held a number of positions in the U.S. Department of Education, and taught program evaluation and research methods at George Washington University and Stanford University, respectively. The major focus of her work is evaluation of education programs, with experience in federal education policy, programs for students placed at risk, school reform, and teachers' professional development. She has conducted national evaluations of the Elementary and Secondary Education Act Title I and the Eisenhower Professional Development Program (for mathematics and science teachers), has studied district and school reform efforts aimed at reducing gaps in student outcomes, and has evaluated policy initiatives related to charter schools and the uses of educational technologies. She holds an M.A. in counseling psychology, an M.A. in sociology, and a Ph.D. in the sociology of education, all from Stanford University.

Carl A. Cohn is a clinical professor and codirector of the Urban Leadership Program at Claremont Graduate University and president of Urban School Imagineers, an educational consulting firm. Previously he served as superintendent of schools in the San Diego Unified School District, and he earlier served in that position for the Long Beach Unified School District, both in California. He has also held positions as a clinical professor at the University of Southern California and a federal court monitor for the special education consent decree in the Los Angeles school system. His tenure in Long Beach culminated with his winning the McGraw Prize in 2002 and the district winning the Broad Prize in 2003. He has worked as a faculty advisor for both the Broad Superintendents Academy and the Harvard Urban Superintendents Program, and he currently serves on the boards of the American College Testing, Inc., the Freedom Writers Foundation, the Center for Reform of School Systems, and EdSource. He holds a B.A. in philosophy from St. John's College, an M.A. in counseling from Chapman University, and an Ed.D. in administrative and policy studies from the University of California, Los Angeles.

Leslie T. Fenwick is the dean of the Howard University School of Education and a tenured professor of educational policy. She has nearly 20 years of experience in higher education, public policy, philanthropy, and urban PK-12 schools. Dr. Fenwick held consecutive appointments at Harvard University as a visiting scholar in education and a visiting fellow prior to serving as a program officer at the Southern Education Foundation. Fenwick's commentary articles have appeared in *Education Week* and her published research focuses on superintendency and principalship, educational equity (particularly as it relates to race) and the minority teacher pipeline, and the link between school reform and community revitalization. A former elementary and junior high school teacher, principal and legislative aide on school reform for the State of Ohio Senate, Fenwick earned a B.S. degree in education from the Curry School of Education at the University of Virginia and a Ph.D. in educational policy and leadership from The Ohio State University. Dr. Fenwick is a member of the National Advisory Board for the George Lucas Educational Foundation and also serves on the boards of the American Association of Colleges for Teacher Education and the Council of Academic Deans from Research Education Institutions.

Michael J. Feuer is the dean at the Graduate School of Education and Human Development at George Washington University. Previously, he served as the executive director of the Division of Behavioral and Social Sciences and Education of the National Research Council (NRC) of the National Academies, where he was responsible for a broad portfolio of studies and other activities aimed at improved economic, social, and education policy making. He was the first director of the NRC's Center for Education and the founding director of the Board on Testing and Assessment. Prior to his work at the NRC, he was a senior analyst and project director at the Office of Technology Assessment. He has been the Burton and Inglis Lecturer at Harvard University. He is a member of the National Academy of Education. He holds a B.A. (magna cum laude) from Queens College of the City University of New York and an M.A. from the Wharton School and a Ph.D. in public policy, both from the University of Pennsylvania.

Jon Fullerton is the executive director of the Center for Education Policy Research at Harvard University. Previously, he served as the director of budget and financial policy for the Board of Education of the Los Angeles Unified School District. In this capacity, he provided independent evaluations of district reforms and helped to ensure that the district's budget was aligned with board priorities. Other positions—reflecting his broad interests in designing and implementing organizational change—include serving as vice president of strategy, evaluation, research, and policy at the Urban Education Partnership in Los Angeles and at as a strategy consultant at McKinsey & Company, in both the education and private sectors. He holds a Ph.D. in government and an A.B. in social studies, both from Harvard University.

Fernando A. Guerra is director of health for the San Antonio Metropolitan Health District and a long-time practicing pediatrician. He is also a clinical professor of pediatrics at the University of Texas Health Science Center at San Antonio and an adjunct professor in public health at the Air Force School of Aerospace Medicine at Brooks Air Force Base and at the University of Texas School of Public Health, Houston. He has served on the federal advisory committees for immunization practices, and vaccines, infant mortality, as well as the Federal Advisory Committee for the National Children's Study. He is currently serving on the board of trustees of the Urban Institute, as chairman of the board of the Children's Environmental Health Institute, and as a member of the Committee on Biomedical Ethics for the March of Dimes. He is a fellow of the American Academy of Pediatrics, and a member of the New York Academy of Medicine, the Texas Academy of Medicine, Science, and Engineering, and the Institute of Medicine, and he was a founding scholar of the Public Health Leadership Institute. He holds a B.A. from the University of Texas, Austin, an M.D. the University of Texas Medical Branch, Galveston; and an M.P.H. from the Harvard School of Public Health.

Jonathan Gueverra serves as the chief executive officer of the Community College of the District of Columbia. Previously he was the provost for the Alexandria Campus of Northern Virginia Community College, one of the largest community colleges in the country. He also continues to work with doctoral students at Lesley University and Morgan State University, where he has taught undergraduate courses in accounting, management, and human resources, as well as graduate courses in leadership and strategic management. He has served on numerous boards, including those of the Massachusetts Business Educators Association, New England Educational

Assessment Network, Lesley University, ITT Technical Institute, and the Commonwealth Soccer Officials Association. Has has also implemented and coordinated Volunteer Income Tax Assistance programs to help low-income, elderly, and non-native English speakers. He has received a lifetime achievement award for his role in developing service learning programs at Wentworth Institute of Technology. He holds a B.A. from Providence College and an M.B.A. and an Ed.D. from the University of Massachusetts.

Jonathan Guryan is an associate professor of human development and social policy and of economics, and a faculty fellow with the Institute for Policy Research at Northwestern University. He is also a faculty research fellow at the National Bureau of Economic Research and serves as a research consultant for the Federal Reserve Bank of Chicago. Previously, he was on the faculty of the University of Chicago's Booth School of Business. His work spans various topics related to labor markets, education policy, and social interaction. His research interests include the causes and consequences of racial inequality, the causes of truancy and school dropout decisions, the labor market for teachers, social interactions in the workplace, occupational licensure, and lottery gambling. He also studies race and discrimination in the labor market and in education. He is a recipient of the John T. Dunlop Outstanding Scholar Award from the Labor and Employment Relations Association. He received his A.B. in economics from Princeton University and his Ph.D. in economics from the Massachusetts Institute of Technology.

Lorraine McDonnell is a professor of political science at the University of California, Santa Barbara. Her research has focused on the design and implementation of K-12 education policies and their effects on school practice. In recent studies, she examined the politics of student testing, particularly the curricular and political values underlying state assessment policies. Her publications have focused on various aspects of education policy and politics, including teacher unions, the education of immigrant students, and the role of citizen deliberation. McDonnell served for 7 years on the National Research Council's (NRC's) Board on Testing and Assessment, and is currently a member of the NRC's advisory committee for the Division of Behavioral and Social Sciences and Education. She was the 2008-2009 president of the American Educational Research Association and is a member of the National Academy of Education. She is also national associate of the National Academy of Sciences. She has a Ph.D. in political science from Stanford University.

C. Kent McGuire recently became president and chief executive officer of the Southern Education Foundation. Previously, he was the dean of the College of Education at Temple University and a professor in the university's Educational Administration Program in the Department of Educational Leadership and Policy Studies. Before working at Temple, he was senior vice president at MDRC, where his responsibilities included leadership of the education, children, and youth division. In the Clinton Administration, he served as assistant secretary of education, the senior officer for the department's research and development agency. He also has served as education program officer for the Pew Charitable Trusts and education program director for the Eli Lilly Endowment, as well as assistant professor at the University of Colorado and senior policy analyst for the Education Commission of the States. His current research interests focus on education administration and policy and organizational change. He holds a B.A. in economics from the University of Michigan, an M.A. in education administration and policy from Columbia University Teachers College, and a Ph.D. in public administration from the University of Colorado, Boulder.

Maxine Singer is president emeritus of the Carnegie Institution of Washington. She previously held positions at the National Institutes of Health and the National Cancer Institute, where she remains as a scientist emeritus. At the Carnegie Institution, she established the Carnegie Academy for Science Education whose goal is to enhance learning of science and mathematics for DC public school teachers and students. Her work has ranged over several areas of nucleic acid biochemistry and molecular biology. She was one of the organizers of the Asilomar Conference on Recombinant DNA. She has been a member of the board of directors of Johnson & Johnson, a trustee of the Yale University Corporation, and a director of the Whitehead Institute. She is a member of the National Academy of Sciences and a recipient of its public welfare medal. She is also a member of the Pontifical Academy of Sciences. Her several awards for public service include the Distinguished Presidential Rank Award, and the National Medal of Science, the nation's highest scientific honor She has received honorary degrees from, among others, Brandeis University, Dartmouth College, Williams College, New York University, Swarthmore College, Harvard University, and Yale University. She holds an A.B. (with high honors) from Swarthmore College and a Ph.D. in biochemistry from Yale University.

William F. Tate IV is the Edward Mallinckrodt Distinguished University Professor in Arts & Sciences at Washington University in St. Louis. He also directs the Center for the Study of Regional Competitiveness in Science and Technology and serves as chair of the Department of Education at the university, where he holds academic and research appointments in the Center for Applied Statistics, Institute for Public Health, urban studies, and medical education. He is a past president of the American Educational Research

Association. He has served as a scholar in residence and as assistant superintendent for mathematics and science in the Dallas Independent School District. He has concentrated his research efforts in four areas: (1) social determinants of mathematics, engineering, technology, and science attainment and disparities; (2) adolescent development and health; (3) political economy of urban metropolitan regions; and (4) leadership in public-private human services alliances and research collaborations. He received his B.S. in economics from Northern Illinois University, his M.A.T. from the University of Texas, Dallas, and his Ph.D. from the University of Maryland. He is completing postdoctoral training in psychiatric epidemiology in the Department of Psychiatry at the Washington University Medical School.